A RAPE AND KILL

The man's long strides were too much for petite, twenty-three-year-old Toni Gibbs to outrun. He slammed her to the cold, dry earth, then dragged her to the abandoned, burned-out school bus and ripped off her clothes. He pushed her shoulders down into the dirty floorboard, then rammed himself into her unyielding body, savagely raping her in a blind rage.

Finally the attack stopped. But the man wasn't done. He plunged a sharp knife blade deep into Toni's slim body again and again—three stab wounds to the back, three more to the chest.

His rage spent, the man quickly gathered up his victim's clothes and stuffed them under the floorboard of the rusted-out bus before fleeing.

Toni Gibbs crawled from the bus shell. One hundred yards away, she died.

Other books by Patricia Springer

BLOOD RUSH
FLESH AND BLOOD
MAIL ORDER MURDER
A LOVE TO DIE FOR

BODY HUNTER

Patricia Springer

PINNACLE BOOKS
Kensington Publishing Corp.
http://www.pinnaclebooks.com

Some names have been changed to protect the privacy of individuals connected to this story.

PINNACLE BOOKS are published by

Kensington Publishing Corp.
850 Third Avenue
New York, NY 10022

All Kensington Titles, Imprints, and Distributed Lines are available at special quantity discounts for bulk purchases for sales promotions, premiums, fund-raising, and educational or institutional use. Special book excerpts or customized printings can also be created to fit specific needs. For details, write or phone the office of the Kensington special sales manager: Kensington Publishing Corp., 850 Third Avenue, New York, NY 10022, attn: Special Sales Department, Phone: 1-800-221-2647.

Pinnacle and the P logo Reg. U.S. Pat. & TM Off.

First Printing: August 2001
10 9 8 7 6 5 4 3 2 1

Printed in the United States of America

*This book is dedicated to four fabulous women
who through their friendships and talents
have enriched my life beyond measure.
Tina Church, LaRee Bryant, Melody Milam Potter,
and Jan Blankenship*

ACKNOWLEDGMENTS

For those of us who attempt to take the unbelievable actions of others and make them understandable, there are many people who assist in our quest. Some have helped with investigations, some with technical advice, and then there are those who have opened their souls so that we may realize their pain and know their everlasting love for their sons and daughters, brothers and sisters, lovers and friends. To all, I say a heartfelt "thank you."

Thanks to Julie Pruitt, station manager, Scott Coppenbarger, news director, Dana Byerley, reporter, and Harold Ferguson, cameraman, of KFDX-TV in Wichita Falls; Carroll Wilson, editor, Sharon Chance, reporter, and Jill Sexton Smolko, of the *Times Record News;* Brad Duncan, Fred Duncan, and Dave Collard of Olney Door and Screen Company; Dana Rice, investigator, and Dorie Glickman, attorney-at-law with the Office of the Public Defender, Wichita County; Leslie Ryan-Hash, court reporter, 30th District Court; John Little, investigator for the Wichita County District Attorney's Office; Jan Blankenship, LPC, and Dr. Melody Potter, Ph.D.; Tina Church of TC Investigations; James Cron, certified latent print examiner; Bryce and Tina Wardrip; Richard Nunley; Floyd and Paulette Jackson; and Wilma Hooker.

As always my grateful appreciation to Karen Haas and LaRee Bryant for making my words work.

And lastly, gratitude to Faryion Wardrip for his exclusive death-row interview, as well as his candor.

Part I

Part I

Chapter One

December 21, 1984

The cold December air chilled twenty-year-old Terry Sims and her friend Leza Boone as they walked to the parking lot of Bethania Regional Health Care Center in Wichita Falls, Texas. Terry's dark brown hair blew gently in the breeze and, as the cold night air could cut like a surgeon's knife, her coat was pulled tightly over her pink uniform. Terry, who aspired to be a doctor, had been working at Bethania for two years.

The young health-care workers laughed and talked about their plans for Christmas as they drove to the home of close friends to exchange gifts. Terry was in the Christmas spirit. She had given two boxes of chocolates to coworkers before she finished her three-to-eleven P.M. shift. It was 11:25 by the time Terry and Leza arrived at their friends' home and nearly an hour later before they left for Leza's rented house on Bell Street.

"I need you to help me study for finals and help me stay awake," Leza told Terry, who occasionally spent the night at her friend's house while both women, students at Midwestern State University, studied for exams.

Leza was scheduled to work a second shift at the hospital. She dropped Terry off at the small white, frame house and drove Terry's car back to work while her own vehicle, out of gas, sat in the driveway in front of the single detached garage to the left of the house.

Terry unlocked the front door with Leza's keys. A narrow awning-style roof protected the entrance from a drizzling rain. The glare from the front porch light was the only lumination into the darkened structure. It was 12:30 A.M. The air conditioner protruding from the front window was silent. Winter had replaced the blistering hot Texas summer. Nature's coldness filled the room, along with peaceful silence.

In the darkened shadows and dripping rain, a man huddled inside his wet coat and watched from across the street. He noticed Terry Sims slowly close the door behind her and Leza speed away.

The stranger had been aimlessly walking the streets of his Wichita Falls neighborhood. He'd shot up some drugs and should have been feeling a radical high but, instead, all he sensed was hostility. But that was nothing new.

He hated everyone. He hated his family. He hated himself.

He wanted to lash out, to hurt someone.

As his anger mushroomed, the drugs clouded his thinking. Soon the anger took over.

Earlier that evening, he had encountered two or three people, persons he didn't know, but for some unfathomable reason had desired to harm. The overt aggression had bubbled to the surface like pudding coming to a boil. The destructive emotions had thickened as the long night wore on.

Drenched from the persistent rain, the stranger decided to head home. Perhaps his rage would have lessened by the time he walked the four blocks back to his apartment. Then he noticed Terry Sims on the front porch of the small house on Bell Street. He watched her as she entered the house alone.

Moments later the tranquility of the empty residence was broken by a loud knock at the front door. As Terry Sims gently opened the wooden closure, she could see a tall, thin man standing between her and the screen door he had pushed ajar. Rainwater dripped from his shaggy brown hair and beaded on his scruffy beard.

Before Sims could react, the man thrust his way into the house. The morning newspaper, protected from the rain in a knotted plastic bag, was wedged in the folds of the door mat that had been jammed between the screen and wooden door in the intruder's rush to enter. The alarm system had been turned off.

"I want to talk to you," the intruder blurted out, his deep-set blue eyes wild with rage.

Terry's petite body quivered, and her eyes widened in fear.

"I need to talk to someone!" he shouted. His eyes were aglow with fire. His voice filled with wrath.

Sims looked toward the door, looking for a way out of the house, away from the mad man who had busted into the house. She lunged for the door.

The six-foot, six-inch, two-hundred-twenty-pound man grabbed Sims and tossed her petite five-foot, three-inch, ninety-four-pound body across the room like a child discarding a rag doll. He pounded his large fists into her slim body, struck her across her heart-shaped face. He screamed obscenities.

Terry was defenseless. She fought instinctually, but her efforts were no more effective than trying to swim upstream in a strong downstream current. Knocked to the floor, she struggled to reach the coffee table where her school books and a *Webster's New Collegiate Diction-*

ary lay ready for study. Nearby sat a red candle surrounded by small poinsettias to celebrate the Christmas season.

The inside of Sims's upper lip began to swell. The bridge of her narrow nose turned red as her glasses fell to the floor. Strike after brutal strike left its mark on her pale, frightened face. The brown eyes that had danced with Christmas excitement only an hour earlier flashed with pain. She begged for mercy.

Terry's small body fell against the brown-and-cream-striped sofa. Cushions tumbled to the floor. She bumped against a magazine-filled basket as she fell forward. The glossy pages of magazines cradled in the brown wicker hopper were smeared with her red blood.

The assailant yanked the pink flowered smock over Sims's head and tossed it inside-out under the cluttered coffee table. Then he dragged her squirming body across the brown shag carpeting to the adjacent bedroom.

The stinging rug burns were seemingly ignored as Terry Sims fought to escape her batterer.

Taking a four-inch knife from his jacket pocket, the man began to poke Terry's chest with the blade's tip. The wounds barely broke the skin of his victim, but they provoked the reaction he was looking for. A reaction he relished. The young nurse was visibly terrified and momentarily paralyzed with fear. Her attacker felt a sense of domination and control he had never had before.

Instinct ostensibly overcame reason and Terry Sims grabbed for the knife the man gripped in his right hand. The sharp blade severed the little finger of her right hand and sliced deep into the four fingers of her left hand. Flesh hung from the bone. Her shrill, agonizing cries echoed throughout the small dwelling and remained confined there. No one heard her screams.

The overpowering man slung Sims's body on top of tan plaid sheets warmed by the heated waterbed mattress. Then he began tearing at her clothes. Her pink shirt, which had been covered by her smock, fell to the floor, along with her blood-stained bra tangled within the shirt fabric.

The spirited woman would not give up, or give in to her attacker. She continued to battle, slapping at her attacker's arms, thrashing at him wildly with her legs.

Between the water bed and the brown paneled bedroom wall lay a yellow electrical cord. The man quickly seized the cord and cut a section to bind Sims's hands behind her back. Securely tied, she had no chance of fighting off her attacker, or of reaching the Slimline phone on the headboard of the bed to call for help.

Terry Sims was rendered defenseless.

The attacker yanked Terry's white Nike tennis shoes from her feet with his bloodstained hands. The shoes made a muffled thud as they dropped to the floor, the ties still neatly bowed. While the man tore the pink uniform pants and underwear from the woman's body, blood from her wounds seeped onto the bedsheets. Terry's frightened expression was frozen across her battered face.

The anger that roared within the unknown assailant like a hungry lion looking for prey had not dissipated. It was not Terry Sims who lay on the bed in front of him, but someone else. Someone who ignited the rage inside him.

The man seized Sims's head and forced the pretty young nurse's face over his genitalia, demanding that she perform oral sex. Tears streamed down her face as she reluctantly widened her mouth to encircle him. His large hands pressed against her head as he thrust his hips back and forth until he reached climax. But his anger was not satisfied with the orgasm. With Sims's uniform pants and underwear still encircling her ankles, the intruder shoved her back down on the bed. Then he roughly wrenched her legs apart, climbed on her small quivering body, and plunged himself inside her. Ferociously, demeaningly, he raped her.

But neither of the violent sexual acts satisfied the rapist. His anger ran too strong, the well of hostility within him too deep.

He dragged Terry's bruised and bleeding body to the small bathroom across the hall with no more effort than it took to carry a toddler. Bending Sims's torso over the edge of the white porcelain tub, he escalated the brutal attack. Stab wound after stab wound riddled her body. The four-inch blade ripped into her freckled back once, twice, three times, leaving wide, gaping wounds on the upper right side near her shoulder blade. Seven stab wounds penetrated her narrow chest, along with several smaller cuts near her modest breasts. A quick slashing motion caught Terry's left upper arm, ripping the skin open in a wide cut.

Sims slumped to the reddish-brown, vinyl-covered floor. Her hair was wet and matted with her own blood, and scarlet streaks marred the front of the bathtub, splattered the square bath tiles, and puddled on the tub's porcelain ledge and the white bathroom chest. Blood flowed from each of the wounds and pooled beneath Terry's battered body. Her head near the kitty litter box, she lay on her left side, her right knee elevated toward her chest. Her hands remained bound behind her by the yellow cord. Except for a thin gold necklace, two small gold studs, one in each earlobe, and two gold rings, she was nude.

The fight was finally gone from Terry Sims. Seventeen vicious knife wounds had pierced her pale flesh. She gasped for air one last time as her lungs filled with blood. Terry Sims was dead.

The violent intruder slipped away from the house on Bell Street and walked back to his apartment. He lay across the bed and closed his eyes. Disbelief filled his mind.

No, he thought. *There is no way I could have killed that girl.*

He had no reason to attack the young nurse. No reason to beat, rape, and stab her.

The vicious aggressor began the process of convincing himself he hadn't really killed Terry Sims.

Leza Boone finished her second shift at Bethania Health Center at 7:15 A.M. on December 21, 1984. Tired and anxious to start studying for finals, Leza drove directly to her rented house on Bell Street where she expected Terry Sims to be waiting.

Leza's knock on the door went unanswered. She thought her friend must have fallen asleep. She knocked again, but there was still no answer. The door, equipped with automatic locks that secured the entrance when closed, wouldn't open. Leza walked two doors down to the landlord's house and borrowed his spare key.

The duplicate key released the lock and Leza walked in to find the living room in disarray. She sucked in a quick breath.

"Terry," Leza called, her voice shaking. "Terry, are you here?" she yelled louder.

A cold chill of fear ran over Leza's body.

Cautiously, she walked through the small, frame house, noticing tossed cushions, Terry's glasses on the floor, and a dark stain that was not there when she'd left for work the day before.

As Leza reached the bathroom door, she stopped suddenly, freezing in horror. A pool of bright red blood was puddled on the floor. Leza ran screaming from the house, frantically waving her arms in the air.

Neighbors looked out their windows at the sounds of Leza's cries. It was 7:20 A.M.

"Something's really wrong! I'm scared!" Leza breathlessly told her landlord. Near hysteria, she told him of the disheveled living room and the blood on the bare bathroom floor. They immediately phoned the police.

The landlord and his wife followed Leza back to the seemingly empty house and went inside to check on Terry while Leza paced anxiously on the front porch.

The moment Leza saw her landlord's ashen face as he emerged from her home, she knew something horrible had happened to Terry. She cried deep, racking sobs.

Wichita Falls police officers arrived at the Bell Street house and immediately secured the area. Detectives searched the house. They found a bloody Kleenex on the coffee table, the victim's purse and wallet scattered across the waterbed, and Terry Sims's bloody body on the bathroom floor.

Cleaning products scattered around the bathroom and towels taken from the rod caused detectives to wonder if the killer had attempted to clean up the crime scene. If he had, it was obvious from the amount of blood splattered on most of the small room's surfaces that the task had been too large. The killer must have given up any futile efforts to wash away the traces of his evil act.

The glum detectives approached Leza. The men confirmed her worst fears—Terry Sims had been murdered.

Chapter Two

January 19, 1985

It had been nearly a month since the gruesome death of Terry Sims. The killer had found a new job and attempted to put the grim events of the murder behind him. He had vowed that it would never happen again. After reading news reports that Sims knew karate and that it was believed that the killing might be gang related, he had convinced himself that Sims had been murdered by someone else.

Now employed, the gangly man pushed a damp mop down the corridor of the Wichita General Hospital. He'd been working as a hospital orderly for several weeks, cleaning up the messes made by others. His life was the one disorder he couldn't seem to straighten out.

Although he blocked the murder from his mind, he couldn't impede his ever-increasing feelings of hostility. It was as though he were back on that circular track in junior high school, running faster and faster. His relationships continued to be a source of frustration and irritation; thus his drug and alcohol use escalated, leading to even more feelings of disappointment. The circle of uncontrollable rage seemed to have no beginning and no end.

Although the orderly thought the housekeeping job beneath him, he emptied trash from a hall receptacle as he watched Toni Gibbs, a beautiful twenty-three-year-old nurse, make her rounds. He had first noticed Toni shortly after beginning work. Her bright flashing eyes and beaming smile lit up a room. Her white nurse's cap, anchored with bobby pins, held her brown hair streaked with gold in place. Toni was small, no more than five-feet, one-inch tall. She weighed a mere ninety-four pounds.

The orderly had wanted to get to know Toni Gibbs better, but she'd brushed him off. His family, Terry Sims, now Toni Gibbs. Everyone seemed to reject him.

He left the hospital after his three-to-eleven P.M. shift and walked the streets of Wichita Falls. The city of one hundred thousand was mere miles from the Oklahoma border. The economy of Wichita County was driven by oil and agriculture, Sheppard Air Force Base, and Midwestern State University.

As Wichita Falls boomed, the young hospital worker sank deeper into financial distress. His feeling of disappointment with his life turned to fury as he screamed to the sky, hollered at the trees, and cursed God. By the time daylight was breaking over the eastern horizon, he was high, drunk, and walking back toward Wichita General.

Toni Gibbs had completed her eight-hour shift. Tired and ready to head home, she drove her 1984, white Z28 Camaro out of the hospital parking lot. In the beams of her headlights, she saw a tall slim man walking along the hospital grounds. It was the new hospital orderly.

"Hi," Toni said, her window only partially open in an effort to keep out the cold January air.

"Hi," the man replied in a low, sullen tone.

"Do you need a ride?" Toni asked.

"Yeah." He climbed into the passenger side of the two-door sports coupe.

Toni Gibbs's kindness had no effect on his angry mood. As the man stared at Toni guiding her car down the nearly deserted city street, an angry fire burned in his belly. His internal hostility shifted to the pretty young registered nurse beside him.

"Drive out U.S. 281," he demanded.

Toni Gibbs's surprised expression altered her attractive features.

"Drive!" he shouted.

Toni obeyed, nervously, guiding her vehicle past a green-and-white sign denoting the Wichita Falls city limits toward U.S. 281 and into neighboring Archer County. Suddenly, the man grabbed her dark jacket and jerked her toward him. The car swerved.

"I want to talk to you!" he yelled. "I need to talk to you!"

But it wasn't Toni Gibbs the man wanted to talk to; it was someone else. As he stared at Toni, he saw another face glaring back at him. Someone else's disappointed eyes piercing him.

The sparkle was gone from Toni's own beautiful eyes, replaced with frantic fear.

The man continued to pull and jerk on Gibbs's jacket. Her tiny body bounced around the interior of her car like a BB in a hand-held maze game, slamming into the driver-side door, then against her attacker until she lost control of the vehicle and veered off the road.

Once stopped, Gibbs sat behind the wheel, gasping from the near crash, her breathing quick and shallow.

The assailant gripped her jacket tightly as he instructed her to drive the car down a dirt road.

"Stop!" he demanded when he spotted a construction site in the otherwise desolate area. "Stop the car!"

The vehicle came to rest on the lonely Archer County road. Still enraged, the man tightened his grip on Toni's jacket, using his greater strength as he resumed slinging her about inside the car. Her head smashed against the headrest, then the steering wheel. Her aggressor began to tear at her clothes.

"I hate you!" he screamed. "I hate you! I hate everybody!"

Frightened, she screamed, "Why? Why do you hate me?"

Toni didn't understand that she wasn't the person the man hated. His displaced anger toward someone else was now directed at her. The pretty young nurse just happened to be in the wrong place at the wrong time.

Like Terry Sims, Toni Gibbs was a fighter. She reached for the door handle of her Camaro and quickly flung it open. Just as she began to flee her captor, a sharp, searing pain tore into her flesh as the cold steel of a knife blade slashed her soft skin. She bolted from the car and made a run for it. A run for her life.

Gibbs's feet moved quickly, but the man's long strides were too much for her. He had soon caught up with Toni in the open pasture north of the dirt road. He slammed her to the cold dry earth, her body hitting the ground with a painful jarring impact. Then he dragged her through an open field blanketed in knee-high grasses. When he reached a burned-out school bus abandoned between sprawling mesquite trees, he ripped the clothes from his victim's body.

Shivering from the cold and the fear, Toni began to cry. Then the abuser topped Toni's petite frame with his own overpowering physique.

The man might have been in complete physical control, but his emotions raged unrestricted. The pretty, pain-laced face beneath him wasn't that of Toni Gibbs. He saw someone else's cool accusing stare. Pushing her shoulders down into the dirty floorboards of the old bus, he rammed himself into Gibbs's unyielding body, savagely raping her. Each painful lunge of his pelvis against hers produced pain, anguish, and heightened fear. Toni's screams echoed in the shell of the rusting bus as the man's rage rampaged on. To rape his victim was not enough. He had to humiliate her. Degrade her. The angry man spun Toni over on her stomach and with as much force as he had used to rape her, he sodomized her.

He had made Toni completely powerless, making himself the absolute ruler over her. He was energized by the power, not by the sex. His complete mastery over Toni, the pain he inflicted on her was the greatest domination he had ever felt.

Toni Gibbs screamed from the pain. Tears of suffering stained her cheeks. Finally, the attack stopped. For several moments there was peace. Toni lay quietly. The hospital orderly she had attempted to befriend lay beside her, taking in depthless, rapid breaths.

Moments later, Toni's back abruptly arched from the same searing pain she first felt in the car. Again and again the hot burn of the sharp knife blade was plunged deep into her slim body. Three stab wounds to the back, three more to the chest. The lifeblood drained quickly from her body.

The attacker kneeled beside Toni, again panting from exhaustion. He forced himself to take short deep breaths as he struggled to regain control. As each breath lengthened, his anger diminished.

Calm at last, he stared disbelievingly at his victim.

The man quickly gathered up Gibbs's clothes and hurriedly stuffed the red-stained white uniform, bra, and panties under the floorboards of the rusted-out vehicle.

Desperation overtook him. He had to get back to Wichita Falls. Away from the smell of death. Away from the unbearable sound of Toni Gibbs gasping for air.

The man climbed behind the wheel of the white Camaro, moved the seat all the way back to accommodate his lengthy legs, and headed back down U.S. 281 toward Wichita Falls. When he passed the high golden arches of McDonald's, he turned the car down a side street, and pulled to the curb at the intersection of Van Buren and McGregor Streets. He abandoned the vehicle and walked less than one half mile back to his apartment.

While her attacker fled the scene, Toni Gibbs struggled to live. She crawled from the bus shell into the open field, pulling herself along the ground by desperately grasping clumps of brush. One hundred yards away, she died.

Chapter Three

After an eight-hour break, Toni Gibbs was expected to return at 10:45 P.M. for a second shift at Wichita Falls Hospital. The Midwestern State University graduate failed to report.

"Something must be wrong," the nursing supervisor told her staff. "It's not like Toni to not show up. I'm calling her brother."

Jeff Gibbs was told that his sister was missing from work. Jeff telephoned his older brother in New Mexico and in a matter of hours, Walden Gibbs was in Wichita Falls. He and Jeff began the search for Toni.

The Gibbs brothers first stopped at the Rain Tree Apartments on Barnett Street where Toni lived. There was no sign of Toni or her white Camaro. Although the apartment seemed in order, they feared the worst. Toni's recent words rang in Jeff's ears.

"I've gotten some obscene phone calls recently," she'd told him. "Sometimes he talks nasty, sometimes he just breathes. If I've been out somewhere, he'll call and tell me what I was wearing. I want to get a tap put on my phone."

Jeff had been distressed by the calls and when Toni asked what type of weapon to buy, he'd purchased her a can of mace. He made certain she knew how to use it and insisted she carry the canister with her whenever she walked alone.

Jeff was scared. His hands trembled as he dialed the phone. "I want to report a missing person," he told the police.

Jeff's next call was even more difficult to make. He had to tell his parents in New Mexico that their only daughter was missing. As soon as they heard the news, Donnie and W. L. Gibbs left for Wichita Falls.

At ten o'clock in the morning, two days after her disappearance, Toni Gibbs's car was found in the two thousand block of Van Buren Street where her attacker had parked it on the morning of the murder. The Camaro's wheels rested close to the curb, a few feet from the outstretched branches of a large, leaf-barren tree. Toni's purse, with her driver's license still inside, was found under the passenger-side front seat, but her keys were missing. Although there was no sign of foul play, police processed the car for fingerprints and fibers. They took samples of a small stain on the front driver's seat and small smears of a red substance on both the inside and outside door handles on the driver's side. Stains they feared might be blood.

"Suggesting that she up and left is ridiculous," Donnie and W. L. Gibbs told reporters when asked if it was possible that Toni had merely left town without leaving word. Mr. Gibbs braved the bitter cold, his bald head bare, to speak to the press. His small wife nestled close to him as he informed the media that they were offering a one-thousand-dollar reward for information about their daughter.

Johnny Tidwell of KLUR radio joined the Gibbs in their efforts to entice persons who might have information about Toni to call in. He set up a reward fund at American National Bank. "We hope to raise ten thousand dollars," Tidwell told listeners.

Wearily, a tall, lanky man listened to news reports as he lay on his bed, staring at the ceiling. Sleep came, then restlessness and confusion.

Had it all been a bad dream? Newscasters speculated that a nurse at Wichita Falls Hospital named Toni Gibbs had been abducted from her apartment on Barnett Street and was missing. He knew he hadn't been way out on Barnett at her apartment.

It wasn't me, he thought. *Thank God, it wasn't me.*

He shook his head, trying to dislodge the image of Toni Gibbs, her bruised and bloody body, her clothes, the bus. But the mental picture remained with him. Haunted him.

As the killer contemplated his role in Toni Gibbs's disappearance, more than three hundred volunteers joined the Gibbses' search for Toni, some on horseback to cover fields laden with mesquite trees and two-foot-tall milo stalks. Others drove back roads and open fields. Helicopters patrolled the area where Gibbs lived.

Many of the searchers were from Midwestern State University, where the pretty young nurse had been a student. Sorority and fraternity members joined with other students from across campus.

"I have to help look for her," John Little had told a friend. "I was at a fraternity party where she was not long ago. We all need to help look." Little's attitude reflected that of many others.

"A lot of nurses are frightened. One nurse has been killed, another is missing," Major Charles Trainham of the Wichita Falls police told the press. In an attempt to reassure residents, he added, "We have twelve investigators checking leads."

But police efforts failed to calm the fears of nurses in the north Texas city. More than twenty nurses at Bethania Regional Health Care Center had reported receiving harassing phone calls. The number had increased since Terry Sims's murder. Staff requests for escorts had tripled. Now with the mysterious disappearance of Toni Gibbs, the Wichita Falls nursing community was in a near panic. Police attempted to quell their fears by assuring them that there was no connection between the murder of Sims and the disappearance of Gibbs.

By January 31, twelve days after Toni Gibbs was last seen, there were no solid leads in the case. The Gibbs were doing all they could to find their only daughter. They posted reward flyers and granted interviews in hopes of triggering a response. More than sixteen thousand dollars had poured into a Clayton, New Mexico, bank reward fund. Born and raised in Clayton, Toni was as well thought of as her caring parents.

Although they'd vowed to remain in Wichita Falls until their daughter was found, W. L. and Donnie Gibbs were finally forced to return to Clayton. They would wait there for word about Toni. Wait and pray.

Wichita Falls police continued to follow every lead. Several persons claiming to have psychic powers called and offered to help, but it wasn't until four weeks after Toni's disappearance that a break in the case finally came.

Charlie Hayes steered his Texas Electric Service pickup truck through the metal gate of a barbed-wire fence and across the open pasture just off West Jentsch Road in Archer County. It was about two-thirty in the afternoon when he headed toward a transformer that needed inspection. He slowed his truck as something in the brown grasses caught his eye.

What is that? Hayes said to himself, squinting for a better look. *Looks like a mannequin.*

Hayes climbed out of his pickup and walked toward the still figure nestled in the weeds. Then he abruptly stopped in his tracks.

It was no mannequin, but the nude body of a young woman lying faceup and sprawled on the ground.

Hayes's breath quickened as his heart raced and his body shuddered. He hurriedly returned to his truck and headed for the nearest phone. He had to call the police.

Shortly after, the field, which had been leased out for cattle grazing land, was surrounded by law enforcement officers from Wichita Falls and Archer County. Bill Guress of the Wichita Falls Police Department, Ed Daniels of the Archer County Sheriff's Department, and Trooper Miller of the Department of Public Safety arrived on the scene together. They immediately had a four-hundred-square-yard area around the abandoned rear section of the school bus sealed off with red barrier tape. Two men were instructed to make crime-scene drawings and the evidence recovery team began searching with metal detectors and documenting the scene with video equipment. A list of all officers at the scene was made. Other than those working the crime scene, no one was allowed near the area.

Guress, Edwards, and Miller walked past the burned-out bus with broken windows, going twenty-five yards south to where the body lay.

Guress scanned the scene. "You can't see this body unless you know it's here, or you just happen on it," Guress said, walking through the tall grasses.

Toni's hands and arms were above her head, her face turned to her left. Her blond hair blended into the dried grass. Guress could clearly see that there were gaping wounds to her chest and a large bruise on her left hip. From her left arm pit to her elbow, Toni's arm had been chewed to the bone, just as a portion of her left lower calf had been eaten away. Guress, a large man, bent down for a closer look at red markings on her thighs and breasts.

"Those are paw marks," Guress said. "Looks like animals have eaten part of her left upper arm and left calf. She's been out here for some time."

While Guress, Daniels, and Miller studied the victim's body, two crime-scene investigators were busy making detailed drawings of the scene. The sketch included U.S. 281 as it intersected with West Jentsch Road. Mesquite bushes at the entrance to the property, the metal gate, barbed-wire fence, and even two Bic pens found near the gate were added to the detailed illustration. The bus and two mesquite trees to the east, a large mesquite tree nearly fifteen feet to the southwest of the bus, a fiberglass tube found in the weeds, a utility pole, an abandoned shed, and Toni Gibbs's body were all in the picture.

Guress walked down the slight slope to the bus. There was no motor, no wheels. The metal form tilted to the driver's side. It was nothing more than a shell with some pipes thrown on the floorboards, along with other debris. The top and sides were rusted.

From the open end of the bus, Guress could see something white. Further inspection revealed a nurse's uniform lying on the dry dirt under the floorboards. It was covered with red stains. A white bra, still clasped, was found among the pipes inside the bus.

Splatters and droplets of what looked like blood dotted the inside walls of the bus. The directions of the blood spots were erratic, with cast-off blood on both the left and right sides of the interior.

"There was a lot of violence in this bus," Guress remarked, shaking his head.

C. D. Cox, Justice of the Peace in Archer City, arrived on the scene to officially pronounce Toni Gibbs dead. He ordered an autopsy, then released her badly disfigured body to All's Funeral Home.

Crime-scene investigators made plaster casts of depressions near the bus and at the field entrance. The indentations included tire tracks left in the dry mud near the bus.

Everything that could be done was being done at the crime scene to help find out how Toni Gibbs died and to produce a lead to her killer's identity. Guress knew the most difficult part of the process needed to be handled immediately. The Gibbses would have to be told—Toni was dead.

"I suppose I probably knew while I was in Wichita Falls, but I didn't give up and I didn't just fall apart," Mrs. Gibbs told reporters after being informed her daughter was dead.

"Part of our lives is gone now. She was just so very, very dear to us. I just wish you could have known her," she added, dabbing a tissue to her tear-filled eyes.

More than four hundred people filled the pews of the Lamar Baptist Church in Wichita Falls for a memorial service to honor Toni. She was popular and well liked, both in New Mexico, where she was a Clayton High School homecoming queen, varsity cheerleader, and a member of the National Honor Society, and the First Baptist Church, as well as in Wichita Falls, where she graduated from Midwestern State University. MSU received a portion of the reward money collected in Toni's name to use for student scholarships, as did West Texas State University.

"She had a sincere love of mankind and was easily upset when others were criticized or being hurt. She loved with a spirit of loyalty and generosity all who knew her," the Reverend Sandy Sandlin said. Sandlin prayed for protection of other potential victims.

But public unrest was high on the heels of another brutal murder, and women decided to rely on themselves, not God and the law to protect them. Gun shops' sales soared.

"Many, many people are now carrying some form of self-defense, from nail files to hat pins. Can you blame them?" Joe Tom White, chapter president of the Texas Weapon Collectors Association, said.

An unidentified nurse summed up the feeling in the North Texas community: "Everybody is scared shitless. Out buying guns. Afraid to walk to work."

No one knew if there would be another victim—or who it might be. Just as they had no idea who the killer or killers were.

Four days after Toni Gibbs's body was found in Archer County, the young hospital orderly quit his job at the Wichita Falls General Hospital.

Chapter Four

March 24, 1985

Now unemployed, the former hospital orderly traveled south from Wichita Falls to Fort Worth in search of work. He checked into a Travel Lodge near downtown, a small motel full of drug dealers. Instead of finding work, he found more dope. He bought drugs, shot up, and kept shooting up.

In Fort Worth, he was lonelier than ever. The unskilled, out-of-work laborer commandeered a car from the parking lot of the Travel Lodge and went to a club on East Lancaster Street. He sat at the bar, drank, felt sorry for himself, and tried to drown out the memories of Terry Sims and Toni Gibbs.

Debra Taylor and Ken, her thirty-one-year-old husband of five years, had been partying Sunday night with friends at their Fort Worth home. They ate dinner, drank beer, sang songs as a friend strummed on his guitar, and had a good time. By midnight, Ken Taylor was tired. Seven-year-old Tarrah, Debra's daughter by a first marriage, and Jennifer, age four, had been asleep for hours.

"Come on, let's go to the club," Debra urged.

"No, Debra, it's late and I'm tired," Ken grumbled, running a hand through his copper-colored hair.

Debra's brother-in-law, who lived with the couple and their two children, and all her friends declined Debra's invitation. Angry and determined to keep the party mood going, the twenty-five-year-old housewife wasn't about to be denied. She was ready to go out. Ready to have more fun. She told everyone at the party that she was going to bed. Then, just after midnight, she slipped away, saying nothing to anyone at the house. Debra walked to a nearby neighborhood bar on East Lancaster.

The tall stranger who sat next to Debra at the bar was instantly attracted to the pretty, brown-haired woman with a narrow face, thinly plucked brows, and delicate features. Her broad smile exposed beautiful white teeth and emphasized her high cheekbones. Her blue denim bib overalls hugged her nicely shaped body.

"Hi. What's your name?" the man asked.

"Debra, Debra Taylor."

The friendly stranger bought Debra a drink, talked awhile, then asked her to dance.

Debra's small hand was dwarfed by the man's large palm and long fingers. He slid his arm around her small waist. Debra's five-foot-four, one-hundred-ten-pound body was pressed firmly to the six-foot-six frame of her partner. They moved across the dance floor in unison, body rubbing against body. Her partner's hot, stale beer breath ruffled Debra's fine hair.

After a couple of dances, Debra was ready to go home. Ken was probably fast asleep in their bed and she was ready to join him. Her dance partner offered her a ride.

As the couple rounded the bar to the parking lot

at the back of the building, the stranger made his move on her. He grabbed her and forced his lips onto hers as his hands groped at her body.

"No!" Debra shouted, as she pulled away and slapped him across the face. A drink and a dance were acceptable; intimate contact was not.

Something in the man snapped. The same fury that had filled his mind and possessed his body on two previous occasions again invaded his being. It consumed him. In his mind, power, anger, repression, frustration, killing, and sex were inextricably bound. He lashed out at the pretty, small-framed woman who had rejected him just like the others.

His hands moved as rapidly as a flag whipping in the cool spring breeze. He struck her on one side of her face, then the other. He hurled her about, then shoved her to the cracked pavement. Debra's head pounded against the black surface as she fell, flecks of asphalt sticking to her hair. Within seconds, the attacker's long, thin forearm was jammed tightly against Debra Taylor's throat. He pressed against the struggling young woman with all his might. He choked the breath from her lungs, the life from her body. Debra Taylor went limp.

Glancing quickly around the empty parking lot, the perpetrator hastily tossed the body of his latest victim in the car he had stolen from the motel parking lot. He sped down the interstate and hurriedly took the first exit at Randall Mill Road. The area was fairly desolate with no buildings except for one apartment unit under construction.

The man lifted Debra's small body from the car with ease and carried it to a clump of trees about one hundred and seventy-five feet from the road. He stripped Debra of her clothing. On his way back to the car, he dropped the clothes in a neat pile about eighty feet from the body in the dense underbrush of the remote area.

The killer returned to the confines of his motel room. He was alone with his anger and the memories of three women—all dead.

While Debra Taylor had been gliding across the dance floor with the long-legged stranger, her friends and family believed she was asleep in her room.

"Well, I'm ready to call it a night," Ken Taylor announced to his guests. He went to the bedroom he shared with his wife, only to find it empty. Debra's purse lay on the dresser and her sweater hung in the closet. It was a cool evening, she couldn't have gone far without a sweater or her purse. Ken Taylor lay on the bed, wondering where Debra could have gone.

The next morning, Ken Taylor awoke to find himself alone. His wife hadn't come home. After spending most of the day checking with family and friends, finding no one had seen or heard from Debra since midnight, Ken's concern turned to fear. His wife was missing. He phoned the police on Monday evening.

Ken Taylor told police he couldn't imagine where Debra had gone. It was unusual for her to leave that late at night, especially without her purse. They had made plans for the upcoming weekend—special plans, for a birthday celebration. Debra would turn twenty-six on Friday, Jennifer five on Sunday, and Tarrah eight a few days later. Debra would never miss such a significant event.

Debra's good friend Angela Myal agreed with Ken. It was unlike Debra not to let someone know where she was. Her friend's mysterious disappearance frightened Angela. She decided not to sit around and wait for the police. She had to take action.

Angela went door to door in the neighborhood, showing Debra's picture and asking people if they had seen her. Myal hoped to find something to explain Debra's disappearance.

One of the many stops Angela made was to a little local bar close to the Taylors' house.

"Do you recognize this woman?" Myla asked the waitresses.

The women expressed surprise at how closely Debra resembled one of their own servers, but no one remembered seeing the pretty blond mother of two at the bar.

March 27, four days after Debra's disappearance, Ken Taylor was reading the morning edition of the *Fort Worth Star-Telegram.* Sally Field had won the Academy Award for her performance in *Places in the Heart,* a movie filmed in part in North Texas. The next headline turned Ken's uneasy feeling to anxiety as he read $50,000 POSTED IN MURDERS OF WOMEN. His distress fast forwarded to panic as he read the article, which described the murders of eight Fort Worth women within a few months prior to Debra's disappearance.

The Fort Worth Crime Commission, the Fort Worth Chamber of Commerce, the Fort Worth Citizens Organization Against Crime, and the Rotary Club of Fort Worth had joined resources to offer the fifty-thousand-dollar reward for information leading to the conviction of the perpetrator or perpetrators in the mysterious deaths. The incentive was sweetened by the addition of another fifty thousand dollars by one of the girls' fathers.

Ken's stomach turned sour as he thought of Debra. Was she safe?

* * *

Construction along the Loop 820 corridor that surrounded the cowtown city of Fort Worth was rapidly increasing. With the ascent of apartments and businesses, access roads were being cleared and paved to transport commuters to and from the city's newest freeway. SRO Asphalt Company was one of the contractors working in the eastern portion of Tarrant County. They began the project on Monday, March 25.

On Friday, two of the SRO workers needed a bathroom break. With no facilities nearby, they left the job at the paving site just west of Randall Mill Road and walked to a thick clump of trees about two hundred feet from the roadway to relieve themselves. As they stood concealed in the thick underbrush, they noticed something unusual. Something that hadn't been noticed in the four days they had been working in the area.

The two men walked through the thick foliage for a closer look. The pale figure, faceup, spread-eagled amongst the thick brush and trees, was that of a nude woman.

The men gasped. The face of the still figure was grotesquely blackened, akin to something seen in a horror film. They rushed from the grove of trees to call for help.

When Detective Ray Sharp of the Fort Worth Police Department arrived, the area had been taped off to preserve evidence. With no way to get a car down to the crime scene, Sharp walked to where the body had been spotted.

She must have been led to the location or carried down here. The growth is too thick for a car to make it through, and I don't see any car tracks, Sharp thought to himself as he trudged through the thick vegetation.

When he reached the body, Sharp made mental

notes: young white female, probably in her early twenties. He circled the corpse, observing leaves and other vegetation that had adhered to the cold, stiff remains. His soft brown hair blew gently in the southerly wind.

There was no way of knowing how long the woman had been dead. From the amount of advanced decomposition, Sharp knew that the body had been at the secluded location for several days. Temperatures had been in the high seventies and low eighties. The body was bloated and the skin of her face and torso was discolored. Sharp drew in a deep breath and closed his eyes momentarily before he again studied the face of the victim. Her lips were swollen, exposing her front teeth and gums. Her eye sockets were misshapen, and the black color of decomposition extended into her scalp. She was unidentifiable.

Sharp made certain that brown paper bags were slipped over the hands and forearms of the Jane Doe. It was imperative to preserve any evidence on her hands or under her nails that might help in identifying her killer.

About fifty feet from the victim, detectives found a pile of clothes. It was not known if they belonged to the dead woman, but the shirt and blue denim overalls would be inspected for possible evidence.

Dr. Nizam Peerwani, Tarrant County Medical Examiner, arrived at the scene. The physician made a preliminary examination of the body.

"I think it's a recent death," Peerwani said in a thick East Indian accent. "I can't make a conclusive determination until I do an autopsy or make a final identification."

While the body was being transported to the medical examiner's office, detectives reviewed recent reports of missing persons. Ken Taylor's report of his missing wife was among them.

"Mr. Taylor, we've found a body out near Loop 820 and Randall Mill Road in east Fort Worth. We think it might be your wife. Can you come down to the morgue and take a look?" an officer asked Ken.

It was the phone call Ken Taylor had dreaded receiving. He prayed on the way to meet with police that it wasn't Debra who had been found, but he knew in his heart that something had to have happened to his wife, or she would be home.

As Taylor was guided toward a stainless-steel table in the cold confines of the Fort Worth city morgue, his heartbeat quickened and his body began to tremble. Dread flooded him, replaced with repulsion at the sight of the hideous figure he knew was that of his beautiful wife.

"I'm sure it's Debra," Taylor said, tears of sorrow and regret flowing free down his ruddy cheeks. "That's the necklace I gave her for Christmas, and those are her wedding rings."

The jewelry was all of Debra that Ken recognized. He couldn't see her sparkling green eyes, her sandy-colored hair, or her perfectly shaped lips. They were gone. The lifeless, deformed figure on the table was not the spirited wife he knew, the woman he loved. It was the mere shell of a once-vibrant woman.

Debra Taylor would have turned twenty-six on the day her body was found in eastern Fort Worth. The next day, instead of celebrating her birthday, family members gathered at the Taylor home to plan a funeral.

Ken held his daughters close to him. He did all he could to comfort them, but his pain was so intense that he found it difficult to suppress his own grief in front of the children.

Later that day, surrounded by family, Ken hung up the telephone at his home.

"That was the medical examiner's office," Ken said, his voice breaking. "They've identified Debra through dental records. It's no surprise. I knew it was her when I saw her yesterday. She was wearing the necklace I gave her for Christmas and her wedding rings."

As friends and family discussed the disappearance and death of Debra, they spoke of the more than twenty women in the Fort Worth area who had been killed or were missing in the past six months. Another body, in a separate location from Debra's, had been found the same day. None of the slayings had been resolved.

"We've got an animal running loose on the streets in this town. I hope to God somebody somewhere saw something so we can stop this guy," Ken said.

Police refused to speculate about who Debra's killer might be—but they had an idea. They had never heard of the two women killed in Wichita Falls and they'd never heard of Ricky Lee Green, a serial killer on the loose in north Texas who was slaying young women during that time period.

But they knew Ken Taylor. Clinging to an old cop theory—that murder victims were usually killed by someone close to them—they were convinced Taylor had something to do with the death of his wife.

Ken Taylor's nightmare wasn't over.

Ken Taylor's nightmare had only just begun.

A few days later, a loud knock at the door interrupted Ken's private thoughts of Debra.

"We have a search warrant," the detectives standing on his porch told Ken as he opened the front door of his Fort Worth home.

"What for?" Ken asked, bewildered.

There was no answer from the officers who pushed

past Taylor and began sifting through his personal belongings, scrutinizing his life.

"What are you looking for?" Taylor demanded.

"Anything that tells us what happened to your wife," the detective replied.

Taylor swore he saw a sneer on the officer's face, but why? He hadn't done anything to Debra. He didn't know who killed her. Two polygraphs had proven that he didn't know who had taken his wife's life. Yet, this was the third time the police had searched his home. What could they be looking for that they hadn't found before?

Taylor was baffled. He soon learned the reason for the searches, and the accusing looks on the officers' faces.

"We need you to come downtown with us to answer some questions," Taylor was told.

"But I've answered all your questions. What more can I tell you?" Taylor asked.

"We just need to clear up some facts. We'll meet you at the station."

Taylor dutifully followed the officers to the Fort Worth police station where he endured yet another round of questioning, as well as a third lie detector test.

He was tired. Weary from the nights of lost sleep over Debra's disappearance. Spent from the ordeal of identifying her body and planning her funeral. He sat at the table in the interview room at the police station, wondering what could possibly happen next.

"Taylor, we know you killed your wife. Why don't you just go ahead and tell us about it?" the detective asked matter-of-factly.

"No. No. I didn't kill my wife. You must be crazy," Taylor stated firmly. "I would never hurt Debra."

"We've talked to your brother-in-law and others that

were at the party the night your wife disappeared. They never saw her leave the house. They tell us you were arguing."

"Yeah, we had an argument. She wanted to go out and I didn't. I guess she decided to go out anyway. No one saw her leave. I don't know where she went," Taylor explained. His exasperation was beginning to show.

"Her family seems to think you could have had something to do with her death," the detective said.

The accusation cut deep into Ken's heart. He loved Debra's family, had accepted Tarrah as his own child, and even agreed to his brother-in-law's living in their house. Ken couldn't believe his in-laws would be of the opinion that he could have anything to do with Debra's death.

The allegations hurt Ken, but worried him more. If the police were convinced that he had killed Debra, had they stopped looking for the real killer? And if so, would he ever be found?

Chapter Five

The murderer of Sims, Gibbs, and Taylor returned to Wichita Falls shortly after Taylor's killing. Fort Worth hadn't brought him the employment he sought, only more fury and violence. He had rented an apartment on Bell Street, one of only four in the small, two-story redbrick building.

At the apartment he often ran into Ellen Blau, a twenty-one-year-old, spirited Midwestern State University student. Ellen, who visited her best friend, Janie Ball, and her husband, Danny, in apartment A, never failed to smile and say hello to the tall, ill-kempt neighbor. He also frequently ran into Ellen outside the Subs 'N Suds where she worked, only two doors down from the Pizza Inn where he was employed. Ellen thought the lanky man a bit peculiar, somewhat of a nuisance, but basically harmless.

Janie didn't agree. Her neighbor gave her the creeps. She had watched the way he stared at Ellen as she came and went from the Ball's apartment. Her five-foot, three-inch, one-hundred-twenty-pound friend was dwarfed by the large man.

"He's weird, Ellen," Janie said. "If he is out of his apartment when you come by, don't stop to talk to him. Come right up."

Something about the athletically built man made
Janie Ball uneasy and she knew Ellen was a nonjudgmental person, friendly to everyone. Janie had often
wished she was more like Ellen. Her gleaming smile
and dancing, deep-brown eyes naturally drew people
to her. But Ellen's accepting manner also frightened
Janie.

Ellen Blau had told Janie about breaking up with
the mechanic she'd left her family home in New Jersey
to be near. Blau had finally gotten fed up with him
when he wouldn't find a job.

Ellen's choice of places to live and the company she
kept after the breakup had concerned Janie, as well
as other friends. Once she left the metal trailer she
had shared with the mechanic, Blau moved into a dilapidated house where rats scurried around the backyard storage shed among boxes of Ellen's clothes, and
the kitchen table was littered with pork-and-beans cans
growing gray hair.

Ellen Blau had once lived with the friend of an old
boyfriend whose chosen occupations included repos-
sessing cars and strip-dancing. He had taken Ellen on
"a job" to repossess a car without even telling her
what they were doing.

Friends had warned Blau about the company she
kept and about accepting rides with strangers. One
friend had even alerted her. "They're going to find
you in a field dead if you don't stop that crap." But
the warnings went unheeded. She trusted everybody
and she loved everything.

While living with girlfriends in a rented house on
York Street, Ellen had kept a dog in her room, a mutt
named Little Bear. The dog eventually had pups and
the whole bunch lived in Ellen's small room.

As hard as the stray dogs were to take, Blau's roommates drew the line when she brought home two guys

that needed "a roof to sleep under," as Ellen had put it. After the men had eaten the girls' food and dominated the television programming, the roommates demanded Ellen tell them to leave. Ellen didn't seem to understand her roommates' frustrations. Her heart was so big, she just wanted to help others. She accepted everyone she met into her life, regardless of their differences. It was one of the things Janie Ball admired most about Ellen, and one of the things she feared as well.

Ball knew without a doubt that Ellen Blau was an intelligent woman. She had attended the Country Day School in Saddle River, New Jersey, before attending the Choate School, a prestigious Connecticut prep school attended by John F. Kennedy, Jr. At Country Day, Ellen Blau's file was filled with certificates of excellence, no recorded discipline problems, and notations of her willingness to volunteer for extracurricular jobs.

Bob Kuhlman, the headmaster at Country Day, had once remarked that Ellen was a child with a wonderful attitude.

"She was able to read people very well," Kuhlman said. "Her first impression of a person was usually the right one."

Blau eventually transferred to the Choate School, spending her tenth and eleventh grades there. The private, four-hundred-acre coeducation boarding and day school for grades nine through twelve was chosen by the Blaus for its excellent curriculum. At Choate, a two-hour drive from both Boston and New York City, the Blaus hoped Ellen would be inspired by the school's attempt to have students think critically and communicate clearly; understand various methods of intellectual inquiry; recognize the interconnections of learning; work independently and in partnership with others; develop a global perspective on cultural, social, political, and environmental issues; appreciate the importance of beauty and grace in her life; and achieve distinction in her individual interests and talents.

The Blaus offered Ellen the finest in education, hoping she would use it to become the best woman she could be. But Ellen didn't feel like she fit in. It was a community of privilege she wasn't used to dealing with. Ellen was more accustomed to finishing her homework and going to her room to listen to a good album. She soon acquired the nickname "Rowdy Blau," or R.B. for short. Most students were obsessed with material things, but Ellen's interest was in helping women, not making a fortune. She had hoped to be an obstetrician/gynecologist.

On one of her rule-breaking trips into town from the Choate campus, "Rowdy Blau" met a man named Jeff. He was a simple guy, who always wore coveralls and was six years older than Ellen. Jeff was a terrible speller and Ellen would frequently try to correct him. She basically became a mother to her socially challenged suitor.

When Blau returned home for the summer, Jeff followed in his trailer. Against orders from her parents, Ellen saw Jeff every day. They began planning a move to Texas where Jeff's brother was stationed at Sheppard Air Force Base in Wichita Falls. Without a word to her parents, Ellen and Jeff left New Jersey bound for Texas.

The Blaus had no idea where Ellen had gone. Only by luck had they found her. Mr. Blau called Wichita Falls police, asked them to hold her until he arrived, then flew to Texas and forced her to return to their New Jersey home.

After making a deal with her parents that she could return to Texas to be with Jeff after she completed school, Blau enrolled in Ramsey High School. It was a bargain the Blaus didn't think they would have to keep, believing time and distance would dampen Ellen's infatuation. But after her 1982 graduation, Ellen returned to Wichita Falls. There she enrolled at Midwestern State University, taking basic studies and working at Bennigan's Restaurant. Within six months she and Jeff had broken up.

It was at Bennigan's that Ellen met Janie Ball. Although Janie, at twenty-eight, was seven years older, she and Ellen became fast friends.

Not owning a car, Ellen Blau rode a bicycle everywhere she went. To work, home, even in the rain, she rode the city streets of Wichita Falls on her trusty bike she nicknamed "Trigger." When not riding her bike, Ellen would readily accept rides with anyone willing to give her a lift.

Janie Ball often wondered how Ellen could be so smart and yet so blind to the kinds of people she accepted rides with.

A hard worker, Ellen left Bennigan's to take a better job at the Subs 'N Suds on Burkburnett Road near Sheppard Air Force Base on the outskirts of town. She had also been able to buy a new Volkswagen Rabbit convertible.

On the night of September 20, 1985, Ellen Blau locked the doors of the casual dining establishment about ten-thirty P.M. She shared a drink with a coworker, and the restaurant manager, at the Pizza Inn next door. Ellen's boyfriend, a Navy diver temporarily stationed at Sheppard Air Force Base, accompanied them.

An argument broke out between the coworker and Ellen's boyfriend. To keep the peace, Ellen decided it was time to take him back to his base dormitory. They said good night; then she returned to the Pizza Inn.

At midnight, when the restaurant closed, the trio of Subs 'N Suds workers stood talking in the parking lot for another twenty minutes.

"I'm going home," Blau told her friends. She was expected to re-open the restaurant at nine the following morning. Never one to shirk her duty, Ellen planned to be there early. She pulled out of the parking lot and headed south on Burkburnett Road, back toward Wichita Falls.

Ten minutes later, Blau's Volkswagen Rabbit was seen circling the parking lot at the Country Store on Burkburnett Road. She stopped at the convenience store briefly.

As Ellen turned the key in the door of her green Volkswagen Rabbit, a familiar man approached. She was congenial, but cool.

"I'd like to talk to you," he said.

"I really need to get home. I have to be back early in the morning," Ellen said with nervousness in her voice. She shifted uneasily from one foot to the other.

"But I need to talk!" the man said more forcefully. His eyes were glazed and his balance unsteady.

Blau fumbled with the keys, then quickly unlocked the driver-side door of her new car. But before she could put the key into the ignition, the man had forced his way into the seat beside her.

"I just want you to listen to me," he said, taking a sip from the beer bottle he carried. Then his tone turned demanding and he shouted, "Drive!"

As Ellen steered her car toward the city limits of Wichita Falls, the man began telling her his problems: his troubles with his family, his drug and alcohol addictions, and his feelings of anger that had tormented him since childhood.

"My parents never listened to what I had to say," he told Blau. "I'd tell them I was sad, cried all the time, but they always said it was a phase I'd grow out of."

Ellen stared straight ahead, not saying a word.

"But I never grew out of it. I started using drugs and alcohol to cover it up, but it doesn't help," he said, his speech slurred.

Blau fidgeted with the steering wheel, twisting her hands around the leather wrap, tapping her fingers on the wheel.

"Listen to me!" he demanded. "You aren't listening to me!"

Shouting directions at Ellen, the man directed her to drive down East Road to a secluded field in rural Wichita County. As soon as Ellen cut the engine of the Rabbit, the intruder was on her, raging out of control.

He grabbed her by her long, naturally curly, dark-brown hair and jerked her toward him. He slapped her, punched her, then took a knife from his pocket and stabbed her.

Ellen battled to get away. With the pain of the burning knife wound driving her, she grabbed for the door handle. She frantically fled the car with the tall, slender man not far behind.

The attacker caught up with Blau by the wall of a stock pond, near a cluster of mesquite trees. He snatched her by her bloodstained cotton T-shirt and jerked her backward. His long fingers dug into her slim arms. He squeezed her tight, screaming obscenities.

Ellen fought the best she could, but her attacker had the power. He had the control. Ellen's light body was thrown to the ground as her clothes were ripped from her body and tossed aside. Blau's blue jeans, with one leg turned inside out, her tennis shoes, shirt, bra, and one sock were scattered on the ground nearby.

Her shivering from the cool September air turned to fearful shakes.

"Why wouldn't you listen to me?" the man screamed in anger. "Why didn't you care about what I was saying?"

Ellen's assailant hovered over her. Each brutalizing strike of his fist caused excruciating pain. Ellen's face swelled, her body ached as he pummeled her over and over. Then the batterer's long forearm pressed hard against her throat. Unable to breathe, her legs and arms thrashed wildly in the air. Within seconds, Ellen's limp limbs fell to the ground. Her fight was gone, but the perpetrator continued to apply pressure. It would take more than ten minutes before life had been totally stripped from Ellen Blau.

The man, his shirt wet with sweat, stood over the body of his newest victim. His breaths were deep, his energy spent. He stared down at the dark-haired girl he had barely known. A calmness went through his body. The rage was gone.

The killer walked to the Volkswagen parked on the dirt road not far from Blau's body. He drove back to town, parking near the apartment complex where he and Ellen's best friend lived.

Physically and emotionally exhausted, he lay in his bed and stared up at the ceiling. Tears came to his eyes as he thought of the woman he'd left nude in the rural field. They ran down his cheeks as his thoughts turned to someone else. He pressed his eyes shut tightly and shook his head. His frustration and displaced anger had claimed another victim.

Chapter Six

Janie Ball was frightened. Ellen Blau had failed to come home overnight. Ellen had begun living with the Balls when she had finally given in to Janie's insistence and left her Polk Street apartment where the roof leaked and she kept getting bit by spiders. During this time, when Ellen was "in between" apartments, she shared space in the Balls' infant son's room while she saved money to move into her own place.

Just that morning, Blau had put down a deposit on an apartment. She was scheduled to move the next weekend. Ball remembered Ellen thinking out loud, figuring out how much of her paycheck would be going for rent.

It wasn't like Ellen not to come home, and certainly not like her not to call if she was going to be late.

Janie Ball ran her fingers through her light brown hair as her mind turned to the headlines in recent months. WOMEN MISSING. WOMEN KILLED. Janie began frantically making calls, trying to find Ellen.

Janie's distress heightened when a call came in from the bread delivery man who serviced the Subs 'N Suds.

"Is Ellen there?" the delivery man asked. "I saw her car down the street, parked in the side parking lot of The Country Store at Burkburnett and Puckett, near Sheppard Air Force Base."

Janie Ball knew exactly where the store was located. Sheppard was on the outskirts of Wichita Falls. A technical training center, Sheppard hosted the only NATO pilot-training program in the world. The Country Store was close by.

"I'll be right there," Ball replied. She hurriedly drove to The Country Store and immediately located Blau's car.

Janie opened the driver-side door and looked inside for any clue as to where Ellen might be. Seeing what looked like blood on the front seat of the unlocked, green VW Rabbit, Janie came close to hysteria. She immediately called her husband.

"The car is parked on the side of the store. The keys are in it. Her purse is in it. The shirt she was wearing last night is in it, along with a broken beer bottle. And something that looks like a trace of blood on the front seat," Janie Ball frantically told her husband. "She was very responsible. I can't figure it out. It's a mystery."

Although police cautioned them not to jump to conclusions, friends began to gather together to form a search party. Ellen Blau had to be found.

As police began to investigate Blau's disappearance as they would any other missing person's report, Janie Ball had one thousand posters printed and asked citizens of Wichita Falls to join the search.

"We just want to find her," Janie told reporters tearfully. Her best friend was gone without a trace. She intended to do everything she could to find her.

The Wichita Falls police weren't prepared to rule Ellen Blau's disappearance a homicide. There were no signs of a struggle. No clues leading to a theory of abduction. No body.

Six SWAT team members searched the area where the abandoned car was found, but there was nothing that suggested Ellen hadn't left the car voluntarily. The car was impounded and processed for clues but, again, leads were elusive. And even though the case had many similarities to the murder of Toni Gibbs, an abandoned car found with her purse, keys, and blood on the interior, authorities still believed they were dealing with separate killers.

Rima Blau, Ellen's mother, had arrived in Wichita Falls from Shelton, Connecticut, soon after she had received news of Ellen's disappearance. She was tired. Her eyes were drawn, the lines in her face deepened by concern. Ellen's father had been forced to remain in Connecticut to operate his business. Ellen's brother had stayed behind with their father, leaving Rima Blau alone in an unfamiliar city. She welcomed the generosity of Janie and Danny Ball, staying at their apartment while she waited for word about her daughter. There wasn't much she could do, but waiting in Texas was better than being in a vacuum of silence in Connecticut. At least in Texas she could talk to Ellen's friends and to the police. She would know what was being done to find her daughter.

"I'm just trying to understand everything," she told Janie, her New England accent laced with confusion.

Janie Ball put her arms around the attractive, dark-haired woman. She loved Ellen like a sister, but she couldn't imagine what Mrs. Blau must be going through. She was facing a mother's worst fears. Although Mrs. Blau was greatly distraught, she refused to believe anything bad had happened to her daughter.

"She's very practical by nature," Mrs. Blau told Janie. "She has a very strong sense of responsibility.

She knows the meaning and purpose of doing a job well. She was an A student in high school."

Mrs. Blau couldn't help but reflect on the future she had hoped would be her daughter's. But the headstrong young woman had left home three years earlier to pursue a relationship that had only lasted six months. By then, Ellen had made friends in Wichita Falls and decided to remain and attend school at Midwestern State. She knew the importance of education and wanted a degree.

"If I don't go back to school, my mind is going to get stagnant," she had told her mother.

Ellen's mother recalled her daughter's stubbornness, which had started at birth. She had been weeks overdue, not coming until mid-March after Rima Blau's father died. Her mother had been told by doctors that it was nature's way of taking care of her until the loss of her father passed. She knew now it was just the beginning of her daughter's strong-willed presence.

Through the years the headstrong young woman had shown courage in pursuing whatever interested her, even if it had meant conflict with her parents. Rima Blau now wished that she could have somehow talked Ellen into staying at the Choate School. She wished her daughter had never come to Wichita Falls.

Making every effort to help find Ellen, Mrs. Blau spent hours with the police. She left disappointed when she was told, "There's nothing to go on at this time." Though she was assured that five men had been assigned to the case, Rima Blau wondered if enough was being done to find Ellen.

The people closest to Ellen did the most for the despairing mother. Ellen's friends visited with Mrs. Blau while she stood vigil and made phone calls. Subs 'N Suds' management offered a one-thousand-dollar reward to anyone with information about Ellen, and the owner of the restaurant added an additional one thousand dollars.

"She's the best we ever had," Curtis Cates, the manager, said of his valued worker after announcing the reward. "Everybody's been a little more careful. We walk all the girls to their cars each night. I think they follow each other home as well."

Ellen's cousin, Kathleen Beller, a former actress on the ABC-TV show *Dynasty,* called LA police for advice; they in turn called Wichita Falls police for information. LA detectives were told there were no real leads in the puzzling disappearance of Ellen Blau. The family's frustrations mounted.

Even with all the displays of concern, police played it by the rules. Knowing that ninety percent of all crimes with victims are committed by friends or family, they questioned everyone. Everyone close to Ellen was given a lie detector test.

Fourteen police recruits and a borrowed helicopter diligently searched a field off Puckett Road, near where Ellen's car had been found. They came up empty handed. Finally, police made a desperate plea to citizens to call Crime Stoppers with any information concerning the missing woman. The two thousand dollars offered by the Subs 'N Suds was combined with four thousand dollars from the Blau family as an incentive for someone to come forward.

Tall grasses obscured the view of many of the open fields along rural Wichita County roads. The brown vegetation, dried from the scorching temperatures of the hot Texas summer, was being mowed by county road crews between the barbed-wire fence line and East Road. The driver of one of the high-

seated tractors stopped and looked toward a mesquite tree not far from the fence line. His tractor
motor idled roughly as he studied the indistinguish-
able form lying about twenty feet from the fence.
The early afternoon sun shone brightly on the figure
as recognition struck the driver.

It was a body. Hardly discernible as a human form,
but nonetheless a body.

When Wichita County Sheriff's Deputy Tom Callahan arrived on the scene, he was led through the
brush and a blanket of wild flowers to a badly decomposed body lying under the willowy branches of a mesquite tree close by the wall of a stock pond. The body
was nude, except for one white sock, banded at the
top with two yellow stripes. Flies swarmed around the
decaying corpse that had been reduced to an almost
skeletal state. Coyotes and other scavengers had added
to the mutilation.

Callahan, his eyes shaded from the sun by the
large brim of his Stetson hat, studied the blackish,
swollen corpse. The body rested facedown on the na-
tive grass, the head turned to the left. The legs were
extended and crossed at the knees. The buttocks was
partially eaten away, as well as the victim's right arm
that extended beyond her head. The skull was void
of hair or flesh. Time, exposure to the elements, and
wild animals had made it impossible to determine
in the field if the person found by the county work
crew was a man or a woman. It was a ghoulish sight
that made even the former military policeman Callahan cringe.

Close by, a pair of blue jeans with one leg inside-
out, tennis shoes, one sock, a bra, and a yellow-and-
white T-shirt were found. Callahan looked closely at
the blouse.

What's written on the front? Callahan asked himself.

He moved closer, his western boots squishing in the mud surrounding the pond.

"Beach party 1985," the deputy read out loud.

Callahan ordered a guard be posted at the scene to secure the area, which was just north of Sheppard Air Force Base. The natural barriers, hills and ponds, kept sightseers and reporters from tracking through potential evidence.

Although the body was found outside the jurisdiction of the Wichita Falls police, county Sheriff Bill Burrow notified them that an unidentified body had been found. Missing Person's investigators immediately thought of Ellen Blau. The three-week time frame in which Blau had been missing matched the condition of the body Sheriff Burrow described. They telephoned Janie Ball and asked her to meet them at the police station.

"Mrs. Ball, a body has been found out in the county. We can't make a positive identification until an autopsy is completed. That will take about ten days. We want you to take a look at this and tell us if you recognize it," investigators told Ball, handing her a shiny object.

Janie gasped as tears began to flow from her eyes. She held the fine gold chain in her hand. It was the necklace Ellen always wore. She clutched the emblem of the praying hands to her lips as she sobbed.

The decayed body was shipped to the Southwest Institute of Forensic Sciences (SWIF) in Dallas for an autopsy. Wichita Falls, like many of the 254 counties in Texas, did not have their own medical examiner. SWIF was faced with the responsibility of determining the cause of death for twelve to fifteen victims a day. Toxicology tests (which showed no drugs present in Ellen Blau's system), microscopic exams, and transcribing reports were all time consuming. Using SWIF resulted in time delays that not only affected law-enforcement personnel, but the families of victims as well.

Finally, the report on the Wichita Falls body was complete. Through dental records, the victim was positively identified as being Ellen Blau.

"Ellen Blau died of undetermined homicidal violence. We don't know exactly what caused her death," Sheriff Burrow told the press. "The precise mechanism cannot be determined. Because of the condition of the body, it is speculated that she was killed the day she disappeared."

Three factors were used by SWIF to determine a homicide had occurred. The remote location where the body was found; the fact that the woman's clothes had apparently been removed by force and strewn around the field; and evident signs of a struggle. Blau's watch had been found a long way from her body and bloodstains were also found some distance away.

Although it was feared as soon as the body was found that it was Ellen's, Janie Ball and the Blau family hopelessly had prayed that it would not be her. They'd held on to the false expectation that Ellen was okay and would be walking into the Ball apartment wearing the fun-loving grin she was best known for. Now they had to accept her death.

"We won't rest until the killer is found. We don't feel like it's the end at all," Murray Blau told reporters by phone from his Shelton, Connecticut, home.

"It's in the hands of the police and sheriff's department now. We feel confident they're doing all the things that have to be done. We hope this will be brought to a hasty conclusion. I feel the good people of Wichita Falls are equally concerned."

There was nothing left for the Blaus to do in Wichita Falls. Ellen's body was shipped back to Connecticut.

Investigators had hoped for a speedy resolution to the case, but they lacked a prime suspect. More than thirty people had been interviewed, most of them polygraphed, and they were no closer to solving the case.

Callahan and other investigators continued to work diligently. They followed up on every call from panicked citizens, grieving friends, and even weirdos.

One man, after being interviewed, shaved his head and sent an envelope containing his hair to Callahan. One self-proclaimed Ninja warrior called with information tying Blau's death to a Japanese warrior cult. It became a roller-coaster ride of false leads and hopeful breakthroughs.

Then there were calls from reporters who tried to find links between Blau's death and the murders of Sims and Gibbs. Investigators shunned the idea.

"We think that it was a person who knew her. It wasn't a random thing," Callahan told the press.

Therefore, three different agencies continued to work three separate homicides looking for three individual killers.

Part II

Chapter Seven

February 15, 1985

A motorcycle slowly passed the field where Toni Gibbs's decomposing body had been found earlier in the day. The man atop the chopper-style cycle made several passes, watching with concentrated interest the activity surrounding the crime scene. After what would be his last pass, twenty-four-year-old Danny Laughlin roared the engine and sped off, his brown, shoulder-length hair blowing behind him and a smile unmistakably covering his handsome face.

Danny Laughlin worked as a bar-back at the Stardust Club in Wichita Falls. He didn't take orders, mix drinks, or mingle with the patrons. Laughlin's job was to mop up the bar and make certain that clean glasses were always within an arm's reach of the bartenders. Occasionally he performed as a male stripper. The handsome young Laughlin had a tight body and seductive moves that female clubgoers appreciated. He also had an overzealous need for attention.

Laughlin had drawn suspicion to himself as he walked his pet wolf in the field near where Gibbs's brutalized body was discovered, as well as his constant motorcycle passes by the crime scene. But not until he denied to a Wichita County grand jury that he had committed the burglary of a Southwestern Bell Telephone office because, "I was in a field out near U.S. 281 and West Jentsch Road at the time," the area where Gibbs's body had later been found, was Laughlin considered a suspect in the murder. Police believed that if Laughlin was in that field, then he must have been there to kill the pretty young nurse.

Witnesses' statements seemed to support the police investigators' theory. Laughlin had been seen in the vicinity of the murder and he seemed to have had an extraordinary curiosity concerning the homicide. In addition, Laughlin himself raised suspicions. He knew information that hadn't been released to the press—information known only to the killer. Police were certain they had their murderer. They focused all their attention on building a case against Danny Laughlin, abandoning any further search and refusing to entertain any notion that the Gibbs's murder could be connected to Sims and Blau.

Laughlin spent the next six months in jail awaiting trial. He frequently wrote to his mother describing harassment by jail guards and his fear of prosecution for a murder he continued to deny.

"They've taken DNA samples from me three times," Danny complained to his mother. "They keep coming in my cell asking for hair, blood, and semen. I know I didn't do it. If those tests match, they've been tampered with."

Wilma Hooker wept when she read her son's letters. Trouble had always followed Danny. It began as early as kindergarten, when Danny had been kicked out for misbehaving and happened again in the fifth grade when he was confined to a mental hospital. He had only moved to Texas from Kansas City a short time before Gibbs's murder to protect his sister, a victim of domestic violence. But the pain in Wilma's heart knew the trouble Danny faced in Texas was worse than anything he had yet experienced. She hoped he could hold up under the strain.

"They keep asking me to write out a confession, but I won't. I'm getting really scared," Laughlin wrote his mother. "The guards keep telling me the State is going to give me a lethal injection and give a lethal injection to my dog. If I'm convicted and they do execute me, I want you, sis, and Mr. Katz to be there."

Danny Laughlin's spirit continued to weaken as he waited for trial in an Archer County Jail cell. He talked with other inmates about the crime. He talked to anyone who would listen.

April 8, 1986

Danny Laughlin strolled into the Gainsville courthouse with a legal pad and black-bound Bible tucked in his right hand. The young defendant was clean shaven, with a new short haircut, and a seemingly unconcerned grin on his face. In his white, long-sleeve shirt and neatly pressed khaki pants, Laughlin barely resembled the motorcycle-riding bar-back/dancer arrested months earlier for the death of Toni Gibbs. He walked with an air of confidence, joked with law enforcement officials, then seated himself next to his defense attorney.

On a change of venue, two hundred potential Cook County jurors had been called for the capital murder trial. They packed into the 1910 beaux-arts–style courthouse located in the center of the town square. The impressive brick and limestone building, one of only a few Texas courthouses built in the twentieth century, featured terra-cotta ornamentation, eagle brackets, and a copper-clad dome. It was the site selected to bear the responsibility of accommodating the Laughlin trial in an unbiased manner.

Wichita Falls District Attorney Barry Macha joined Archer County District Attorney Jack McGaughey in prosecuting Laughlin. Once a twelve-member panel had been seated, the two experienced prosecutors began laying out their case.

"Laughlin met Miss Gibbs at the Stardust Club where he worked, and there he made sexual advances toward her," Macha told jurors, setting up the theory that Gibbs had been killed for rejecting Laughlin's advances.

The lighthearted mood Laughlin had taken into court quickly turned to anger. He had told Roger Williams, his court-appointed attorney, that he hadn't known Gibbs personally, but only by sight. The two had only spoken once, briefly in passing at the club. Now the prosecution was portraying him as a cast-off suitor. Laughlin was furious.

Wilma Hooker sat behind her son, her outward composure masking the emotional turmoil inside. Wilma had ridden a bus from Arizona to Texas to be at her son's trial. An unknown benefactor from nearby Olney, Texas, was paying her motel bill. It was a financial strain to be in Gainsville, but Wilma would have made any sacrifice to be there for Danny. She remembered the day she had received a phone call from a stranger in Texas notifying her that Danny had been arrested for murder. She hadn't believed it then, and she didn't believe it now.

The medical examiner from the Southwest Institute of Forensic Sciences explained to jurors about the multiple contusions and bruises on the upper chest of Toni Gibbs. Dark bruises on her left thigh and the left side of her chest were also pointed out. Then, with the aid of graphic photos, the medical examiner showed jurors a one-inch-long, incised wound on the left thumb, stab wounds on Gibbs's chest, and three stab wounds on her back.

Jurors flinched as they stared at the color photos of a young woman's body, ravaged not only by the rage of an out-of-control killer, but also by the ravenous appetites of wild animals. Their eyes drifted from the carnage in the pictures to the man accused of committing the crime.

When Texas Ranger Gerth told jurors that, when questioned, Laughlin had mentioned something about an arm and a leg being eaten off the body, Laughlin's mood descended further into the depths of despondency. "That information had not been released publicly and was knowledge only the killer would have," Gerth stated.

Nikkie Standifer, a CertainTeed Corporation employee and key prosecution witness, testified that she had seen Laughlin in the Archer County field where Miss Gibbs's body was found, prior to its discovery. "It was either on February ninth or tenth," Standifer said.

The prosecutor reminded jurors that Gibbs's body had not been found until February 15.

Laughlin shook his head and mumbled under his breath in frustration. During the morning recess he stomped out of the courtroom. He didn't like the way his trial had started. Macha was twisting the facts, spinning the truth.

When Harry Harrison was called to the stand, Laughlin's mood changed from despair to wrath. He loathed Harrison. Laughlin had first met the career criminal while they were both incarcerated in the Archer County jail. Laughlin's eyes followed Harrison as he sashayed confidently to the witness chair.

"We had just finished eating breakfast and talking

about our military service," Harrison said as he began to talk about his association with Laughlin. Harrison then dropped a courtroom bomb.

"He said he held a knife to her [Gibbs's] throat and held her in the missionary position. When he got through [raping her], he stabbed her and then turned her over and sodomized her. After that, he started crying and said he had found the Lord since then and God would forgive him," Harrison said, with a slight grin of satisfaction directed at Laughlin.

Laughlin was infuriated. He made little effort to hide his aggravation and almost everyone in the courtroom knew he was close to losing control.

"Have you been promised anything by the District Attorney's office in exchange for your testimony?" Defense Attorney Roger Williams asked Harrison.

Although Harrison denied agreeing to any such exchange of information for favors from the DA's office, it was later learned that seventeen charges against Harrison had been expunged from his record.

When Phil "Rocket" Guerieri testified that Laughlin had told him there was no reason to keep looking for the missing nurse, Laughlin again expressed his anger. He vigorously wrote on his yellow legal pad and underlined something so strongly that paper ripped and heads turned in his direction.

Roger Williams turned and spoke quietly to his client, who nodded and sat back peacefully.

The last of a jailhouse trio to testify against Laughlin was Glen Lowrance. He told jurors that Laughlin had told him in the county jail, "I know I'm guilty, but I've got this case beat and I'll be out in two weeks and write to you."

Danny Laughlin remained silent, his head drooped. His mother sat behind him, a hot flash of resentment surging through her body. *Lies, all lies,* she thought.

Wilma Hooker was unfaltering in her belief that Danny didn't kill Toni Gibbs. No one could convince her he had, but it was up to Roger Williams to convince the jury of her son's innocence.

Danny Laughlin had been riding a wave of emotions during the first days of the trial. His initial confidence had slipped away like seaweed drawn back into the ocean. But Laughlin's mood was elevated to a new high when Bob Estrada, a criminal defense attorney hired by a friend of Laughlin, entered the courtroom and took his seat beside his new client and Roger Williams. By the time Williams had finished questioning the first defense witness, Laughlin had resumed his self-assured attitude. His renewed confidence spread to his mother, whose mood had likewise taken a surge upward.

Joyce Gregory, a former bartender at the Stardust, told the jury that Laughlin's job behind the bar would leave him little time to talk to patrons of the club. Her description of Laughlin's work cast doubt that he would have had the opportunity to "hit on" Gibbs at the popular Wichita Falls watering hole. Gregory also stated that she was with Laughlin from about eleven-thirty A.M. until later in the afternoon on the day Gibbs was reported missing.

"I was helping him move into his Fillmore Street apartment and riding around in his pickup truck," Gregory said. "He took me home about five-thirty that afternoon. Then I saw him again later that night at work."

The partial alibi that Gregory was providing for Laughlin infuriated Barry Macha. The tall, handsome district attorney was on his feet ready to attack the witness and her relationship to the defendant on cross-examination.

"You spent quite a bit of time together," Macha said

smartly. "In fact, you spent so much time together it caused you and your boyfriend to break up, didn't it?"

"That's true," Gregory said, "but we were just close friends."

"Didn't you previously tell the grand jury that Laughlin took you home at three or four? Is your memory better today or better then?" Macha demanded angrily.

"It's better today," Gregory said matter-of-factly.

"It's better with age? Like fine wine?" Macha asked sarcastically.

Macha's tone of voice had Williams before the judge objecting to Macha's badgering of the witness.

District Judge Frank Douthitt warned Macha; then Gregory was dismissed.

Lisa Jones, another former Stardust employee, reiterated Gregory's testimony that Laughlin, as part of his job, did not have contact with bar patrons. She also testified Laughlin arrived at work at six-thirty P.M. on January 19.

Laughlin allowed himself a slight smile of satisfaction and his body took on a posture of increased comfort. Things were beginning to go his way.

Bill Blanton, a supervisor for CertainTeed Corporation, slowly walked to the witness chair. Blanton refuted Nikkie Standifer's testimony. The key prosecution witness had testified that she saw Laughlin in the Archer County field where Miss Gibbs's body was before it was discovered by authorities, and that the sighting had taken place on February 9 or 10. Standifer added that she was sure of the dates because she didn't think she had worked either day of that weekend. Blanton disagreed, telling the jury that Standifer had been at work on both days.

Blanton's testimony cast doubt on Standifer's credibility as to when, or even if, she had seen Danny Laughlin in the Archer County field.

Williams, Estrada, and Laughlin were confident as court recessed. Williams hoped to wind up his case the following day. Laughlin left the courthouse in the same talkative mood he had entered with on the first day of the trial. He was scheduled to take the stand the following day. Laughlin looked forward to telling his side of the story. Telling the truth.

The next day, Danny Laughlin sauntered to the witness stand with self-assurance. His shoulders back and head erect, he was the picture of confidence. Laughlin's dark eyes met his mother's and they exchanged smiles.

Laughlin's attorney asked him to explain to the jury what he was doing on the morning of January 19, 1985.

"Joyce Gregory and I did laundry; then we went back to my new apartment on Fillmore Street," Laughlin said.

"What did Joyce do?" Williams asked.

"She was hanging pictures for me," Laughlin answered.

The defendant then explained that he and Gregory later went to a flea market on Holliday Street, then up Midwestern Parkway.

"We drove through the Burger King and I got a root beer and Joyce got a Coke," Laughlin said. "We cruised Kemp Boulevard and then I took Joyce home. I got home by five-thirty P.M. to get ready to go to work."

"What were you doing on February tenth, Mr. Laughlin?" Williams asked.

Laughlin shifted uneasily in his chair. He would have to tell the jury about breaking into the telephone office and stealing the money box. But being convicted of theft was better than being found guilty of murder.

"I entered a Southwestern Bell office in Wichita Falls and stole a money-changer box. I got the code to open the door to the building from someone who worked there. I'd been working for a maintenance company in the office for a while.

"I loaded the heavy box in my pickup truck to take it out of town to break into it. I went out on a county road and broke into the box.

"After taking the money, I left it there and was chased part of the way back to Wichita Falls by someone who saw me," Laughlin explained.

Williams walked to the witness stand and leaned closer to his client. Looking Laughlin in the eye, Williams asked, "Did you tell Harry Harrison that you killed Miss Gibbs?"

"No!" Laughlin said loudly. "In fact, Harrison was so nervous that day in the jail that I tried to calm him down by reading scriptures to him."

"Danny, how did you know facts about Gibbs's murder?" Williams asked.

"I knew police information about the crime by reading reports one day in a captain's office. I was left there for about a half hour when he was out.

"I bragged to friends about knowing details of her death, to look like I knew something. When I talked about the killing and said I might have been in that field at one time with my dog, people acted interested. I just kept talking," Laughlin explained.

"Did you ever say you killed Toni Gibbs?" Williams asked.

"Not one time," Laughlin replied. "Not one time did I ever imply I was the killer. I never admitted nothing."

Williams had one final question for his client. After

a dramatic pause, Williams asked, "Danny, tell the ladies and gentlemen of the jury—did you kill Toni Gibbs?"

"No, I did not. I had nothing to do with it," Laughlin said emphatically.

After final arguments were presented from both prosecutors and the defense, the case was turned over to the jury for deliberations. It was a difficult case with very differing opinions. Argumentative shouts could be heard from the jury room. At times even muffled sobs rose from behind the closed door. As time continued to pass, prosecutors became increasingly uneasy and defense attorneys more certain that their client would be found not guilty.

The jury finally emerged from the confined quarters, some with tear-streaked faces, others with wearied looks. They had worked for fourteen hours over a two-day period to reach a decision. But they were hopelessly deadlocked eleven to one for acquittal. Judge Douthitt declared a mistrial and Laughlin left the courthouse with his attorneys.

Although he was not found innocent of the vicious murder of Toni Gibbs, Laughlin saw the hung jury as a victory.

"I thank the Man right here," Laughlin said, smiling, pointing at the Bible he had carried into the courtroom each day of the trial. "If they let me, I imagine I would give people some hugs. Anyway, I'd like to thank the jury."

Laughlin's attorney blasted the State's witnesses. "They never made a case until they scrounged up the jailhouse witnesses," Williams told reporters outside the courtroom. "Would you make any important decision in your life based on what those gentlemen told you?"

District Attorney Barry Macha was not only disappointed, but furious with the outcome. Convinced that he had prosecuted the right man, he pledged to retry Laughlin for Gibbs's murder. Local law enforcement agreed, virtually shutting down any further investigation of Gibbs's killing. Their tunnel vision saw only one man responsible for the brutal killing—Danny Laughlin.

Chapter Eight

May 6, 1986

Tina Kimbrew chased after her black toy poodle as he slipped past her at the door and made a break for the street. Still dressed in her nightgown, the cute, slim, twenty-one-year-old had been sleeping late after her night shift as waitress and bartender at Baron's Lounge at the Sheraton Hotel.

"Come here, Nicole!" Tina said sternly to the feisty pup. She grabbed the quick-footed dog and carried her back to her apartment.

Minutes later, neighbors saw a tall, thin man, wearing a blue-and-white baseball cap, knock on Tina's front door.

The gangly man was coming down from a drug-induced high. He needed a fix. He knew Tina and thought she might be able to supply him with the narcotics he craved.

Tina had met the man at the Stardust country-and-western club where he had worked as a bouncer and Danny Laughlin had once worked as a bar-back. Originally from Vernon, Texas, Tina had recently moved to Wichita Falls from Odessa, Texas, where she had been attending private school. She and her visitor had dated a couple of times, but it was nothing more than a casual relationship. Tina cordially opened the door to him.

The young woman's pleasant disposition changed as soon as the door closed behind the unkempt man. He grabbed her, forcing his lips to hers. Tina pulled away, pushing against his chest to release his viselike grip. Her dark brown hair swung swiftly to the side as her head rang with the impact of the man's open hand against her cheek. Kimbrew stumbled backward, falling against a brown wicker table. The next blow was her attacker's fist connecting with Tina's right eye. It throbbed from the impact. Her knees buckled and she dropped to the floor.

In seconds, the man she thought to be her friend was on top of her, slapping her, punching her face with quick-tempered blows. The right side of both her top and bottom lips swelled, immediately discoloring from the blood that rose just below the surface. She fought to regain her footing, clawing her way to the sofa. Tina Kimbrew pulled at the cushions to help her stand, but they tumbled to the carpet as her aggressor knocked her down.

The incensed man pulled at Tina's underpants, jerking them from her body. She continued to fight. Although he was more than one hundred pounds heavier and over a foot taller, Tina was determined to ward off the assault. The man's greatest advantage was his intense anger. Rage that drove him to seek domination. To have complete control.

Kimbrew pressed her elbows into the carpeted surface of the living room as she attempted to rise. The man pushed her back and slipped his hands around her neck, squeezing firmly. The thin gold necklace that encircled her throat pressed into her flesh, scraping the surface raw. Tina's elbows dug deeply into the rug's abrasive fibers.

Kimbrew continued to struggle. The man slung his forearm over her nose and mouth, compressing tightly. Her small frame flailed beneath the strength of her attacker for no more than a few seconds. The blood vessels to her brain collapsed. Her eyes held but a flicker of light until the continued pressure on her throat extinguished it like a candle being snuffed out. She sank into total blackness.

The man who had once called Tina Kimbrew his friend gaped at her lifeless body in disbelief. Quickly he fled the Park Regency Apartments and the sight of the white-gowned body stretched across the brown carpet. He returned to his own apartment. No one was there. He felt all alone. A familiar feeling, one he had felt since he was a kid. No one to talk to. No one to listen to his problems.

He lay across his bed, staring at the ceiling. In the swirls of the textured dome he saw the face of Tina Kimbrew staring back at him. Closing his eyes was useless; he could still see her looking at him with questioning eyes. "Why?" she seemed to ask. He couldn't tell her. He didn't know why. All he knew was that he needed to get away. Out of Wichita Falls.

The ocean, he thought. *I'd like to see the ocean.*

Shelly Kelly and Tina Kimbrew were close—more like sisters than cousins. They had seen each other frequently since Kimbrew's move to Wichita Falls from Odessa three months earlier. Kelly had expected to see Tina at the Wichita Falls hospital where Tina's mother was recovering from back surgery, but Tina hadn't shown up since the night before. It was three P.M. when Shelly phoned Tina's apartment.

"There's no answer," Shelly told her grandmother who had accompanied her and her two-year-old daughter, Amy, to the hospital.

"We need to go by her apartment and check on her. She needs to come see her mom," Mildred Kimbrew said.

Kelly drove to the Park Regency Apartments on Seymour Road where Tina Kimbrew lived alone. She noticed Tina's car parked out front.

"There's no answer," Shelly told her grandmother. "She must have gotten a ride with someone. Her car's here."

Amy's angelic face was a mess from the candy she had been given at the hospital. Kelly decided to clean the child's dirty hands before heading home.

"Let's go inside and clean Amy up," she said.

As Shelly turned the spare key Tina had given her grandmother in the lock of the apartment, she was met at the door by Tina's poodle, Nicole, jumping and barking loudly.

She glanced to the right, inside the apartment, noticing that a table and lamp had been knocked over.

"Look what that dog did to this apartment," Shelly said irritably. One leg of the wicker table had been broken, a gold glass ashtray with cigarette butts was spilled on the carpet, and a can of Sergant's flea powder had been dumped on the floor. Beside the sofa was a plastic tumbler and a Styrofoam cup from the Sonic Drive-In.

As Kelly moved farther into the seemingly empty room, she noticed her cousin lying motionless on the floor.

She must be unconscious. Maybe she fell, Shelly thought to herself as she moved closer to Tina.

Tina was lying on her back, next to a brown floral pillow that had been pulled from the sofa. Her dark brown hair was drawn above her head and spread across the lighter brown carpeting. She wore a white-lace nightgown that was pulled above her waist. Her underpants lay nearby.

Stunned, Shelly grabbed Amy and backed up slowly to rest against the wall. She could only stare at her cousin's face in horror. Frozen with fear, Shelly couldn't move. She could hardly breathe.

Mildred Kimbrew rushed to Tina, shaking her gently in an attempt to wake her up. Bruises marred the familiar pretty face.

"Shelly, she's dead! I can't look at her like this. Let's get something to cover her up," the older woman said, shaking.

Shelly rushed to the bedroom and returned with a pink, blue, and white floral sheet. She draped the fabric over Tina and called the police.

Detective Steve Pruitt was on his way home when he received the radio call.

"There's a report of a deceased person at the Park Regency Apartments." The dispatcher's voice broke through Pruitt's thoughts.

Pruitt, an investigator in the Crimes Against Persons Division of the Wichita Falls Police Department, turned his car around and headed toward the apartments. When he arrived on the scene, Officer Allen was inside, checking the victim on the floor for signs of life.

Allen looked up at Pruitt as he entered the room. He shook his head slightly, lowering his eyes to the pale woman on the floor in front of him.

Pruitt removed the sheet covering the corpse. He looked at Tina Kimbrew's body carefully, making mental notes: light-colored nightgown, bruising on face, neck, and legs, exposed genitals, panties close to the body on the floor.

"Who put the sheet over the victim?" Pruitt asked.

"I did. But I didn't touch anything. I didn't know what to do," Shelly Kelly said through her tears.

Pruitt feared that the presence of the victim's relatives would hamper the investigation. They very well could have contaminated the crime scene. He moved to get Kelly, Amy, and Mrs. Kimbrew out of the apartment as quickly as possible.

Tina Kimbrew was the fourth woman killed in Wichita Falls in eighteen months. Everything had to be done to insure a thorough investigation. This was one murder Pruitt intended to see did not go unsolved.

Neighbors told investigators they had seen a man leaving the apartment about five hours before her body was discovered. The man was described as six-feet, two-inches tall, lanky, dark hair, and wearing a blue-and-white baseball cap. Police released the description to the press, adding, "We'd sure like to talk to him."

The chief of police knew that was an understatement. Four young women had been murdered in the Wichita Falls area. Four killers were on the loose. Maybe they would get lucky with this one.

Chapter Nine

A tall, shaggy-haired man stood on the seawall in Galveston, Texas. A cool breeze from the Gulf of Mexico blew across his weary face as he stared into the vastness of the open sea. The dark waters mirrored his mood. Riddled with guilt, he felt as though he had been plunged beneath the gulf's surf and was drowning in a sea of despair.

Back in Wichita Falls, friends of Tina Kimbrew couldn't believe Tina was dead.

"She was funny. Always a jokester," Tim Nardi, general manager of the Sheraton Hotel, told reporters. "This is such a shock. You don't think about these things until they happen in your own backyard."

Tina was remembered by all her friends as being a really sweet, nice girl. Her killer remembered her the same way. That memory drove him deeper into despondency.

In Vernon, Texas, north of Wichita Falls, Elaine and Robert Kimbrew felt the same darkened hopelessness. Their only child was dead. The pain in Elaine's heart was sharper than the surgeon's instrument used to mend her back only days before.

Tina had been a gift from God. Elaine and Robert had been told early in their marriage that they would never have children. Then, in what they believed was a true miracle, Tina was conceived. It had been a touch-and-go pregnancy, but Elaine was determined to deliver their child.

In what could be described as a difficult delivery, Robert was faced with the decision of saving the life of his wife or saving his child. But by the grace of God, and the skill of a special doctor, both mother and daughter pulled through. The birth had created an extraordinary bond between them.

Robert, a small man in stature with a big heart filled with love for his daughter, had been brought to his knees by Tina's death. Likewise, his wife's grief was inconsolable. Swallowed by the blackness of their loss, the Kimbrews sank into the depths of depression.

The same feelings of depression and despair gripped Tina Kimbrew's killer as he stood on the concrete seawall in Galveston. His personal failures plunged him into hopelessness. He thought of all the people he had disappointed and deceived. His victims. Their families. His own family.

Exhausted from the more than four-hundred-mile trip from his North Texas home to the southern Texas coastal island, he checked into a local, low-rate motel. It had been a week since the murder of Tina Kimbrew. Fatigue embraced him. Guilt consumed him. He couldn't sleep. He reached for the phone on the nightstand and dialed the local emergency number.

"I'm going to kill myself," he told the Galveston 911 operator.

Within minutes, officers were at his door.

"Why would you want to kill yourself?" one of the officers asked the man who sat on the wrinkled, faded bedspread of his motel room.

"I killed someone in Wichita Falls," the somber

man said. He lowered his head, cradling it in his hands.

"Who did you kill?" another officer asked.

"Tina Kimbrew," he responded. "I went to Tina's apartment on May sixth. She was wearing a light-colored nightgown when she answered the door. I went inside to get drugs."

The questioning officer glanced at his partner. The young policemen knew instantly what had to be done. The man was immediately placed in protective custody.

Within hours of hearing from the Galveston Police, Detective Steve Pruitt had secured an arrest warrant from Justice of the Peace Arthur Williams for Faryion Edward Wardrip. According to the warrant, Wardrip had said he knew Kimbrew and had gone to her apartment the day the body was discovered. Pruitt and another officer drove to the Gulf Coast city to pick up their prisoner.

"I didn't mean to kill her. It was an accident. She was my friend," Wardrip said in a sad tone as he rode in the rear seat of the police car.

"You don't have to say anything," Pruitt advised Wardrip. "You'll get an attorney in Wichita Falls."

"I just went to get drugs. I didn't mean to do it," Wardrip said, as though he had an uncontrollable need to explain the murder.

Pruitt was cautious not to ask Wardrip any direct questions about the Kimbrew murder for fear of violating his rights. Wardrip would be arraigned in magistrate court in Wichita Falls. If he was indeed their killer, Pruitt wasn't about to mess up the case on a technicality.

Deciding to stick to casual conversation, Pruitt asked, "Did you know Ellen Blau?"

"Yes," Wardrip said. "I knew Ellen."

Pruitt knew that Ellen Blau's killing was one of the

unsolved murders that had made young women in the
Wichita Falls area fearful in the few preceding months.
The Blau case was officially under the jurisdiction of
the Wichita County Sheriff's Department. Pruitt made
a mental note. *Call the sheriff and tell him he might want
to interview Wardrip about Blau.*

Pruitt decided to avoid any further questions about
Blau and didn't ask about the Archer County case of
Toni Gibbs or the Wichita Falls death of Terry Sims.
Pruitt, like other interdepartmental detectives, continued to believe there was no relationship between the
murders of any of the four women who had been killed
in the far North Texas area. And there was certainly no
reason to suspect Wardrip, who hadn't been mentioned
as a suspect.

As the county-issued car rolled down the interstate
highway, Wardrip thought to himself, *I'm going to
prison. But I can't be there for the rest of my life. I just can't.
I couldn't take it.*

He remained tight-lipped in the rear seat, his head
resting on the seat back.

"Why were you in Galveston?" Pruitt asked, inter-
rupting Faryion's fearful thoughts.

"I wanted to see the Gulf of Mexico," Wardrip replied.

Within hours of arriving back in Wichita Falls,
twenty-seven-year-old Faryion Edward Wardrip was arraigned for the murder of Tina Kimbrew. Dressed in
blue jeans, secured at the waist by a leather belt with
a large, oval, metal buckle, Wardrip stood beside his
public defender, Christine Harris, before the magistrate court judge. The open collar of his wrinkled
short-sleeve, plaid shirt revealed the top of a white T-
shirt. Scuff marks marred his light-colored cowboy

boots. Wardrip's brown hair was full and unruly. The stubble of growth on his cheeks and chin made it apparent he hadn't shaved in days. His brown mustache was as shaggy and unkempt as his hair. Wardrip looked tired. His eyelids drooped as he stood slumped before the judge.

"Hold your hands out, palms up," the booking officer instructed.

"I don't know how I got those cuts on my hands," Wardrip said.

Police officers carefully documented the cuts on Wardrip's long, thin fingers and large hands.

A witness identified the clothing Wardrip was wearing at the time of his arrest as looking like the clothes worn by a man seen going into Kimbrew's apartment about eleven-thirty the morning of the murder. It was one of the last times Tina Kimbrew had been seen alive.

Detective Pruitt called Tom Callahan of the Wichita Falls Sheriff's Department and informed him of Wardrip's confession to the murder of Tina Kimbrew and his statement that he had known Ellen Blau. It was all Pruitt could do. The Blau case was in the jurisdiction of the county sheriff. It was up to Callahan and the sheriff to follow up.

News of the arrest of Faryion Wardrip for the murder of Tina Kimbrew spread rapidly through Wichita Falls. Three days after Wardrip's arrest, Thomas Eugene Granger, a friend of Wardrip's, contacted the Wichita Falls Police with astonishing news.

"I have information about Faryion Wardrip," Granger told them. "He had a connection with all those girls who were killed.

"He worked at General Hospital at the time of Gibbs's and Sims's murders and knew them both. Wardrip also lived across the street from the Subs 'N Suds

on Sheppard Access. Wardrip quit the General right
after the Gibbs killing and moved away right after the
girl at Subs 'N Suds was killed. He moved out on Airport Drive.

"Wardrip had a black-handled knife with a double
edge that was six inches long. He liked boot knives,"
Granger said.

Granger's statement was placed in a file to be passed
up the chain of command, but somehow the statement
never became part of the official investigative file on
the unsolved murders. This was partially because
Wichita Falls Police and the Wichita County district
attorney continued to believe that they were after
more than one perpetrator. The DA's office was still
convinced that Danny Laughlin was responsible for
killing Toni Gibbs. It was as though the DA and police
had tunnel vision. Laughlin was their prime suspect
and had failed a polygraph. Therefore, they disregarded or ignored evidence that pointed to any other
person. Granger's statement stalled in the system. No
one apparently ever investigated his claim that Wardrip may have had something to do with not only Kimbrew, whom he had confessed to killing, but the
murders of Sims, Gibbs, and Blau as well. Information
that may have solved the murders had fallen through
the cracks.

Disturbed by the police's apparent disinterest in
Wardrip as a suspect, Granger went to work for Ray
Cannedy, a Wichita Falls private investigator. Although
the links between Wardrip and the unsolved murders
were only circumstantial, it convinced the private investigators that Wardrip should be considered a suspect in all the killings. Granger and Cannedy took
their report to the police.

"I just went around asking people that both of us
knew, where he lived, where he worked. I was basically

looking into his past," Granger told police. "I was thinking, 'My God. This guy had the opportunity each time.' And he killed one girl already. He was at all the sites."

Police dutifully took Cannedy's and Granger's report, but Granger could see that their suspicions were falling on deaf ears.

Back at Cannedy's office, Granger let off steam.

"They looked at us like we were a bunch of idiots!" Granger shouted. "It upsets me. He's getting away with all this stuff and no one is looking into it."

Granger had cause for frustration. Even after his second statement to authorities, Wardrip was disregarded as a suspect in any of the other three women's deaths.

Police steadfastly stood by proven police procedures as a team of officers investigated the unsolved cases. They recanvassed the areas and talked again to neighbors, acquaintances, coworkers, and family. The chief of police was confident in his officers' abilities as he boasted of a homicide clearance rate that recorded nine out of eleven cases solved in 1985.

The Ellen Blau murder was one of the two unsolved cases.

Chapter Ten

The realization of what he had done and how his family was going to take the news of his confession to murder ate away at Faryion Wardrip. He had to soften the blow. Make up some excuse for his actions.

"Bryce, I killed her," Wardrip told his younger brother from the Wichita Falls jail. "I had given her more than one hundred thousand dollars of drugs to sell. I went to her apartment, there were no drugs and no money. I told her I'd give her a couple of hours to get the money; then I called my connection in Mexico. He told me to take care of her, then go to Mexico. He told me I'd be okay. But he set me up and I was arrested."

Bryce was overwhelmed by his brother's confession. Faryion hadn't always been admirable, especially when he was on drugs, but Bryce couldn't imagine that his brother could possibly be a killer.

Although Faryion Edward Wardrip was the fourth child of nine born to Diana and George Wardrip of Marion, Indiana, he often felt as though he were an only child. He frequently had feelings of depression and loneliness. As a boy, he'd cried easily. When he'd tried to reach out for help, he'd been told it was merely a phase he would soon grow out of.

School hadn't offered much more than his family in the way of support. Classmates made fun of Wardrip's hand-me-down clothing and he experienced a sense of worthlessness compared to more affluent students. Wardrip wanted to fit in, but he always felt he had come from the "wrong side of the tracks." His father worked in a local factory; his mother was a homemaker responsible for raising the nine Wardrip children. Although there was always food on the table, clothes on their backs, and toys for their enjoyment, Faryion Wardrip wanted more. He wanted the respect of others. In his mind he failed to live up to the wealthy, macho American ideal. He felt like a failure.

Increasing his feelings of inadequacy, Wardrip had a history of academic failure due to a learning disability. He spent the majority of his academic years in special-education classes. The lack of success in school had created in Wardrip a sense of low self-esteem, and no vision for the future. His melancholy spirit and sense of disconnection with his family grew with each passing year. He felt he was falling into an abyss of despair from which he couldn't emerge. His frustrations were manifested in rebellious, unacceptable ways.

At thirteen, young Wardrip was arrested for shoplifting. The juvenile court believed justice would be best served by the youthful offender picking beans in a Marion, Indiana, downtown community garden. It hadn't seemed like much of a punishment to Wardrip, who actually enjoyed harvesting the crops each Saturday. He walked the rows of beans, stripping them from their vines with a new-found sense of accomplishment.

Later, stealing a bicycle from a neighbor's yard and not getting caught hadn't taught Wardrip any lessons either. Young Wardrip thought he was indestructible. Unaccountable.

At fourteen, Wardrip began to drink a little alcohol, smoke a little pot. As he aged, Wardrip graduated to harder, more destructive drugs. Acid took him on trips far away from the frustrations of school and family. He would argue with his father, take a hit of that day's drug-of-choice, then argue with his father even more. It had become a vicious circle.

Wardrip's only school successes came in athletic venues rather than in the classroom. He was a competitive swimmer, played basketball, and ran track. However, his small sports victories didn't make up for his great classroom failures. Feelings of inadequacies became a cloak Wardrip wore throughout the seasons.

Wardrip's bomb of discontent detonated at home. He and his father seemed to be at odds most of the time. The younger Wardrip's anger, stuffed just below the surface, had grown like a snowball gaining momentum as it tumbled down a steep slope. The avalanche of emotions erupted when George Wardrip finally demanded that his oldest son move out of his house.

Faryion Wardrip had been seventeen years old at the time. His father had paid a couple of hundred dollars for his son's first car. When the car was missing for several days, George Wardrip demanded to know where it was.

"My friend blew his engine in his truck so I pulled the engine out of my car and stuck it in his truck," young Wardrip explained, wondering why his father was so irritated.

George Wardrip was more than irritated, he was furious. It had been one more example of Faryion's irresponsibility.

"Go upstairs and pack your stuff. I want you out," George Wardrip said angrily.

His son walked up the stairs of the Wardrip home, packed his clothes in paper bags, and walked out the front door. He couldn't believe his parents were throwing him out. None of the other Wardrip children had ever been asked to leave the family home. Tears rose in his eyes.

"Faryion, come back," his mother called from the front porch.

Relief flooded her son. *They were just trying to scare me. They aren't really throwing me out,* Faryion thought.

He turned and walked happily back to the house. Relief relaxed his tense shoulders and put a bounce in his step.

"Give me your key," his mother said, her hand outstretched.

"Ya'll mean it?" the stunned teen asked.

"Yes, we mean it," his father said.

Their son handed the house key to his mother, turned, and walked away. Clutching the sacks of clothes tightly, he cried like a baby. It was time for him to set his own course.

Faryion Wardrip dropped out of high school, having only completed the tenth grade. He was restless and on his own. He spent the majority of his time taking a hit from a marijuana joint or experimenting with speed. He needed a direction to his life, a focus.

The army seemed the key to Wardrip's problem. He enlisted in the Indiana National Guard and was shipped off to boot camp. But instead of helping him develop a positive attitude, the discipline and structured regiment was too much for Wardrip to handle. He didn't like drills or orders. He made it through the grueling six-week program with the aid of a few joints and a handful of black mollies. Then Wardrip was shipped back to Indiana to serve his meager commitment of one weekend a month and two weeks during the summers.

The pledge he had taken to protect his country was all but forgotten when he stepped foot in his home state. For months he failed to show up for monthly maneuvers. Finally, the army released him with a "less than honorable" discharge.

Wardrip bounced from job to job. He didn't work to build a career. He worked to buy drugs.

George Wardrip moved his family to Texas in search of work. Faryion tagged along, adrift in a sea of indecision and irresponsibility.

While living in Wichita Falls, Wardrip met Johnna Jackson at a local club. The short, plump, dark-haired girl took an instant liking to the tall, lanky Wardrip. Within a short time they were married.

It was a rocky union from the beginning. Wardrip couldn't keep a steady job and Johnna was content to lounge on the sofa, watch television, and have babies. He wondered where the fun-loving girl he met in the bar had gone and when Johnna had turned into a wallflower, someone who didn't speak until spoken to. He had encouraged her to get a job, but she didn't want to work. Her greatest ambition was to be a mother and housewife. That would have been okay with Wardrip if the bills didn't need to be paid. There were responsibilities—obligations he himself neglected in favor of an instant high. He needed Johnna to help out. He needed her to listen to him, to hear his concerns. But instead, she shut him out, barely speaking to him when he was home. When she did listen, he felt as though she never really heard what he was saying.

The old familiar anger of his youth returned. The

drugs took over his thinking. He wanted to lash out. Johnna became a convenient target.

They fought often about his inability to keep a job, and his failure to provide for his family. He more often than not used their money for drugs, not food.

Johnna's mother and stepfather attempted to help. They had let the struggling couple move in with them on several occasions. Floyd Jackson had even given Faryion five thousand dollars to help them out, but within two weeks it was gone. Smoked up or shot up, Wardrip couldn't remember. Floyd had been furious.

"Faryion is the type of person who would climb a tree to tell a lie rather than stand on the ground to tell the truth," Floyd told his wife. "He's lied about almost everything and every story has come back to haunt him. It's like when he told us he ran into a sign post; then we found out a friend had beat the hell out of him."

Wardrip had worked ten different jobs during Johnna's first pregnancy. Then, trying to appease the Jacksons and regain Johnna's trust, Wardrip had taken a job at Wichita General. He thought he was too good to be pushing a mop and quit soon after a young nurse named Toni Gibbs was found murdered in an Archer County field.

He tried fast-food jobs, working at a Pizza Inn near Sheppard Air Force Base, then quit as suddenly as he had at Wichita General.

During his latest unemployment streak, the Jacksons had taken Johnna and Wardrip's two children into their home, but refused to let Faryion live with them. It had been an ugly scene. Jackson had tired of paying their rent, and buying their groceries while his son-in-law bounced from job to job. He finally put his foot down.

"I'll come get you and the kids," Jackson told

Johnna, "but Faryion is not coming back to our home."

Johnna had talked with her husband and he reluctantly agreed.

Jackson had arrived at his daughter's and son-in-law's apartment, ready to pack up Johnna and the kids to take them home. Faryion was nowhere in sight, then suddenly appeared as they were almost ready to leave.

"Hi," Wardrip said, obviously high from a fresh dose of drugs. He bitterly sneered at his father-in-law. "You can't take my family."

Without warning Wardrip grabbed his baby daughter, refusing to give her up.

"You don't have any money," Jackson said. "Johnna and the kids need a place to live."

Jackson's reasoning fell on deaf ears. Wardrip was angry. Mad at Jackson for being right. Furious at himself for putting drugs before his family.

Suddenly, Wardrip tossed the baby in the air toward Paulette Jackson. The loving grandmother caught her, then pressed her protectively to her breast.

"I always wanted a piece of you," Wardrip sneered at Jackson, taking a step forward.

Before Wardrip could react, Jackson hit his son-in-law squarely in the face. Wardrip's knees buckled and he slumped to the ground.

"I'm going to get help," Wardrip said, his large hand covering his face. He bolted up the stairs.

Floyd, Paulette, Johnna, and the children were in the Jacksons' car pulling away from the apartment when Wardrip reappeared, a butcher knife grasped in his right hand. He angrily waved the weapon in the air at his departing father-in-law.

A short time later, Wardrip showed up at the Jacksons' home.

"Come out here!" Wardrip shouted from the porch.

Jackson opened the door, a .357 Magnum in his hand. Police sirens screeched in the background as Wardrip fled.

After three years of a rocky marriage, Johnna filed for divorce. Wardrip loved his wife, but at the same time hated her. He didn't understand why she couldn't help him or why she couldn't stick it out. The anger inside him grew to an intense, overbearing level. He wanted to hurt her. Hurt her as much as he felt hurt. But Johnna was the mother of his children; there was no way he would ever harm her.

In the midst of his intense anger, frustration, and drug-induced stupor, Wardrip had happened upon Tina Kimbrew. It hadn't been Tina's pretty face that looked up at him with terror in its eyes, it had been Johnna's. It wasn't Tina he had strangled the life out of. It had been Johnna.

As Bryce Wardrip hung up the phone after talking to his older brother, he shook his head. He couldn't believe his brother had committed murder. There had only been one time in recent years that he had seen his brother display any violent behavior.

Bryce had been at his brother's and sister-in-law's apartment when Faryion struck Johnna, blackening her eye.

"If you want to be a man, take on a man," Bryce had barked at his brother. The two Wardrip brothers commenced to "get it on," as Bryce later described the incident.

But Wardrip wasn't in jail for a domestic spat that ended in a black eye. This was murder.

"We were both on drugs. It just got out of hand," Wardrip said. "Bryce, you have to tell Mom and Dad."

A knot the size of a Texas horse apple formed in Bryce's stomach. How on earth was he going to tell his mother and father that one of their children had just confessed to murder?

Chapter Eleven

A withdrawn Faryion Wardrip sat at a table in the Wichita County courthouse as members of the grand jury filed in and took their seats. The district attorney was prepared to present evidence against Wardrip, but the jury would determine whether the facts and accusations presented by the prosecutor warranted an indictment and eventual trial of the accused for the murder of Tina Kimbrew.

District Attorney Barry Macha reviewed for the panel a copy of the arrest warrant which indicated that Faryion Wardrip admitted knowing Tina Kimbrew and having gone to her apartment the day her body was discovered. The warrant also cited a witness who had identified Waldrip's clothing as that worn by a man seen going into Kimbrew's apartment at eleven-thirty A.M., the last time Tina had been seen alive.

In a written document, Wardrip stated that he had gone to Tina Kimbrew's apartment to solicit drugs and that she had answered the door wearing a light-colored nightgown. He asserted that murder had not been on his mind.

"I didn't mean to kill her. I just went to get drugs. It was an accident—she was my friend," Wardrip's statement read.

A somber and seemingly remorseful Faryion Wardrip dropped his head and averted his eyes from the jury. He was indeed sorry for the death of Tina Kimbrew. He knew he would probably spend some time in prison, but he couldn't bear the thought of spending the rest of his life there.

The evidence, the confession, the witnesses' statements all asserted that Wardrip was the killer. The grand jury had no recourse but to indict him for the murder of Tina Kimbrew. A bond of seventy-five thousand dollars was set.

In a separate action, having nothing to do with the case against Wardrip, the same grand jury also considered evidence in the murder of Ellen Blau. It was the third time in June of 1986 that jurors reviewed the case. There was no new information. No solid suspects. The investigation had been hampered by the lack of physical evidence, including the cause of death. The jury wasn't privy to the statements by private investigators Granger and Cannedy concerning their suspicions of the man the jury had just indicted for the murder of Tina Kimbrew. They were unaware that Wardrip had told Wichita Falls officers that he knew Ellen Blau. For lack of any specific information concerning the identity of Ellen Blau's killer, the grand jury took no action. Grand jurors were disappointed at the stalemate in the Blau case, but pleased that they had indicted at least one of the killers of young women in and around Wichita Falls. Faryion Wardrip would stand trial for the murder of Tina Kimbrew and Danny Laughlin would be retried for the murder of Toni Gibbs. Jurors only hoped the killer or killers of Sims and Blau would soon be apprehended.

* * *

George Wardrip and his wife, Diana, were devastated by their son's indictment. The couple tearfully clung to one another for strength in facing some of their darkest days. They had known for some time that their son was troubled—his drug and alcohol addictions had signaled that—but they couldn't conceive that Faryion had taken the life of another person. In their minds he wasn't a killer. He was good with kids, often served as the mediator in family disputes, and was a fun-loving jokester. Even with his addictions, how could their son be capable of killing someone?

The Wardrips finally had to accept the fact that Faryion had indeed taken the life of Tina Kimbrew. But they vowed not to abandon him. They visited him in jail, sent money for commissary items like snack foods and toiletries, and kept in touch by phone. They would do all they could to help Faryion out of the dismal pit of sin he had plummeted into.

In December 1986, Faryion Wardrip, after pleading guilty to the murder of Tina Kimbrew, was sentenced to thirty-five years in the Texas Department of Criminal Justice (TDCJ) institutional division. Thirtieth District Court Judge Calvin Ashley pronounced the sentence after Faryion's public defender, Christine Harris, and District Attorney Barry Macha informed the court of a plea agreement between their two offices.

"Faryion's always been willing to take responsibility for Tina's death. It's just been a matter of what the sentence will be," Harris told reporters following the sentencing.

Wardrip had informed his attorney of his desire to turn his life around and to pursue an education while in prison.

"He has one of the better attitudes I've ever seen

as far as the outlook of what he's facing," Harris said. The young attorney was convinced that her client would seize all the opportunities afforded him at TDCJ.

Wardrip had successfully persuaded his attorney that he sought change in his life; convincing her to go to bat for him. Wardrip knew that after serving only a portion of his sentence, unlike Tina Kimbrew, he would be able to go home again.

The tall pine trees along Interstate 45 reached toward the sky like prisoners grasping for freedom. Wardrip watched the stately pines, covered at the base of their trunks with a drape of blue bonnets, yellow black-eyed Susans, and red Indian paintbrushes, pass by his window. The Texas wildflowers and regal pines reminded him of Christmas trees hugged by colorful tree skirts. He was on his way to Huntsville, headquarters for the largest state-operated prison system in the United States.

Wardrip's first stop was at the diagnostic unit, where he was given both physical and psychological assessments, as well as a haircut and shave. Under the TDCJ rules, male offenders had to be clean shaven and had to keep their hair trimmed up the back of their necks and head, and neatly cut around the ears.

Wardrip's longish-brown hair fell to the floor as the prison barber gave him a TDCJ-issue trim. It reminded Wardrip of his brief and not so memorable time in the army.

Once Wardrip had been judged physically sound, except for diabetes that was under control, the TDCJ psychologist began a battery of tests.

Wardrip sat at the table across from the counselor. His dark hair was neatly parted and combed to the left, the close cut making his face appear longer and thinner than before. Without the scraggly beard and mustache, Wardrip was somewhat handsome.

"This is the block design test," the female psychologist said, spreading blocks and a board in front of Wardrip. "I want you to put each of the blocks in the proper hole. This is a timed test. Do you understand?"

Wardrip nodded. The psychologist pressed the button on the chrome-plated stopwatch. Wardrip worked with lightning speed, his long, thin fingers maneuvering the blocks into the proper slots. He completed the task in under six seconds.

"That's the fastest I've ever had anyone put the blocks in the correct slots," the psychologist said, smiling. "Do you mind doing it again?"

Wardrip, who had rarely been praised, was elated by the compliment. "Sure," he said.

Again the button on the chrome watch was compressed and the sweeping hand on the watch began to move.

"Six seconds," she said again.

Wardrip swelled with pride. "What's this test for?" he asked.

"It's to determine your space perception and planning skills," she said. "To be able to put the patterns together so we can determine how your brain works. It'll help in determining what kind of work you are best suited for. In your case, you are very mechanically minded and are probably artistic."

"That's right," Wardrip said proudly. "I'm an artist."

Wardrip finally received his TDCJ classification and was assigned to one of the more than one hundred facilities operated by the Texas Department of Criminal Justice. At twenty-seven, Wardrip was one of just under a hundred thousand inmates incarcerated in

the TDCJ system and he fell into the twenty-eight percent of Caucasians.

Wardrip sat in his cell staring at the institutional
green walls. He knew he had to do something to
change his circumstances. He wanted to be free of
confinement. He had a choice. He could become bitter and resentful toward the system, as many of his
fellow prisoners had obviously become, or he could
work toward making the most of the time he had to
serve. He glanced at the black-bound Bible on the bed
beside him. Someone had left the book in his cell
shortly after he had arrived. He picked up the Bible
and began to read.

Passages surged through Wardrip like bolts of
lightning striking a rod.

*"For God so loved the world that he gave His only begotten
Son, that whosoever believeth in Him should not perish, but
have everlasting life."*

*"And shall come forth; they that have done good, unto
the resurrection of life; and they that have done evil, unto
the resurrection of damnation."*

*"If ye continue in my word, then are ye my disciples indeed;
And ye shall know the truth, and the truth shall make you
free."*

Wardrip rested the open book in his lap. *If I know
the truth, the truth will make me free,* he thought. He
wanted to be free, released from the burdens of his
sins and the nightmares of seeing Tina Kimbrew's
face in his restless sleep. And most of all he wanted
free of the steel bars that restricted him. He read
on.

*"You are the light of the world. . . . Let your light shine
before men in such a way that they may see your good works
and glorify your Father who is in Heaven."*

That was it. Wardrip knew what he had to do to
turn his life around.

June 1992

Although Faryion Wardrip was safely behind bars, Danny Laughlin nervously waited to find out when, or if, Barry Macha would take him back to court for Toni Gibbs's murder, and Ken Taylor continued to be harassed by the Fort Worth Police Department and shunned by his family, the victim count continued to climb.

The family of Terry Sims agonized over her death. Their world had been shattered. Their loss was intensified by the lack of information on the unsolved killing. Who could have done such a horrible thing? And why? The questions were constantly asked by the Sims.

There appeared no reason for the senseless slaying.

"She wasn't a girl who walked the streets in a short skirt and makeup. She was the opposite of that," her agonized mother said. "She loved to help people. She worked with autistic children and visited patients in the hospital in her free time."

The family couldn't understand why someone would take the life of a person like Terry. No one understood.

Sims's mother cried for her daughter every day. The steady stream of tears seemed to have no beginning, and no end. They were a visible manifestation of her intense grief.

Terry's death shattered the family unit. The Simses divorced as a result of Terry's murder, neither parent able to cope with the loss. Mrs. Sims went through several periods she described as "not being well." Depression ravaged her spirit. "It doesn't get easier with time," she told friends mournfully.

The investigations of the murders of Sims, Blau, and Taylor continued separately without success. Every lead was being investigated. The search for the killers was not isolated to the North Texas area; suspects out-side their geographical locations were also scrutinized.

When a man in Tucson, Arizona, raped three women, then killed himself, Wichita Falls lawmen investigated possible relationships between the man and any of the local victims. It turned out to be yet another in a growing list of dead ends.

Frustration ran through each agency department. Their defeat seemed to narrow their tunnel vision even further and reinforce their notions that they were searching for several killers. They feared that the murderers could erupt again at any time and claim the lives of more young women.

Toni Sims was the only victim who attracted interagency cooperation, but only because she had been abducted in Wichita County and killed in Archer County.

In a darkened Wichita Falls garage, Archer County deputies sprayed Luminol on the rusted bus abandoned not far from the body of Toni Gibbs.

The chemical causes bloodstains, otherwise undetectable, to be visible to the naked eye. Sheriff Pippin of Archer County knew it was literally like "fishing in the dark," but he had to give it a shot. Luminol testing had not been an investigative tool available when Gibbs was murdered seven years earlier. Although Pippin had little belief that the test would yield any evidence as to who had committed the murder, he hoped that it might help paint a picture of what happened to Gibbs on the night she died.

The shell of the bus had been transported to a long, silver-metal building and nestled between antique trucks and retired Wichita Falls fire vehicles. The chemical test required a darkened location to be best effective, so deputies covered the windows with carpet and wooden boards. The deputies were looking for some thin strand of evidence that would reignite the investigation.

Within seconds of the spraying, the walls of the bus exploded in an eerie purplish glow. The ghoulish gleam showed on a door handle and on the right side of the shell, glaring reminders of the young nurse's brutal death.

The investigators, representing Archer County, Wichita County, and the Wichita Falls Police Department, stood in silence as they watched the condemning glow come to life. The experienced lawmen could only imagine the terror that raged through Toni Gibbs when she was held hostage in the dilapidated structure.

Their thoughts turned to Danny Wayne Laughlin, freed by a hung jury instead of being punished for the brutal Gibbs killing. Many, including Wichita County District Attorney Barry Macha, thought they had the right man and had hoped the Luminol would give them enough proof to retry Laughlin.

In truth, Laughlin's life had become a living hell since his implication in the murder of Gibbs. Despite the jury's eleven-to-one vote for acquittal at his 1986 trial, many people continued to look at Laughlin as a killer.

Laughlin's mother, Wilma Hooker, had often complained of her son's treatment. She claimed that every place Laughlin went, he was harassed by the police.

"He would be stopped for minor traffic violations and blatantly called a murderer. Lawmen would go to his place of work and after talking with his supervisors and warning girls he worked with that he might hurt them, Danny would be fired," Hooker complained to the press. Laughlin and his family could not escape the stigma of Danny being an accused murderer.

Laughlin's mother became a victim as much as her

son. She ached from Danny's pain, a hurt she could not ease. Fearful tears tumbled down her cheeks and moistened the pillow under her head each night. Her body trembled, knowing how close Danny had come to a death sentence.

After serving two years in a Texas prison for burglary and perjury convictions, Laughlin was paroled to Hockley County, Texas, a few miles from Levelland, a West Texas city of nearly fourteen thousand. This laidback area of Texas was a comfortable place to live, with oil derricks dotting the horizon and endless rows of cotton, and old-timers who got together in the mornings to drink coffee and talk.

Danny Laughlin lived in peaceful surroundings. He had a porch swing beneath his two big, old shade trees and a bumper sticker on his pickup truck read BEAUTIFUL THINGS HAPPEN WHEN YOU PRAY. But Danny wasn't content.

"The only thing I want is to just be happy and have some peace now," Laughlin said to his soon-to-be father-in-law after their day's work in the oil field. "But I don't think I'll ever have peace of mind as long as someone out there thinks I killed Toni Gibbs."

Although the charges against Laughlin were eventually dropped, prosecutors continued to claim he was Gibbs's killer.

"I don't understand why they don't stand up and say they got the wrong guy," Laughlin said. "The thing that worries me about it is the guy that did it is still out there."

No other women in the Wichita Falls area had fallen prey to the viciousness of the killers at large. Had they moved on to other places, or were not free to kill again?

Laughlin put his muscular arms, a colorful horse

tattoed on each bicep, around his twenty-three-year-old fiancée, Anita Rivas, seated in front of him in the drying summer grass.

"It's my own fault I got into this mess," the parolee said.

Much of the responsibility for his arrest had to be laid at the feet of Laughlin himself, who had bragged about knowing unpublicized facts about the case. Facts he had learned in the sheriff's office while waiting to be booked into the Wichita County jail.

Laughlin knew one thing for sure—he never wanted to return to prison.

"I saw some really bad things. The people down there are pigs," he told his fiancée bitterly.

The scars of prison life were external, as well as internal. His body bore the injuries. His spirit carried the bitterness. He had spent two years in prison after admitting to the burglary he'd committed the day of Gibbs's murder, the burglary that had served as his alibi, and he confessed to perjury. He had decided not to fight the charges after his attorney told him the public was convinced he was guilty of murder.

The one thing Laughlin wanted most was for people to know he had not taken Toni's life.

"I thought about calling Toni's family and telling them I didn't do it, and I'm sorry the police stopped looking for who did," Laughlin told his family.

Danny's mother had the same thought. Time after time she picked up the phone receiver and began to dial the number for Gibbs's parents. *I just want them to know Danny didn't kill their daughter,* Hooker thought as she dialed. But she never completed the call. She never spoke to the Gibbses.

Laughlin eventually married Rivas, whom he had met in a Wichita Falls convenience store where he worked as a clerk. But the stigma of the Gibbs's murder continued to haunt him.

The demons that danced inside Laughlin plagued him and after another brush with the law, Laughlin decided a new start in a new state would be advantageous. He moved to Colorado in hopes of making a clean beginning.

One day, as he spoke to his mother by phone, Danny, in a melancholy mood at the time, talked about his life since the Gibbs's murder. "I'm tired of living like this, Mom. All they need is one little hair that's mine to send me back on murder charges. Besides, I'm worth more dead than alive."

But Danny Laughlin had much to live for. He was elated to be an expectant father, but worried about what his son would think of him with murder suspicions still hanging over his head.

"Mom, if anything ever happens to me, make sure I get my name cleared, because I didn't do that," he told her. If he died, the one thing Danny could leave his son would be a good name and the knowledge that his father had not been guilty of murder.

One week later, and three months before his son, Cody, was born in 1993, Danny Laughlin was killed in a head-on car collision in Cripple Creek, Colorado. The impact was so severe that the mangled mass of twisted steel barely resembled automobiles. At the time of his death, he left behind a legacy shrouded in suspicious shadows, a legacy that would have to be endured by his family.

The son that would never know his father was born in December 1993. Young Cody Laughlin entered the world with as much trauma as his father had left it. With the umbilical cord perilously wrapped around his tiny neck and his heart rate having dropped to a critical thirteen beats per minute from the newborn norm of one hundred to one hundred and fifty, Cody was taken by emergency C-section. But Cody was a survivor. He grew healthy and strong.

Like the Sims and Gibbs families, along with the suffering Laughlins, the Blaus languished from the loss of their daughter. The Blau family still found Ellen's death hard to accept. Murray Blau had to do something. By 1990, the case had been at a stalemate for five years. He decided to renew his offer of a reward.

On September 20 of each year, marking the anniversary of the disappearance of Ellen and on her birthday, an ad ran in the Wichita Falls newspaper.

ELLEN BLAU
MURDERED SEPTEMBER 1985
$10,000 REWARD
for information leading to arrest
and conviction of person
or persons responsible.
Call Wichita County Sheriff's Office
Tel. #

A smiling photo of Ellen was set at the left of the typed advertisement.

The public notices produced no new information concerning Ellen Blau's death. Investigators still believed the killer was someone she knew, and they believed the man had never killed again.

By 1994, it had been almost a decade since the Blaus lost their only daughter. Daily hard work had failed to purge the memory of his loss for Murray Blau. His initial anger had cooled, yet hardened. The pain was somewhat abated, replaced by a feeling of helplessness that became his constant companion.

Blau told a reporter from the Wichita Falls newspaper, "We'll never give up."

He hoped the message would be read by the killer who would realize that one day Murray Blau would have retribution for his daughter. It didn't matter how long it would take. There was no statute of limitations on murder.

Like Murray Blau, Ken Taylor longed for the killer of his wife, Debra, to be found. Taylor had another weighty reason other than retribution for Debra; he sought vindication for himself.

Ken Taylor had lost everything dear to him. His wife of five years was dead, the two little girls he'd watched play on the living-room floor were living away from him, and he was estranged from his in-laws. There was nothing more for Taylor to lose.

His ordeal began on the night he reported Debra missing to Fort Worth police. Taylor had immediately become the prime suspect. Authorities searched his house several times and he had taken three lie-detector tests. For months, detectives followed him like bloodhounds tracking their prey. They even followed him home from his wife's funeral.

After a while, even Debra's supportive family began to waver in their belief of his innocence. They blamed Ken for her disappearance, and ultimately faulted him directly for her death. His father-in-law finally alienated him totally, refusing even to speak to Taylor. Believing in Ken's guilt, his dead wife's family took steps to protect his daughter and stepdaughter. They successfully gained custody. Debra's killer had managed to sever Taylor's only remaining connection with his wife.

* * *

Of the five North Texas victims' families, only Robert and Elaine Kimbrew knew who had killed their only child. Being aware that Faryion Wardrip had taken the life of Tina didn't make it any easier, but it gave them a sense of purpose in the horrible ordeal that they had been living.

The Kimbrews made a vow—they would do all they could to keep Wardrip behind bars as long as possible.

In 1990, four years after Wardrip was classified as a state prisoner and given his TDCJ number, he prepared for his second parole hearing. Robert Kimbrew was furious.

The Texas Board of Pardons and Paroles had failed to notify Kimbrew of the first hearing, held a year earlier. Kimbrew thought the whole process premature.

"Four years is not enough," Kimbrew said. "I don't know what it's going to take to be enough for her mother and me. But four years is not enough." His dark eyes flashed from the adrenaline that rushed through his veins.

With good time and other credits added to Wardrip's actual time, the parole board considered him to have served thirteen years, nine months, and twenty-nine days. Almost forty percent of his thirty-five-year imposed sentence.

"I thought I'd be dead and gone when he got out of prison," Kimbrew said. "I didn't think of how I'd have to deal with the thought of him being out on the streets."

Kimbrew did all he could to ensure that the killer of his daughter remain behind bars. He gathered about two thousand protest letters written by friends and relatives. The mild-mannered, humble man resented having to fight to keep his daughter's killer in prison. He even feared for his own life if Wardrip was released, because of his efforts to keep his daughter's killer behind bars. But Robert Kimbrew had a worthy motive.

"I would feel responsible if I didn't fight the parole board and Wardrip injured another person after his early release," Kimbrew said.

The Kimbrews' efforts were rewarded. Wardrip was denied parole for the second time.

"I don't know if he's as disappointed at not getting out as I am not being able to see my daughter," Kimbrew said.

The one thing Kimbrew wanted to do was face his daughter's killer. He wanted to ask, "What did Tina say? How long did it take for her to die?" He wanted to look Tina's killer in the eye.

The small, quiet, sorrowful father would have his chance. Through the Victim Services division of TDCJ, Robert and Elaine Kimbrew were going to have the opportunity to sit across from Faryion Wardrip and ask him all the questions that had plagued them for years.

Robert hoped to finally have his most important question answered, "Why the hell did you do this?"

Chapter Twelve

For eleven years, Faryion Wardrip immersed himself in prison rehabilitation programs. He began by attending Alcoholics Anonymous and Narcotics Anonymous meetings sponsored by the Institutional Substance Abuse Program, where he shared his experiences with other addicts. From fellow users, he received both strength and hope.

Wardrip wasn't unique for his dependency on drugs and alcohol at TDCJ. Seventy-nine percent of all the male inmates were addicts and almost half of them had committed their crimes while under the influence of alcohol or illegal drugs. But unlike many, Wardrip was determined to kick the habit. Prison made it more difficult to obtain the forbidden substances, but they could be had for a price, either through corrupt, greedy guards, or smuggled in by enabling visitors. Wardrip knew he would have to establish a firm foundation with the tools needed to keep him clean on the streets, whenever his release happened.

The twelve-step programs followed by AA and NA members are a time-tested method of recovery from various obsessive-compulsive behaviors that individuals believe have made their lives unmanageable. Wardrip knew his life had been out of control. He hadn't the will to stop drinking or using drugs. He plunged into the twelve steps, utilizing his newfound Christianity as his mainstay.

Step one had been easy. Wardrip freely admitted that he was powerless over his problem and that his life had become unmanageable.

Steps two and three were also effortless. He believed in God as his Higher Power and willingly turned his life over to Him.

Step four was not as difficult for Wardrip as it was painful. He had to take a moral inventory of himself. The catalogue of offenses made him cringe. There had been so many transgressions, beginning with shoplifting. But his moral inventory plummeted to its darkest depths when he was forced to admit Tina Kimbrew's murder hadn't been a drug deal gone bad as he had tried to make his brother Bryce believe.

Step five was one Wardrip knew he couldn't keep. Oh, he admitted to God and to himself the exact nature of his wrongs, but he couldn't, he wouldn't, admit them to another human being. Spending the rest of his life in prison was an unthinkable possibility.

He prayed to have God remove all his defects of character and humbly asked God to forgive his shortcomings as required in steps six and seven.

Just like step five, Wardrip knew that steps eight and nine would be impossible to achieve. The first part was a snap; he could make the list of all persons he had harmed and, although he was willing to make amends to them, he couldn't. He didn't intend to spend any more time in prison than he had to.

In step ten, Wardrip continued to take personal inventory and when he was wrong, he would promptly admit it.

Wardrip achieved step eleven through prayer and meditation to improve his conscious contact with God, praying only for knowledge of God's will for him and the power to carry that out.

Lastly, in step twelve, Wardrip pledged to carry the message to other codependents, and to practice the principles in all his affairs.

Wardrip knew above all that the twelve steps were not something just done once and he would be miraculously cured. They had to become his way of life. They demanded vigilance, faith, and honest effort every waking hour of every day. Wardrip was willing to work the steps in hopes that he would be able to live life on life's terms with both fortitude and faith. He became obsessed in his preoccupation with the twelve-step system. Seemingly, Faryion Wardrip became the poster inmate for AA, but only Wardrip knew if his transformation was real or a manipulative trick in order to earn early release.

In addition to AA and NA meetings, Wardrip attended anger management classes and worked toward getting his General Education Development (GED) certificate. He had replaced his need for abusive substances with a zealous desire for control of his life.

From the time he was a small boy, Wardrip had been on the defensive whenever other kids called him names, criticized him for his poor school performance, or shamed him for wearing hand-me-downs. As an adult, Wardrip often felt pushed to the point that he had to "take control," either verbally or physically. It was that need for control that had driven him to dominate. To kill.

Wardrip had been a prime candidate for anger management therapy. The percentage of homicides in Texas had been steadily increasing in the 1980s. Wardrip had become one of the horrifying statistics, with fifty percent of all murders white-on-white crimes. Wardrip learned that an anger problem was any behavior that was hurtful to himself or others. He discovered he must recognize when he was becoming angry and how to intervene with prepared strategies when he fell into the depths of depression, adverse reactions, or conflicting incidents. The counselor taught him to focus on identifying his needs and wants and to use assertive, nonaggressive action to satisfy them; and to change learned behaviors of aggression, controlling, brooding, and depression. Most importantly, Wardrip had to learn to separate anger from rage or violence; divide shame and blame issues; to establish limits and boundaries; and to explore risk taking and safety issues. The concept was new for Wardrip, but he worked hard to become a useful, productive citizen. He excessively drove himself to be a perfect person.

Education was part of Wardrip's early release plan. Working through the Windham School, Wardrip was able to complete his high school equivalency certificate. He was lucky. The Windham School, established in 1969, was the first educational program within a statewide prison system. Like some thirty to fifty percent of inmates, Wardrip had a history of academic failure. The Windham School believed that if they helped break the cycle of low literacy skills, they could help stop criminal activity.

Wardrip had resolved to make better choices, to make a better life when released. He diligently studied the five subjects—writing, social studies, science, literature and arts, and mathematics—required for passing the GED. Wardrip's obsessive/compulsive tendencies became focused on his studies, but the underlying personality disorder remained.

There was little time for all that Wardrip had chosen to accomplish. His day started at three-thirty each morning with a general wake-up call. Breakfast was at four-thirty; he reported to work at six A.M. Wardrip, like all offenders in the prison system, with the exception of those on death row, was expected to work in one of the nonpaying jobs supervised by TDCJ personnel. He earned privileges as a result of his good work habits. Those who refused to work lost their rewards and were placed on "cell restriction." That meant they remained in their cells twenty-four hours a day, with no trips to the day room, commissary, or recreation yard. All personal property was taken away while an inmate was on cell restriction.

Wardrip didn't think he could face losing his drawing materials, his schoolbooks, and most importantly, his Bible. He worked hard, studied hard, and stacked up good behavior credits.

Ten years after the 1986 murder of Tina Kimbrew, David Doerfler sat in the visitors' room at the prison unit where Faryion Wardrip was confined, waiting for the convicted killer. He watched scrupulously as the tall, thin inmate took the chair opposite him. Wardrip's white prison-issue shirt was frayed at the collar from frequent washings, but clean and tucked neatly in his white elastic-waist trousers. Across the left breast pocket, Wardrip's TDCJ number was written in indelible black ink.

"Hi, Faryion, I'm David Doerfler. I'm with the Victim Services division of TDCJ. I want to talk to you about participating in the Victim Offender Mediation/Dialogue program," Doerfler said.

"I don't know anything about it," Wardrip replied. The inquisitive look on his face caused a deep vertical wrinkle between his two thick, dark eyebrows.

Doerfler explained that the program, which matched victims with violent offenders for a one-time encounter, was a relatively new program in the Texas prison system and the first of its kind in the country.

"The goal is resolution, not retribution," Doerfler told Wardrip, hoping to ease any reluctance he might have in meeting the Kimbrews face-to-face. "And your participation is strictly voluntary. You will receive nothing in return for your cooperation."

"I want to meet Mr. Kimbrew," Wardrip said, his eyes wide with excitement. "I want to tell him how sorry I am. That I live every day in memory of Tina."

Robert Kimbrew was just as anxious as Wardrip to have an opportunity to sit across the table, man to man, victim to offender. The groundbreaking program at the forefront of victim-offender mediation practices could be a way to help him take back his life. A life wrenched by Tina's violent death. After months of counseling to prepare both the offender and the victim for the meeting, Robert Kimbrew was finally scheduled to meet his daughter's murderer.

It took all the energy Kimbrew could muster to walk through the prison gates and into the area assigned for his mediation with Faryion Wardrip.

For five and a half gut-wrenching hours, Robert Kimbrew told Faryion Wardrip about his daughter. How she had been a special gift from God when he and his wife, Elaine, believed they would be forever childless. He told his daughter's killer about the plans and dreams Tina had shared with him about her future. How Tina had not only been a good daughter to him, but a good friend to many. The father's eyes filled with sadness as he related story after story to his daughter's killer.

The pain of eleven years without Tina showed on the wrinkled brow and tight-pressed lips of the anguished father. His voice cracked at times, then rose to a level of anger and contempt when telling Wardrip the horror he had brought into his life, and exactly how he felt about the killing.

Wardrip looked the anguished father in the eye. "Tina is the only person I've ever harmed," Wardrip said with sincerity and regret in his voice.

Kimbrew's face began to soften, his lips relaxed, and the tension in his shoulders lessened as he noted what appeared to be pain in Wardrip's eyes.

"I was a straight-A student. Popular in school," Wardrip lied. He then told Kimbrew about the drugs, the drinking. How his life had gotten out of hand and how sorrowful he was.

"I'm the youngest of nine children. My family needs me. My dad is dying; that's why I'm wanting to get out of prison. For my dad," Wardrip told Kimbrew, perhaps hoping to manipulate the grieving father into compassion.

Kimbrew stared at Wardrip for a moment. "I've never thought of killing anyone. I wouldn't want to put your mother and father through what I've been through," he said.

Kimbrew reiterated the pain he and Tina's mother had been through. The loss that could never be replaced.

"Robert, I am truly sorry," Wardrip said, with what appeared as genuineness. The convicted killer cast his tear-filled eyes downward.

The older man stared at his daughter's killer. "I hope you think about Tina every day. I don't mean that as punishment, but as a reminder to stay away from the drugs and anger that made you kill my daughter," Kimbrew said, an agonizing edge still in his voice. "When you get out and feel the urge to go back to the drugs, I hope you will find the strength to call me or someone else and stay away from the people who brought you to this ruin."

Wardrip watched Kimbrew in disbelief. The always talkative inmate appeared stunned into speechlessness. How could a man whose daughter was killed offer help to her killer? Wardrip marveled.

"If you get out and you get into trouble and you don't call me, there'll be no mercy," Kimbrew added with a hint of intimidation in his tone.

With tears in his eyes and a lump in his throat, Wardrip told Kimbrew, "Tina was my friend and she changed my life. She gave her life so I could change my life."

Robert Kimbrew stood to leave. Wardrip looked into the grieving father's eyes, knowing that he was responsible for the pain and the tears that filled them.

As Robert Kimbrew reached his hand forward to shake Wardrip's hand, the thirty-nine-year-old inmate stood numbed in amazement. *How can he want to shake my hand?* Wardrip thought.

The killer seized Kimbrew's hand, accepting the gesture of what he believed to be forgiveness. But there was no forgiveness in Robert Kimbrew's heart, only loneliness and heartache. Meeting with Wardrip was probably the hardest thing he had ever done. He had the opportunity to tell Wardrip exactly how he felt. Despite what Wardrip had done, Kimbrew still viewed him as a human being, but he would never be able to forgive him of depriving him of his only child.

Wardrip, on the other hand, was uplifted by the mediation experience. Even though he had lied about almost everything he had told Robert Kimbrew, including his grades, his popularity, his birth-order position in the family, and his father's health, Wardrip had no regrets. He knew that the meeting would help him make it to the outside. He would have the perfect life he dreamed of.

Chapter Thirteen

George Wardrip, six-foot, one-inch tall with dark, deep-set eyes, and salt-and-pepper hair, stood before the Hamilton Street Church of Christ in Olney, Texas, as an impressive figure. He was not there to direct worship, but to humbly address his fellow worshipers. His hands were moist as he adjusted his glasses. His wife, Diana, a short, petite woman, often quiet but full of spunk, sat in the pew beside him. George took a long deep breath, then spoke in a soft, timid voice.

"My son's been in prison. He was convicted of a crime and spent eleven years behind bars. He's going to be out on parole soon. This is our church family and he needs a lot of love and support getting connected to the community," Wardrip said.

Members of the Hamilton Street Church of Christ loved the Wardrip family, which was active in the life of the church. Without hesitation, the congregation overwhelmingly responded to Wardrip's plea. In the spirit of their pioneering ancestors who gathered in Olney in the 1880s for forming trail outfits and branding cattle, the members of the church not only provided their love and prayers to the Wardrips, but guaranteed that clothes, money, and a job awaited their son upon release.

In the meantime, Faryion's mother began preparations for her son's return home, fussing over where he would sleep in their small, rent-subsidized apartment.

"Mom, he's been locked up for eleven years. He doesn't care if he sleeps in the corner," Bryce, her youngest child, told her.

Faryion Wardrip breathed in the fresh air of freedom. Eleven years of confinement in TDCJ facilities had made the thirty-nine-year-old parolee anxious for open fields and the love of his family. Under the Texas parole system he had to have a sponsor who agreed to help him in his efforts to rebuild his life. Wardrip's father had gladly accepted that role, determined to help his eldest son follow a path of redemption.

As elated as George Wardrip was to have his son freed from prison, Robert Kimbrew was equally angered.

"I fought the parole board before they finally gave it to him," Kimbrew told reporters when he heard the news of Wardrip's release. "It never ends, does it? I was hoping he'd get life, but he didn't. The biggest insult I'd ever been paid was the day I found out he was gonna get out after eleven years."

Local authorities had the same gnawing frustration.

"It's a shame that someone gets thirty-five years and gets out in eleven," Sheriff Callahan said. Callahan, a deputy at the time of the murders, had been elevated to sheriff of Wichita County.

"When we prosecute people, it's frustrating to know they don't serve a complete sentence," Archer County Prosecutor Tim Cole commented.

George Wardrip knew in his heart that there would be animosity from some, but it didn't dampen his jubilation that Faryion was on his way home.

With his son beside him, George drove past the green-and-white city limits sign of Olney, Texas.

OLNEY
CITY LIMIT
POP. 3519
HOME OF THE
ONE ARM
DOVE HUNT

Faryion Wardrip smiled to himself. He had heard his family talk about the one-arm dove hunt, but he had never seen the sight of more than one hundred one-armed amputee hunters take to the fields in a competition of shooting expertise.

The big-time annual event was first begun by two "One Arm Jacks," as the two men, both from Olney and both named Jack, liked to call themselves. They wouldn't let their own adversity keep them down and wanted to share their enthusiasm for life with other upper-extremity amputees. The event was supported by locals who donated their time, talents, and money. One-armed hunters from all over the country took part in a glove swap, the one-arm talent show, a cow chip chunkin', a one-arm skeet shoot, golf tournament, pool tournament, horseshoes, a dove hunt, and a ten-cents-a-finger breakfast over the two-day event.

Wardrip saw the dove hunt as a symbol of the kind of townspeople residing in Olney. Annually, for more than twenty-five years, they had offered their hospitality to the disabled. Wardrip felt certain Olney would give him a fresh start. The sleepy little town, nearly forty miles south of Wichita Falls, would be a haven from the memories of his prior crimes. There remained only one problem: an electronic surveillance monitor attached to his leg. As part of his parole, Wardrip was required to wear the monitor at all times. He could only travel from his residence at his parents' apartment to work, or to church and back again. To attend anger-management classes, or any event that might require him to travel outside the Olney city limits, he had to obtain special permission from his parole officer.

Wardrip didn't mind the travel restrictions. His greatest fear was that he would not be accepted by the small community if they knew about his prison time for the savage murder of Tina Kimbrew. He wanted more than anything to be accepted by the people of Olney. He believed that in Olney he could attain his idea of a perfect life.

Wardrip had thought long and hard about what to tell people. He knew the story he told about why he was imprisoned and why he wore a leg monitor had to be believable. He couldn't chance their rejection by telling them the truth about Tina Kimbrew.

Faryion Wardrip walked across the redbrick street, under the porte-cochere, and then through the glass doors of the Hamilton Street Church of Christ. Reverend Scott Clark, a youthful-looking minister who worked part-time at the local nursing home, waited for him inside.

"Welcome, Faryion," Clark said with an outstretched hand.

Wardrip's tall frame was slumped, his head bowed. He wore pants that were far too short for his lanky frame.

He looks like a kid on the playground, anxious about being picked for the game, Scott thought to himself.

Scott led Wardrip into the church sanctuary, where he was introduced to members of the small church community.

"I was convicted of vehicular manslaughter," Wardrip told the people at the Church of Christ. "I got drunk, wrecked my truck, and my fiancée was killed."

The story not only provided a believable cover for his parole status, but moved the congregation to expressions of sympathy. Wardrip's massaging of the truth had won the people over immediately.

In the ensuing weeks, Reverend Clark and Faryion Wardrip had many long talks. The enthusiastic and dedicated Clark found Wardrip to be a man in search of a place to call home. He appeared lonely, disenfranchised. After a wasted youth and eleven years in prison, Wardrip had nothing to call his own. He wore the charity clothing provided by the parishioners, often with the pants legs rolled up because they were too long, and sometimes the hems of his jeans reached only to the tops of his socks. Clark was impressed that his lack of clothing failed to deter Wardrip from church. Clark believed his new friend was a soul in search of God's acceptance.

In less than a month, Wardrip had transformed from a frightened outsider to a confident member of the church brotherhood. He was at the Hamilton Street church nearly every time the doors were open and was baptized by Reverend Clark within weeks of arriving at the Olney parish.

"Olney and this church are truly places of second chances," Wardrip told Clark. "This is home. I feel like I've always been here."

Clark believed in Faryion Wardrip and his professed confession of his sins. On bent knees, the two men bowed their heads as the new convert prayed for redemption.

Wardrip became familiar with scripture. He had studied and participated in prison Bible studies. He also took correspondence courses that taught him more about the book. His obsessive-compulsive personality was directed toward learning more about God and he soon became knowledgeable and articulate concerning the Bible.

"I want to take my turn at helping with the Wednesday night service," Wardrip told Clark.

"You'll have to speak to the elders," Clark said, explaining that it was the church dignitaries who would make the final decision as to whether he would be allowed to participate.

Wardrip went before the elders of the church.

"I want an opportunity to express my acceptance of God's grace to the congregation in worship," he told them.

"You want to lead a prayer, sure, lead a prayer," the elders said.

In their conversation with Wardrip, the leaders of the Hamilton Street Church of Christ learned that not only was the man knowledgeable about Bible facts, but expressive as well. He could handle himself in front of a crowd. He wasn't afraid. But what the church members saw as confidence, his younger brother Bryce saw as arrogance. Bryce had been watching Faryion closely. Because of his failure to confess his true sins, Bryce believed his brother's baptism and church teaching were a farce. Bryce had his doubts that his brother's Christian transformation was real.

Clark, on the other hand, was convinced. "In a small town, people like that don't come along every day," Clark told the elders. "Especially people who seem to understand what it's like to be forgiven."

Clark knew that a lot of people in the religious world had a problem with understanding forgiveness because they hadn't done anything really bad. Clark thought of Jesus at Simon's house where he said, *"This woman washed my feet with her tears and then you, Simon, haven't even given me any water. The one who has been forgiven much, loves much."*

From what Clark heard in Faryion Wardrip's prayers and the stories he wanted to tell of his past, the new parolee wanted God to know he was sorry for his sins. Clark and the elders decided to ask Wardrip if he wanted to teach one of the Wednesday night lessons.

Wardrip was given an outline and a text. He did a good job and was put in the regular teaching rotation, which meant he spoke about every thirteen or fourteen weeks. Then Clark asked Wardrip for a favor.

"I have to be gone for a couple of Wednesday nights," Clark said. "Will you give your testimony to the teenagers?"

"Sure," Wardrip said enthusiastically.

The next Wednesday night, Faryion Wardrip, former drug user and paroled killer, stood before the junior- and senior-high youth of the Hamilton Street Church of Christ.

"You don't want to mess with drugs. You don't want to get messed up with bad friends, because look what happened to my life. **You do**n't want to do that," Wardrip said with emotion.

The overpowering figure of the reformed killer loomed over the young teens. His words of warning about addiction, bad choices, and regrets filled their heads. Wardrip emotionally poured out his heart, revealing his fears for the teens who might follow his path to a life of broken dreams.

The teens were frightened by his strong testimony. Seemingly overnight Wardrip became the Nicky Cruz of Olney. His message was as powerful in the small Texas town as New York's Nicky Cruz's had been in the popular book, *The Cross and the Switchblade.*

Clark and the elders agreed, Wardrip had something important to say to the youth. He became a regular speaker, telling horror stories about his misspent youth. He was plugged into the kids, and they listened with fascination and determination not to follow his self-proclaimed pattern of self-destruction. But in all his testimonies Wardrip always held something back— the truth about Tina Kimbrew.

By the late summer of 1998, Wardrip had adjusted to life in Olney. He had a good job and was active in the Church of Christ, but something was missing. He hadn't put a name to it, but he knew that his life wasn't whole. Then fate took an unexpected emotional turn.

"Faryion, we have a friend who is coming to visit from Oklahoma. We would like for you to meet her," friends told Wardrip.

"Sure, why not?" Wardrip said. His last two romances had ended badly. He had been engaged briefly to a younger woman in the church. He had wined and dined her at his parents' apartment in their absence. Soft music and candlelight set the mood for their romantic interludes. Then there had been Beverly, a young mother of two. He had bought the engagement ring and they were picking a date for their wedding when, for unknown reasons, Reverend Clark suggested they needed a cooling-off period. Beverly broke off the engagement and Wardrip had again been left with a feeling of emptiness.

From what his friends told him, Glenda Kelley was a strong Christian. Someone who would accept him for who he was now, not what he had been in the past.

Glenda Diane Kelley was five years Wardrip's senior. At forty-five years of age, Glenda had led a distraught life. She had been trapped in an emotionally abusive twenty-year marriage. When her husband committed adultery, Glenda walked away from the jewels, the Mercedes, the big home, and followed God. Glenda Kelley and Faryion Wardrip were both lost souls searching for the meaning of life. When they met, it was as if their kindred spirits united.

Wardrip's attraction to Glenda amazed Wardrip's brother Bryce, and even somewhat surprised Wardrip himself. She was not the type of woman he had traditionally been drawn to. At about five-foot-four, with a slim to medium build, Glenda was plain by most standards. Her mousy brown hair was blunt cut in a shoulder-length bob. She wore glasses, little or no makeup, and conservative clothing. Glenda certainly didn't possess the outward beauty or style Wardrip normally found attractive. But Faryion saw more than Glenda's outward appearance.

"She's a flower compared to the cactuses I've dated. She is beautiful. Intelligent. She's perfect. How's a country boy like me going to have a snowball's chance on a hot sidewalk with her?" Wardrip asked a friend.

The attraction was mutual. Glenda Kelley and Wardrip began a long-distance romance.

Shortly after she met Wardrip, Kelley enrolled in a Bible college in Lubbock, Texas. Wardrip was worried. He thought, *She is going to be around a lot of guys going to Bible college to be ministers. She's going to meet a guy a lot classier than I am. A lot more educated. I'm not going to have a chance with her.*

He sat down and wrote her a letter.

Glenda, I know you might be against long distance relationships but I'm just crazy about you. If we just commit to each other we can make this long distance relationship work. You'll come see me and I'll come see you. You can stay in school, but let's commit to each other.

He was nervous about Glenda's response. He never expected her reply.

"Yes, I'll marry you," Glenda said.

Although Wardrip hadn't actually asked Kelley to marry him, he was ecstatic over her affirmative response. He believed she was his gift from God. He would do anything to keep from losing her, including withholding the truth about his shady past and the blood on his hands.

"The semester ends in October," Glenda told him by phone.

"Well, you show up October first, and I'll have an apartment ready. I'll set everything up," he assured her.

Wardrip found a small apartment in the same government-subsidized building where he lived with his parents. He quickly set about paying the deposit, getting the phone turned on, buying furniture, and setting up their first home.

Determined to do it God's way, Glenda lived with the Wardrips in their apartment while Faryion stayed a few doors away in their future home. The soon-to-be newlyweds would have picnics on the carpet of their apartment; then at ten o'clock every evening Wardrip would walk Glenda down to his parents' home where she slept each night.

The couple had planned to marry in December; however, George Wardrip was scheduled to begin radiation treatments for cancer in November. Wanting his father to be present at his wedding, Faryion Wardrip approached Reverend Clark.

"Can you marry us this Saturday night?" Wardrip asked his good friend and pastor.

"Yeah, I guess," Clark said, surprised at the request.

Some of the church members overheard Wardrip and Clark's conversation and set out to make the wedding a memorable one. The couple wanted to make a fresh start, and the congregation wanted to show their support. In a matter of days, singers, flowers, plants, punch, and cake had been ordered for the nuptials of Faryion Wardrip and Glenda Kelley.

While the congregation pulled together a traditional wedding with all the trimmings, Wardrip and Glenda drove to nearby Graham, county seat of Young County, and applied for a marriage license. The application indicated that Faryion Wardrip, born March 6, 1959, in Salem, Indiana, intended to enter into marriage with Glenda Diane Kelley, born January 6, 1953, in Dodge City, Kansas. Wardrip paid the license fee and the couple returned to Olney.

It was three days before the scheduled wedding when Wardrip called his mother to let her know he would be married on Saturday, not in November as first planned. Then he called his brother Bryce and asked if he would stand up for him as best man.

"Have you told Glenda the real reason you're wearing a leg monitor?" Bryce asked his brother.

"No. There's no need for Glenda to know the details," the older Wardrip replied.

Bryce's misgivings about Faryion's conversion and baptism returned. He knew his brother had turned their parents' apartment into "party central" whenever they were away. Now suddenly he was planning marriage. It didn't make sense to Bryce. Reluctantly, he agreed to be the best man, but wondered why Faryion had chosen him.

As kids, Bryce felt abused by Faryion and their older brother, Roy. The older boys had beaten him, thrown darts at him, tied him up and dragged him across the yard. They had even crashed into his Big Wheel, knocking him to the ground. When Bryce tattled to their father, his brothers would smash peanut-butter-

and-jelly sandwiches into his face. But the physical mistreatment was not as traumatic as the emotional torture. The two older brothers would don white sheets and scratch on the screen of Bryce's bedroom window. Terror surged through the youngest Wardrip as he lay still in his bed, afraid to breathe or the ghosts outside would surely get him.

As the Wardrip boys matured, Bryce continued to feel used by his older brother. When Bryce sold Faryion a car for four hundred dollars on a verbal agreement, he never received a dime of the money.

As used and abused as he had felt over the years, Bryce somehow felt obligated to help his brother restore his life. He agreed to be Faryion's best man.

On October 15, 1998, three days after Wardrip and Kelley obtained their marriage license, Bryce and Tina Wardrip's three-year-old and six-year-old daughters walked down the aisle of the Hamilton Street Church of Christ. Outfitted in identical pink floral dresses with large white collars, white tights, and pink bows in their hair, the girls smiled broadly at their daddy and Uncle Faryion as they stood at the front of the altar. The girls carried flower baskets with woven wicker handles. Their four-year-old brother followed them, carrying a white pillow with two shiny gold rings. The rough-and-tumble little boy's white shirt was neatly tucked into the pants of his gray suit.

Only minutes before the ceremony the boy had said, "Daddy, we look like a bunch of monkeys." Bryce agreed. The day before, Bryce and his brother had argued about Bryce's wedding wardrobe.

"I want you to wear a pink shirt and mauve tie," Wardrip had told Bryce.

"I'm not wearing any pink shirt," Bryce had retorted, refusing to wear what he believed to be feminine colors.

Bryce won the argument and stood beside his brother as best man dressed in a light blue shirt and dark sports coat. The groom wore the pink shirt and mauve tie, with a dark blue sports coat, a white rose boutonniere, and the light slacks his bride had insisted on.

A broad grin spanned Wardrip's face as he watched Glenda walk from the rear of the church to where he stood waiting at the front. Wardrip thought Glenda was a vision in her off-white dress and matching jacket. Truly a God-send.

In less than fifteen minutes, Reverend Scott Clark pronounced Faryion Wardrip and Glenda Kelley husband and wife.

There was no honeymoon. Wardrip was restricted by the surveillance monitor attached to his ankle. The new groom promised his bride that in February, less than three months away, they would be honeymooning in some romantic spot. He would have fulfilled his parole obligation and the monitor would be removed.

Wardrip was happier than he had ever been. He believed his marriage was the beginning of the perfect life he had dreamed of for so many years.

Chapter Fourteen

After arriving in Olney, Wardrip had drifted from job to job. It wasn't until his father sought out Frank Duncan at the Olney Door and Screen Company and asked him to help give his son a second chance that Wardrip had a job he liked.

"Frank, you know my boy Faryion is home. He got himself into some trouble and he's been in prison. He needs a job. Frank, I'd be pleased if you'd give him a chance," George Wardrip told the company's owner.

George Wardrip towered over the short, stocky Duncan. As dissimilar as the two men were in physical appearance, they were alike in their love for their sons. George Wardrip was trying to get Faryion back on track, and Duncan was turning over the reins of the family-owned business to his son Brad.

"Sure, George, we've given lots of men with records jobs. Bring him on out and let us talk to him," Duncan said.

The Olney Door and Screen Company was the small town's third-largest employer with thirty-five full-time employees. The manufacturing company produced screen doors for construction coast to coast, with the Department of Housing and Urban Development (HUD) their largest contractor.

Within days, Faryion Wardrip was sitting in the office of Brad Duncan, Fred's son, and president of the screen company.

"Tell me about yourself," Brad said to Wardrip.

With no apparent pause, the ex-con began to tell Brad the same story he had told the members of his Church of Christ congregation. He was convincing in his description of the auto accident, the death of his fiancée, his incarceration, and the ankle monitor he wore. He not only won the job he desired, but also the compassion of his employer. Once again he had manipulated the truth to his advantage.

"Faryion, this is Dave Collard, our purchasing agent," Brad said. "You'll be working with him. He'll show you the ropes."

Collard, a middle-aged man with graying hair and a pleasant smile, took Wardrip under his wing. The two men became instant friends. Wardrip had common sense, people skills, and a work ethic unlike many of the laborers at the factory, qualities that earned greater value for him, not only with Collard, but the Duncans as well.

Within weeks Collard watched from his office as Wardrip drove the forklift to move materials from one location to another in the factory yard. He thought of how quickly Wardrip had adjusted to the work routine. He had taken to purchasing like a fish to water. Wardrip was perfect for the job slot. Collard's only concern was Wardrip's own impatience with himself.

"Faryion, take it easy," Collard had advised when his employee had become angry over an error he had made. "Don't get so upset."

The friendly advice was ignored. Wardrip was a perfectionist, driven to be flawless in his job performance. It was part of his plan. A piece of the puzzle that when complete would reveal a mosaic of what would be his picture of an impeccable life.

Wardrip's apparent change of character had made him a likable employee. He had been well received by the vendors dealing with the company, and Collard hoped to be able to turn most, if not all, of the responsibilities of purchasing over to Wardrip shortly. Collard planned to go back out on the road for outside sales.

It had been a difficult time for Collard. His wife had been ill for some time before she finally lost her fight with cancer.

Wardrip was one of the first people to arrive at Collard's house after hearing the news of his wife's death. In the living room of Collard's house, the two men embraced and cried.

"Dave, I'm so sorry," Wardrip said with tears in his eyes.

"I know, son, I know," Collard said.

In the few months he had been with the company, Wardrip had become like a son to Collard. Collard had watched him grow emotionally and advance professionally. He was equally pleased that Wardrip seemed to be happily married. He thought Glenda's influence had helped to bring Wardrip down to earth. To settle him. But Collard had given Wardrip some good-natured ribbing as well.

Their first Christmas together, the newlyweds had agreed not to pay more than one hundred dollars for gifts to one another. Faryion Wardrip had been upset when he had stuck to the imposed limit and his wife had not, giving him an adorable black poodle puppy as a gift.

"You're in a lot of trouble," Collard had taunted. He enjoyed poking fun at Wardrip. The younger man was good natured and had taken the ribbing well.

"You better watch out, Faryion, she's keeping you on a short leash," Collard had teased when he heard that Wardrip cooked Glenda breakfast every morning, led them in Bible study, then did the dishes.

The cord remained short as Glenda arrived on most days at noon with Faryion's lunch and brought him an occasional morning snack. In addition, she chastised him for working, even if infrequently, on Sunday. But nonetheless, to Collard, Wardrip seemed to be on cloud nine. His life appeared to be working out just as he had expressed to Collard he had hoped it would.

As the two men sat in the factory yard one day, Wardrip stared out to the north, gazing at a tall stand of trees.

"You can't imagine how long it had been since I had seen trees," Wardrip said, remembering the gray, cold walls of the prison unit.

"Huntsville [prison] is a place you don't want to go back to," Collard said.

"I never want to go back," Wardrip said with determination and a bit of fear in his voice.

He had expressed the same fear to Bryce.

"I'm so scared on this program," Wardrip had told his brother. "Even if there's a false report, I can go back."

Bryce mulled over Faryion's statement. His older brother had always thought he was ten feet tall and bullet proof. Since his release from prison, Bryce had seen glimpses of a change.

Glenda seemed to keep him on the straight and narrow, but there was some backsliding that concerned Bryce. At his house, Faryion would watch *Bevis and Butthead* on television, listen to rock and roll, and generally have a good time joking and playing with Bryce's kids. But as soon as Glenda would arrive, his brother changed into a Bible-thumping holy roller. It was something Bryce had difficulty tolerating.

Tina, Bryce's wife, was equally uncomfortable as she watched Glenda tell her brother-in-law where to sit, even how to sit. In general, Glenda made Faryion's brother and sister-in-law uncomfortable in their own home. One day Tina had watched all the henpecking she could stand.

"They have surgery for that," Tina told Glenda curtly.

Glenda's questioning look told Tina her older sister-in-law had no idea what she was talking about.

"To remove the stick up your ass," Tina said.

Part III

Chapter Fifteen

As Faryion Wardrip labored at the door and screen factory, Archer County District Attorney Investigator Paul Smith and Wichita County District Attorney Investigator John Little toiled over the unsolved murder files of Terry Sims, Toni Gibbs, and Ellen Blau. They searched for a common denominator. Something that might tether the fifteen-year-old murders together.

Archer County District Attorney Tim Cole, who had pursued the latest technological advances in DNA testing in the Toni Gibbs case three years earlier, challenged Smith to untangle the mass of information accumulated in the fifteen years since the murders had been committed. Cole had been disappointed and a bit surprised when 1996 DNA tests showed that the original suspect in the Gibbs's killing was not the murderer.

Danny Wayne Laughlin, who had been unsuccessfully tried for Gibbs's murder, was innocent. The findings came too late for Laughlin. His death in a Colorado car crash in 1993 had come three years before the DNA findings that would clear him of the crime he had repeatedly denied.

But while Cole was disappointed with the DNA test findings exonerating Laughlin, the tests revealed a sur-

prising discovery. The semen found in Sims matched
the semen found in Gibbs. For the first time since the
1984/1985 slayings, authorities had linked the two
murders to a single killer. One man.

Cole instructed Smith to reopen the case of Toni
Gibbs for further review.

"Find me a common link between Sims and Gibbs,"
Cole told his investigator.

Because Gibbs had been abducted from Wichita
County and transported to Archer County, the two
governmental entities had decided more than a decade before to work together in searching for the killer. There was no question that their collaboration
would continue. For fifteen years, both DA Cole and
DA Macha kept the murders of the three young
women alive in their minds and hearts. They had
vowed never to give up the search for the vicious killer
who had plagued their region's young women for
eighteen fright-filled months. Each district attorney assigned an investigator to the sole pursuit of finding
the slayer.

Investigators Smith and Little pored over the files,
searching for any clue, anyone who might appear in
the files of Gibbs, Sims, and Blau.

"Here he is again," Little said to Smith as he reviewed Gibbs's file. "His name has popped up in both
Gibbs's and Sims's files."

Then the investigators came across a notation in
one of the cold case files. A notation that stunned the
experienced detectives. A Thomas Granger had gone
to the police twice in 1986 to report his suspicions
that a man he knew had something to do with the
deaths of Sims, Gibbs, and Blau. The first time had
been only three days after he had confessed to killing
another Wichita Falls woman. Evidently the information had been disregarded.

The second time Granger approached police was after he and a private investigator named Ray Cannedy investigated links between the man and the murdered women themselves. They had even prepared a report, which they gave to local police and the FBI.

"We have to consider him a suspect," Little said.

Smith and Little had eliminated more than two dozen men over the two years they had been working on the cold case files of the unsolved murders. Each suspect had been systematically expunged. The man whose name appeared in the files would join that list of former suspects if his DNA sample didn't match the semen samples from the victims. If his sample matched, Smith and Little knew beyond any doubt that they would have their killer.

Since the late 1980s, DNA, a genetic profile or a genetic fingerprint as it's sometimes called, had been perfected and used by law enforcement to identify suspects from hair, blood, semen, or tissue found at the scene of a violent crime. Smith and Little knew that a person could change his name and physical features, but he couldn't change his DNA configuration.

In DNA fingerprinting, DNA is extracted from a sample, such as blood, hair, or saliva, and cut into segments using enzymes. Those segments are sorted by lengths. Segments that contain sequences of repeated DNA bases, which vary greatly from one individual to another, are radioactively tagged, causing them to form a visual pattern. That pattern becomes the person's DNA fingerprint. In criminal investigations, the DNA fingerprint of a suspect is compared to that of evidence found at a crime scene. It could come from such things as hair, blood spatter, any type of biological tissue. Coffee cups, soda cans, toothbrushes, even bubble gum had been used to collect DNA samples from suspects.

It would take as few as fifty human cells to provide trained scientists with a genetic fingerprint with the power to damn a suspect or absolve him. National databases, including one maintained by the FBI, were being set up across the county, but unless their suspect had a felony record and had been required to give a sample, he wouldn't be found among the more than five hundred thousand offenders already profiled by the FBI. If he had been registered, the Wichita County/Archer County case was a prime candidate for the national database system—multiple jurisdictions working in harmony. A unique association for the far North Texas region.

There was another important ingredient that Cole and Little had in their favor. Luckily, the semen samples taken from the bodies of Sims and Gibbs had been frozen and properly preserved at the Southwest Institute of Forensic Sciences in Dallas in hopes that one day a suspect would be found. All Smith and Little had to do was gather a DNA sample from their suspect and have it tested at a forensic lab. Then they would know if their two-year search for a killer was over, or if they would continue the tedious process of poring over the case files for another lead.

But a routine background check on their newest suspect gave Little and Smith cause for optimism.

Little went to his boss's office, trying to hide his optimism. "What would you say," he asked Macha, "if I told you that I think I've got the guy we're looking for, that I can put him in the middle of everything that happened, and that he's already been to prison for murder?"

* * *

"Faryion, this is David," Doerfler said over the phone. "You've been out of the Victim Offender Mediation program for a couple of years now, and out of prison about a year. I want to do a follow-up interview with you. We'll be able to use it at a later date for funding requests."

"Sure. Come on up to Olney. I'll talk to you," Wardrip said.

Doerfler and a female reporter drove from Doerfler's Austin, Texas, office three hundred miles north to Olney. The three sat down at the Olney factory where Wardrip worked and began talking.

"We just want to know how you're doing," Doerfler began. "Tell us about your job, where you live, your life here in Olney."

"I'm married to a good Christian woman," Wardrip began. "Glenda is the love of my life. I am so lucky to have her. She keeps me focused in the right direction. She's older than I am, more stable, although she's been through some bad times as well.

"We live in an apartment in town we share with our poodle.

"I'm teaching Sunday school at the Church of Christ and occasionally leading the Wednesday night services. Glenda also works with the kids at church."

"Sounds like things are going really well for you, Faryion," the woman said.

"They are," Wardrip replied. "I'm a different person than I was all those years ago. I don't even know who that person was. I can't imagine taking the life of anyone."

The murder of Tina Kimbrew remained an appalling reminder of his dark days of alcohol, drugs, and uncontrollable anger.

"What about work? How's the job going?" Doerfler asked.

"Great. I like the work. I have lots of different duties, so it keeps my interest. The Duncans, who own the company, are good people, and Dave Collard is a good friend as well as my boss."

As Wardrip spoke, he subconsciously straightened the papers on the desk and rearranged the pencils in the glass.

"Well, that's about it. I'm glad things are going so well," the woman said.

"They're perfect, just perfect," Wardrip responded.

As the two interviewers made their way back to Austin, the woman spoke to Doerfler.

"The interview with Faryion was really good," she said. "He's on his way. He's done everything perfect. But I'm bothered by one small thing."

"What's that?" Doerfler asked.

"That man is terrified to death," she said. "And I don't know why."

Doerfler agreed. He had sensed Wardrip's anxiety as well, but he couldn't put his finger on why Wardrip appeared so fearful. Faryion seemingly had it all. What could he be so afraid of?

It was agreed that John Little would conduct surveillance on the newest suspect. Tailing him. Watching him. Waiting for an opportunity to collect a DNA specimen undetected.

"We'll either eliminate him and move on, or we can start building a case for the DAs," Little said.

Investigator Little watched the buildings of downtown Wichita Falls shrink in his rear-view mirror as he headed south down Route 79 toward the little town of Olney. Wichita Falls was a thriving metropolis in comparison to the tiny Texas town. The city of one hundred thousand was supported by oil, agriculture,

Sheppard Air Force Base, and Midwestern State University.

Known for their love of the traditional Friday night high-school football game, Wichita Falls hosted the annual Oil Bowl, which matched high school all-stars from Texas against rival all-stars from neighboring Oklahoma. The other major sporting event was the Hotter 'N Hell Hundred, a bicycle competition that annually attracted thousands to the sun-baked roads of the North Texas city in temperatures that well exceeded the one hundred degrees of the event's namesake.

Little was thankful that the February temperatures were far below those of the hot Texas summers. He might be sitting for hours in his car watching his suspect, waiting to seize the opportunity to gather a DNA sample from him.

The man's routine had been fairly easy to follow. He left for work each day at the same time. Ate lunch at the plant, either brown-bagging it or waiting for his wife to deliver a hot meal, attended church on Wednesday nights and Sunday mornings.

That leg monitor has made this easier, Little thought as he stared at the closed front door of the apartment at the Mockingbird Lane apartments. *He can't leave the city without permission and he's limited within the city limits to work and church.* Little knew that if the man were more mobile, it would have been difficult to keep him under observation without being discovered.

North Texas temperatures could be brutally cold in February. The car's heater would provide welcome warmth, but the exhaust from the tail pipe could give him away. Little took no chances. He had been following the suspect for weeks. Watching. Waiting for a chance to get his evidence sample and turn it over to Gene Screen for testing.

In the weeks Little had been following the suspect, he had used a number of different cars to avoid detection. Little felt certain the man was the key to their case. The break that law enforcement, the people of Wichita Falls, and the victims' families had waited for these past fifteen years.

The dark-haired detective slumped down in his vehicle as he observed the front door to the apartment open and the man he had been expecting emerge. The suspect was followed closely by his wife. Little waited until the couple's blue Honda Civic had passed before he started his engine and made the half circle at the end of the cul-de-sac.

Well behind the blue car, Little moved slowly through Olney, past white, frame houses, turning windmills, and barking dogs. Heading north down Main Street, Little passed the Olney Door and Screen factory, watching carefully as the woman pulled the Honda to a stop in front of the factory's double-gated, chain-link fence.

Little turned his car down a side street, doubled back, and parked behind the coin-operated laundromat across Main Street from Olney Door and Screen. He could see the man kiss his wife, then walk into the back entrance of the factory. It was 6:55 A.M. on February 2, 1999.

The detective needed a better vantage point. The laundry building concealed his vehicle, but also obstructed his full view of the factory yard. He needed to move in closer.

Little had thought ahead. He knew he would need to blend in with people arriving to wash and dry their clothing. The investigator had even borrowed a basket of clothes his wife had left in their laundry room at home.

Little entered the concrete-block building and

watched silently through the large, grimy, plate-glass window that spanned the storefront. He wisely began washing, rewashing, drying, and redrying the clothing. Waiting for his chance to secure the coveted DNA sample.

The laundry kept Little warm, as well as gave him a great observation point from which to watch the suspect. He stood near the window and waited. Hoping for an opportunity to gather his evidence.

The suspect went in and out of the factory yard, drove a forklift, and loaded a trailer. Then he disappeared into the factory's main building. Little stared at the door the man had entered. Would he be inside the remainder of the day? Had this been just another wasted day of observation? Little shifted uneasily.

In five minutes, the man emerged from the same door he had entered earlier. It was nine o'clock.

The now familiar blue Honda pulled into the factory parking area and stopped just west of the double fence gates. Within seconds, the warm exhaust smoke that had penetrated the cool crisp morning air vanished.

The tall, lanky figure of a man emerged from the building. *He's taking his coffee break,* Little thought to himself as he watched the familiar figure put a package of crackers in his mouth as he opened the gate, then closed it behind him. He sat in the passenger-side seat of the Honda.

A smile of satisfaction crossed Little's handsome face as he watched his man open the package of cellophane-wrapped cheese crackers and drink from his paper cup. The man seemed at ease. He talked casually with his wife and the small child she was baby-sitting in the backseat of the vehicle, unaware of the probing dark eyes that watched his every move from across the four-lane street.

The cup, Little thought. *He can't leave it in the car.* At one point, he even toyed with the idea of running across the street, reaching through the window to grab the cup, and taking off with it. But Little waited patiently.

After fifteen minutes, the man climbed out of the Civic, said something in parting to his wife, and closed the passenger-side door. Little's eyes were fixed on the tall figure standing by the car. He didn't move. He didn't blink. He stared at the suspect as he set the coffee cup on the car, opened one side of the double gate, leaving the other side open. He took the cup from the hood of the car, and walked back into the yard. Only when the man tossed his crumpled cellophane wrapper and used coffee cup in the blue, fifty-five-gallon barrel inside the gated fence did Little's face register a small but satisfied grin.

Little continued to wait. He watched patiently as the woman drove away in the Honda and her husband climbed aboard a forklift inside the factory gates. For a few minutes, he moved metal poles from the yard into the building at the rear of the compound known as "the pole barn."

It was time for Little to make his move. He walked past the yellow painted sign that read LAUNDRY and strolled casually across Olney's four-lane Main Street dividing the factory from the laundromat, then through the fence gates. He coolly sauntered toward the blue trash barrel.

The suspect, seeing Little inside the yard, climbed down from the forklift.

"Can I help you?" he asked.

"I just need to get a spit cup," Little said, looking up at the man who stood more than four inches taller than him and pointing to the bulge of tobacco in his right cheek.

"A spit cup? Sure, help yourself," he said.

Little's eyes immediately settled on the small, eight-ounce paper cup with the words WILDCARD POKER in red and black lettering on it. The cup still held traces of the cheese crackers his man had been eating only minutes earlier.

The detective discreetly reached into the barrel and lifted the cup, careful not to touch the rim where the suspect's saliva might be present.

Got it, Little thought. *Now all I have to do is get this to Gene Screen for the DNA testing.*

Nodding toward his benefactor in a symbolic gesture of thanks, Little left the factory yard with his evidence in hand.

In a matter of days, Faryion Wardrip would either be completely cleared of any suspicion in the murders of Terry Sims and Toni Gibbs, or he would be charged with capital murder.

Victim Terry Sims, 21.

Victim Toni Gibbs, 23.

Victim Debra Taylor, 25.

Victim Ellen Blau, 21.

Victim Tina Kimbrew, 21.

Kimbrew's body was found in her apartment by relatives.

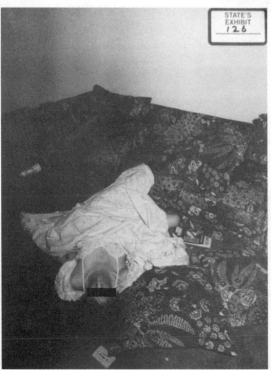

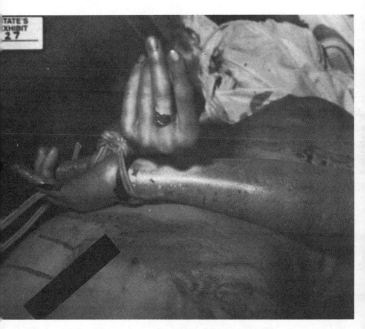

Sims's hands had been bound with an electric cord before she was raped and murdered.

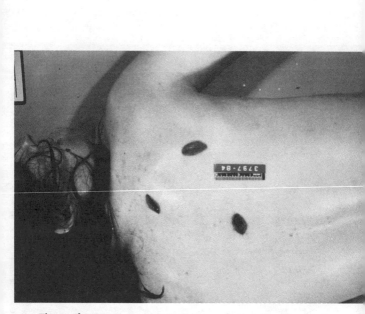

Three of Sims's ten stab wounds were to her back.

Gibbs was raped and left for dead in this rusted school bus.

Gibbs crawled from the bus to die in the grass.

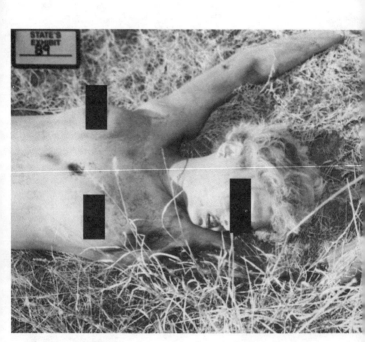

Gibbs's mutilated body was found a month after she disappeared.

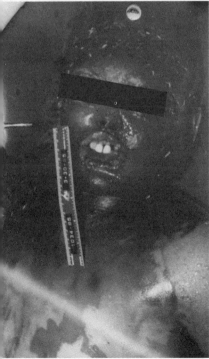

Found in a remote area
of Fort Worth, Texas,
Taylor's decomposing
body had to be
identified through
dental records.

Blau had been missing for three weeks, before her body was found ravaged by animals.

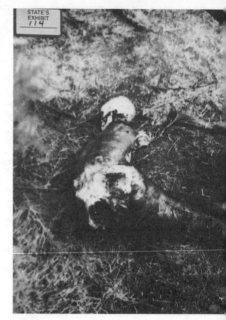

Police found all of the hair and flesh gone from Blau's skull.

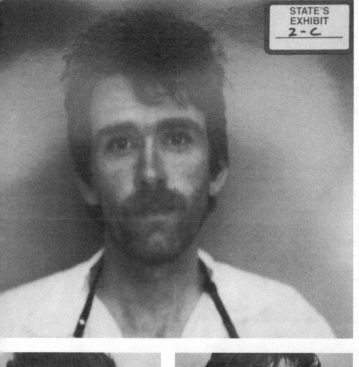

Faryion Wardrip was arrested in 1986
for the murder of Tina Kimbrew.

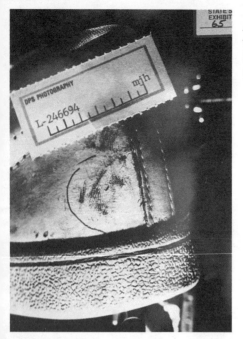

A bloody thumbprint was found on the left heel of Terry Sims's shoe.

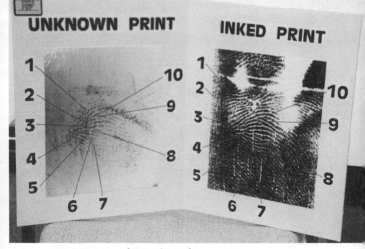

Comparison of Wardrip's fingerprint with the one found on Sims's shoe.

Wardrip's DNA was retrieved by police from his discarded spit cup.

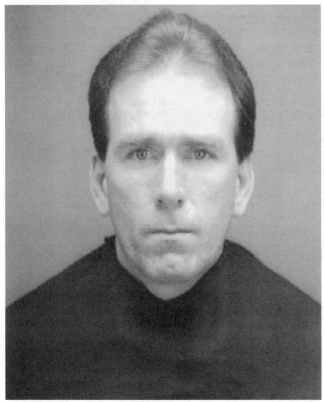

Wardrip was arrested in 1999 for the murder of Terry Sims.

Autopsy diagrams for Sims, Gibbs, and Kimbrew
showed a similar pattern of stab wounds.

Glenda Wardrip sits behind her husband Faryion in court.

Wardrip's brother Bruce after hearing verdict.

Wardrip escorted from courtroom by deputies after hearing death sentence.

Terry Sims's mother, Marsha Bridgens (left), and her sister, Vickie Grimes.

Debra Taylor's husband, Ken.

Tina Kimbrew's mother, Elaine Thornhill.

Toni Gibbs's father, W.L. Gibbs (left), and her brother, Jeff Gibbs.

District Attorney Barry Macha.

Public Defender John Curry.

Assistant Public Defender Dorie Glickman
and Investigator Dana Rice.

Faryion Wardrip on Death Row in Huntsville, Texas in 2000.

Chapter Sixteen

"John, this is Judy Floyd with Gene Screen. I was able to collect a saliva sample from the cup you sent me. I'll be able to make a comparison," the DNA expert told Little, indicating there had been enough of the salivary excretion to perform the test.

"The only way there won't be a match is if I somehow picked up the wrong cup out of that barrel," Little said confidently. Instinctually, the investigator knew Faryion Wardrip was his man. He only needed the technological evidence to prove it.

Little, Smith, and the district attorneys of both Wichita and Archer Counties waited anxiously for the results of the testing. For fifteen years, they had longed for a break in the case, but the next few days of waiting for the test results would be excruciating.

The cases of Sims and Gibbs had been dormant for years. An occasional lead that landed in the DAs' offices would be followed up, but for the most part, the cold cases had remained a mystery.

Floyd sat at her lab table at the Gene Screen facility in Dallas. She carefully took the biological material from the paper cup supplied by John Little and mixed it with chemicals that would break down other cellular materials. She only needed a tiny sample of the DNA, just one hundred to two hundred cells.

The DNA molecules consisted of paired filaments that interlocked like zippers. Each filament, made up of chemical bases, aligned in unique sequences. The DNA was amplified by separating paired filaments and mixing them with short fragments known as primers. When a primer locked on to a particular site on a sample DNA molecule, it triggered production of a longer fragment that matched a piece of the sample. A sample mixed with thirteen primers multiplied into millions of distinctive molecules. Exposed to an electrical current, the molecules sorted into color-coded bands on a gel.

Floyd then began to compare the crime-scene sample taken from the corpse of Terry Sims with Faryion Wardrip's sample. As an expert in the DNA field, Floyd knew it was virtually impossible for an unrelated person to match up perfectly on thirteen different levels. If Wardrip's sample matched, the odds of him being the perpetrator would be overwhelming.

Floyd bent over her microscope to make the comparison.

On February 12, 1999, the fax machine in the Wichita County District Attorney's office screeched the arrival of an incoming fax. The header at the top of the page announced that the communication was from Gene Screen.

More than two dozen suspects had been tested for a DNA match. Some had volunteered and others, like Wardrip, had their DNA collected secretly. Several men identified by the six police agencies who had worked the Sims, Gibbs, and Blau cases were immediately eliminated. Little and Smith waited impatiently to see if Wardrip would be among those whose semen didn't match Sims or Gibbs.

"The individual whose saliva was deposited on the cup cannot be excluded as a contributor in the sperm DNA found on Terry Sims' oral swab. The frequency of occurrence of the genetic profile found in this individual is as follows, 1 in 16,310,932 (Caucasians)," the communication read.

Little grinned with recognition. Recent breakthroughs in DNA testing had set many men free, exonerating them from violent crimes, but the tests had worked in his favor. The results confirmed Wardrip was their man. Little expected to narrow the DNA numbers down with further testing, but they had enough to request a warrant for Wardrip's arrest.

District Attorney Barry Macha was elated with the news that technology had made it possible to identify a killer that had been at large for more than fifteen years, but he knew old-fashioned gumshoe investigative work had come up with Wardrip as a possible suspect. Macha immediately gave credit to his investigator and Paul Smith, the Archer County investigator, for their work. He couldn't have been more pleased with the marriage of proven investigative techniques and recent technological advances.

Little and Smith rushed to get an arrest warrant authorizing the apprehension of Faryion Wardrip for the capital murder of Terry Sims. A separate warrant would have to be obtained for Wardrip's blood sample and fingerprints. They would be compared with crime-scene evidence once the arrest had been made. The investigators wanted Wardrip in custody as soon as possible. The arrest warrant was issued within hours.

* * *

Saturday morning, February 13, 1999, Faryion Wardrip prepared to report to his parole officer in Wichita Falls. This would be the last day he would be encumbered by the surveillance device on his ankle. He had done his time and adhered to the rules of his release for two years. Finally, he would be free—released from the constant reminder of his violent indiscretion and free from the confinement of the device he had come to think of as a ball and chain. Faryion had arranged to take the following week off from work. Now he and Glenda could take the honeymoon they had postponed for nearly four months.

"I'll be back in a couple of hours," Faryion told Glenda as he took the car keys and headed for the door of their apartment. "Then our honeymoon will begin." The newlyweds smiled at one another, kissed; then Faryion was gone.

John Little and Paul Smith talked with probation officer John Dillard in his office in the Wichita County courthouse. Smith occasionally eyed the manila folder he had placed on the desk that separated the probation officer and the investigators. All three men anxiously awaited the arrival of Wardrip: Dillard, for Wardrip's regularly scheduled parole check-in; Smith and Little to make an arrest for the murder of Terry Sims.

Dillard listened as Little and Smith explained the arrest warrant, which included an abundance of circumstantial evidence, such as the fact that Wardrip had lived two blocks from where Sims's body was found, one mile from where Gibbs's car was abandoned, and across the hall from one of Blau's close friends. He'd worked as an orderly in the same hospital as Gibbs, and later two businesses away from where Blau served fast-food on Burkburnett Road.

It was hard for Dillard to recognize the man the investigators described. Wardrip had been a model parolee since his release from prison two years earlier. Wardrip and Dillard had worked out a schedule every week and Wardrip had not strayed from the plan. In addition, Dillard had made surprise visits to check on Wardrip's whereabouts and his activities at work and home.

Wardrip had attended mandatory anger-management classes, Alcoholics Anonymous, and Narcotics Anonymous. He'd even attended meetings for longer than the state required.

"John, I've done everything the state has asked me to do. Can I get the electronic monitor off?" Wardrip had asked Dillard more than once in the two years they had been meeting.

"No, Faryion," Dillard had replied. He knew that it was futile for Wardrip to ask. No one had been released early from the monitoring system since the program had started in 1997. Faryion had to be monitored for the full two years the state had ordered. Oddly, Wardrip's time was now up. The monitor was scheduled to be removed that very day. The day he would be arrested for Sims's murder.

As usual, Wardrip arrived at Dillard's office right on time. He had been punctual for two years; there had been no reason to believe that he would be late that day.

Wardrip's face registered slight confusion as he walked into Dillard's office and saw Little and Smith rising to their feet.

Little and Smith introduced themselves, identifying

their positions with their respective district attorneys' offices. Wardrip, substantially taller than the investigators, watched the men closely.

"We want to talk to you about a few things," Smith said. "Let's go up to the DA's office."

Wardrip's heart sank. This was to have been the beginning of his freedom. He had done everything he could to make things perfect for him and Glenda. He had made more money in the last year than he had any year of his life. His sixteen-thousand-dollar income, added to Glenda's pay, totaled thirty-seven thousand dollars. It was not a lot of money to some people, but to Wardrip it was a great sum. He had even been able to trade in his old beat-up, cream-colored Pontiac for a new car.

Having given his life to God, Faryion believed he was living a blessed life. Nothing could go wrong now. He was so close to the elusive happiness he had sought for years. As soon as the leg monitor was removed, he would have the perfect life he had dreamed of and worked for.

Wardrip sat uncomfortably in the chair in the DA's office. The interview began with the standard reading of the Miranda Warning.

Considered a cornerstone of our civil liberties, the Miranda Warning is named for Ernesto Miranda, an eighth-grade dropout with a criminal record. Miranda had been arrested for raping and kidnapping a mildly retarded eighteen-year-old woman in Phoenix, Arizona. After a two-hour police interrogation, Miranda had signed a written confession. He was never told he had the right to remain silent, to have a lawyer present, or to be protected against self-incrimination. Miranda's sentence was overturned three years later, in

1966, by the Supreme Court. By their ruling, the court established that an accused person has the right to remain silent and that prosecutors may not use statements made by defendants while in custody unless they have been advised of their rights.

Miranda's reprieve was short-lived. He was convicted in a second trial and served eleven years. He was arrested and sent to prison several more times before being fatally stabbed in a barroom fight. His suspected killer was released, ironically having exercised his Miranda Right to remain silent.

Wardrip was familiar with the Miranda Warning, having been read the same rights after his 1986 arrest. But unlike his previous capture, Wardrip was determined to remain silent. He had no intentions of talking to police about Sims, Gibbs, Blau, or Taylor. This time he had too much to lose. He had Glenda. Their life together. His family. His friends. His job.

"Did you know Ellen Blau?" one of the investigators asked.

"No," Wardrip lied.

Little and Smith had agreed they would begin the questioning with the Ellen Blau case. They had the DNA evidence for Sims and Gibbs, but they lacked the physical evidence they needed to connect Wardrip with Blau's death.

"Did you have anything to do with Ellen Blau's death?"

"No," Wardrip answered emphatically.

Questioning continued for some time concerning Wardrip's connection to Blau. The suspect remained defiant in his contention that he had nothing to do with Blau's murder. Then the interview turned to the Sims's and Gibbs's murders.

Just as he had done when asked about Ellen Blau,

Wardrip denied knowing anything about the other two young Wichita Falls women.

"We have DNA evidence linking you to Terry Sims," Little said, watching Wardrip closely for any reaction. But the pronouncement didn't alter Wardrip's denial of knowing Terry Sims or killing her. Finally, Little and Smith decided to forgo any further questioning.

"Am I free to go?" Wardrip asked.

"I'm afraid not," Little said, disappointed that they hadn't gotten any information linking Wardrip to Blau.

"Faryion Wardrip, you are under arrest for the capital murder of Terry Sims," Little informed Wardrip. The investigators decided to let the suspect sit in jail and stew about the capital murder charge. The next step was to get blood samples and fingerprints. With that evidence in hand, the investigators would have the leverage they needed to put pressure on Wardrip and get the confession they wanted.

Wardrip was taken from the third-floor DA's office to the first-floor booking area of the Wichita County Jail. There the sheriff's deputy took first his right hand, then his left, and carefully rolled each of the tips of his long, lean fingers in the black ink, then rolled them on the clean, white fingerprint card.

Wardrip couldn't believe what was happening. He was supposed to be on his way home, free of the remembrances of prison. He had managed to shove the crimes of the past so far back in the recesses of his mind that he hadn't even thought of them since arriving in Olney. It was as though they never existed. He and Glenda had made plans. How could he tell her what was happening? How he could tell her now about the death of Tina Kimbrew? How could he explain why he'd lied? Would she leave him? And what would the news of his arrest do to his family, his ailing father in particular? His breathing became rapid. His hands shook as the deputy handed him a paper towel to wipe the black smudges from his fingertips.

"There's some mistake," Wardrip insisted. "I didn't do what they said."

His statements were ignored.

Wardrip was whisked into a waiting sheriff's car and transported to the hospital where a blood sample was drawn. The blood was then transferred to Judy Floyd at Gene Screen for evaluation and comparison with evidence found at the crime scenes of Sims and Gibbs.

In the confines of his jail cell, Wardrip finally relinquished control of his fear. He jumped up and down on the hard floor of the cell and he screamed to anyone that could hear.

"You people are crazy!" he yelled, pulling on the steel bars of the cell. "I didn't do this thing! I have a good job, a good wife. I'm doing great. I'm not doing anything wrong." Tears streamed down his face.

Wardrip was enraged that after two years of restricted movement and on the very day he would be unbound forever, he had again lost his freedom. He couldn't tell his parents he had again been arrested for murder. He decided to call Bryce.

"Bryce?" Wardrip said into the jail phone. "I've been arrested. I need you to call Mom and Dad."

Bryce Wardrip stared at his wife sitting at the kitchen table. He didn't say a word for several moments. Tina watched the color drain from her husband's face. Finally, he said, "I'll give you the number." His words were edged with bitterness.

"I don't have anything to write with but toothpaste," Wardrip said. "I need you to call them, then call me back later."

Anger began to fester in Bryce. Why did *he* have to always tell their folks bad news? he asked himself.

As disgusted as Bryce was with Faryion, he believed his brother was telling the truth when he said he hadn't killed the Wichita Falls women.

"I stand behind my brother," Bryce later told the press, his expression solemn. He was obviously distraught over the allegations made against his brother.

The following morning, it was Faryion Wardrip's duty to read the scriptures and serve communion to the members of the Hamilton Street Church of Christ. Some members knew why Wardrip was absent; others learned the news from parishioners as they gathered in small groups, speaking in muffled tones. Reverend Clark took over the leadership of the class that Faryion and Glenda Wardrip had been team teaching for several weeks. The Wardrips had been an effective duo. Faryion told their students horror stories of life on the streets as a sinner, while Glenda tempered his stories with her knowledge of the Bible and God's salvation.

On hearing the news of their teacher's arrest, the junior high kids wanted to talk about Wardrip and what he had been accused of doing. Typically, the kids recoiled. They were numbed by the news, not unlike their parents.

Clark spoke to the leaders of the church just prior to the morning worship service, warning them that a reporter from the Wichita Falls newspaper had requested to attend their morning worship service. The reporter, like any other visitor, was welcomed by Clark to worship with his congregation. But the elders were nervous about the visitor's intrusion on their private quandary.

"The reporter's out there from the newspaper.

What are you going to do?" one of the elders asked anxiously just prior to entering the sanctuary.

"Let God work," the young minister replied calmly.

Clark knew he had to address Wardrip's arrest up front. As he looked out upon his congregation, a woman slipped into a pew and whispered to her friend, "Did you see the newspaper? I just can't believe it. I just can't put him [Wardrip] together with what they say he's done."

Clark's congregation waited silently in the pews for him to tell them what to do amidst all the flurry. In their hands, they held the morning service's bulletin, where Faryion Wardrip's name appeared as a participant in the morning worship. He was to read the scriptures as the elders passed out the communion Eucharist.

Moments after Clark took his place at the front of the church, he began to speak. "We've got some business to conduct. If you haven't heard from the media, if you haven't read the newspaper yet, Faryion Wardrip's been arrested for some old murders in Wichita Falls. We need to talk about this."

Clark read prayer requests from Wardrip's family, then asked his congregation to rise up, seize the opportunity, and use it for the church's advantage. "Folks, this is a wide-open opportunity to show everyone what we're made of," Clark said.

Clark had to reaffirm the people's place as a church.

"We are here to offer the Gospel of Jesus Christ and the grace of God and His forgiveness. That is who we are. That is what we do. That's what we've done. We have nothing to be ashamed of. Nothing to hide. That you are here is a testimony to that.

"We are going to put this in God's hands and we're going to pray for this family. And pray for Faryion," Clark said.

"First of all, we're in the business of loving people. . . . All we can offer, all we have to comfort them is the love we have for him and his family." Clark's words brought a resounding "amen" from several churchgoers.

"Each of you will have to make up your own mind," Clark continued. "Don't judge him too harshly."

Clark reminded the people that under our justice system a man, even a once-convicted murderer, is innocent until proven guilty.

"Wait until you hear all the facts before you decide what you think," Clark counseled. "Remember what you know about this man. And let's show everyone how God's family can respond to a crisis like this."

As his fellow church members weighed the impact of his arrest on their congregation, Wardrip was transferred from his jail cell back to the booking area of the jail.

"We need to reprint you, Wardrip," the deputy explained.

The first set of fingerprints taken the previous day were not of the quality needed for comparison. Wardrip couldn't be ruled out as the person who had left a bloody thumbprint on the tennis shoe of Terry Sims, but a clearer print was needed for a positive identification.

As soon as Wardrip's prints had been registered on the new print card, they were sent to the Department of Public Safety's crime lab in Austin to be compared with the print on Sims's shoe.

Wardrip remained in jail while Little and Smith continued their work, shoring up the case against him. The investigators filed a probable cause affidavit with the court. The document consisted of facts and circumstances sufficient to warrant belief that Faryion Wardrip had been responsible for the death of Terry Sims. The record revealed DNA evidence linking Wardrip to Sims. Little then released the affidavit to the press.

The headline of the Wichita Falls *Times Record News* closely resembled one that spanned the front page of the daily paper more than thirteen years earlier. Faryion Wardrip had been arrested for murder.

The newspaper cited the DNA evidence collected from the suspect, which matched the semen found in the bodies of Sims and Gibbs.

"Tests revealed that his DNA was a one-in-sixteenmillion match with semen found in Sims's body," the *Olney Enterprise,* Wardrip's hometown newspaper, stated in their cover story.

Faryion Wardrip sat despondently on his jail bunk, tears falling on the newspaper resting on his knees.

"Wardrip, you have a visitor," the jailer announced.

"Who is it?" Wardrip asked.

"Your wife."

Wardrip longed to see Glenda, to hold her, and at the same time he dreaded facing her. What was he going to tell her? How would he explain the crimes or the fact that he had never bothered to mention them before now? He entered the visiting area filled with apprehension.

Glenda Wardrip's eyes were red from too many tears and too little sleep. She stared at her husband through the glass barrier. Her pale face, reddened eyes, and impassive expression told Wardrip she was in shock.

"Glenda, I'm so sorry," Wardrip said. "I should have told you everything."

Glenda gently shook her head, her brown hair softly swinging from side to side. "No," she said, "I don't want to talk about the past."

As Glenda left the visitor's area, Wardrip thought, *It's all over.* His years of trying to rehabilitate himself. His relationship with his family. The job he loved. Marriage to the woman he adored. All gone. Convinced there was nothing left for him to salvage, Faryion Wardrip called out for a deputy.

"Tell John, that DA guy, I want to talk to him," Faryion said. "And tell him he better get out here before I change my mind."

Chapter Seventeen

John Little was at his desk reviewing the DNA test forwarded to him by Judy Floyd when the phone rang.

"This is Captain Foster at the jail annex," Foster told Little. "A couple of my jailers have advised me that when they were escorting Faryion Wardrip to his cell, he told them he wanted to speak to you."

"Okay, I'll be out there shortly," Little said.

"Wardrip said you better get out here before he changes his mind," Foster said.

Little immediately contacted Paul Smith to meet him at the jail annex in the southern portion of Wichita Falls, then grabbed a tape recorder and writing pad and headed for the door.

Perhaps the newspaper article had done the trick, Little thought. Possibly Wardrip realized they had enough evidence to convict him. Conceivably he could confess.

Little knew better than to get excited about an inmate sending word that he wanted to talk. He would just have to wait and find out what Wardrip had on his mind.

Little and Smith were already in the jail library/study room when Wardrip was escorted in by guards. Wardrip, pale faced and wearing a white jail uniform, was restrained in handcuffs and leg irons. Wardrip appeared depressed and withdrawn, nothing like the confidant person Little had confronted previously. His hair was a mess and his shoulders stooped. He spoke in hushed tones rather than the brash timber of their previous meeting.

"I want to talk," Wardrip said as he sat across from the investigators.

Little nodded to the guard, who unlocked the handcuffs. The prisoner's legs remained shackled.

"That's why we're here," Smith said.

"I visited with my wife this morning. Now I want to talk," Wardrip said.

"On Saturday you advised us that you wanted an attorney," Little said. "We can't speak to you unless you waive your rights."

"I'll waive them," Wardrip responded. He looked tired, defeated.

Once again, Wardrip was given the Miranda Warning, advising him that he was entitled to an attorney and that statements he made could (would) be used against him in a court of law.

Wardrip agreed to the provisions and formally waived his rights. Little started the taperecorder.

"Test, one, two, three, test, one, two, three. Today's date is February the sixteenth, 1999. The time is 10:28 A.M. We are at the Wichita County Sheriff's Office Detention Center at the annex. Present in the room is myself, John Little, I'm an investigator for the DA's office in Wichita County; Paul Smith, investigator for the DA's office in Montague County; and Faryion Edward Wardrip."

Little instructed Wardrip to identify himself on the tape; then the investigator stated their purpose.

"We are here today to talk to Mr. Wardrip about

some unsolved cases from 1984 through 1985," Little said. "You have the right to terminate the interview at any time. Do you understand that?"

"I do," Wardrip said solemnly, but he had no intention of stopping the proceedings. His mind was made up. He would tell Little and Smith everything they wanted to know. The life Wardrip had dreamed of was gone. He knew he couldn't get it back. It was time to confess.

"Faryion, what I would like to do is just kind of go back to the beginning in your own words and start with the events surrounding December 21, 1984, if you would. This would be in reference to the death of Terry Sims," Little prompted.

"I don't recall the dates to be exact. I do know, at that time I was under heavy drugs. Intravenous drugs caused a lot of dysfunctional activities in my life. All it did was create hate in my heart. I was out walking, actually walking home. I had been in a fight with my ex-wife. Drugs had just totally taken control of my life and as I was walking, she [Sims] was at her door. I went up to the door and forced my way in. Well, I just ransacked her, just slung her all over the house in a violent rage. Stripped her down and murdered her," Wardrip said, his voice trailing off as he lowered his head.

"Where were you living at this time, Mr. Wardrip?" Little asked.

"About four blocks up from where the incident happened," Wardrip answered.

"Where were you working at that time?" Little asked.

"I don't think I was working," Wardrip said.

"Can you describe to me how you killed Ms. Sims?" Little asked.

"I think she was stabbed," Wardrip said with a

puzzled look on his face. "It is hard to remember, but she was stabbed. It was such a violent rage I don't recall all the details, but I know I'm responsible for it."

"Do you remember what you did immediately after you committed the crime?" Little asked.

"Walked. Just walked until I finally ended up back at the house. I remember walking. It was raining. I just walked all hours and then somehow I ended up back at the apartment," Wardrip said.

"Who was living at the apartment with you?" Little asked.

"My ex-wife. Johnna. That's the only name I know. She has remarried and moved. I don't know where," Wardrip said.

"Did you have any conversation with Ms. Sims beforehand?" Little asked.

"No."

"Did you know her in any way beforehand?"

"No."

"So you just were walking in the neighborhood and saw her standing there at her door going in," Little stated.

"Yes."

"Did you knock on the door?" Little asked.

Wardrip contemplated the question for a moment, then spoke. "I don't recall. I don't recall."

"Did you have sex with her?"

Wardrip looked surprised. "No, I don't think I had sex. I'm almost pretty sure that I didn't have sex with her. I do remember stripping her down out of anger, but I don't recall having sex with her."

Had Wardrip forgotten the violent sexual assault on Terry Sims, or was he cunning enough to know rape coupled with murder made for a capital offense punishable by death?

"Do you recall what the house looked like that she lived in?" Little asked.

"No, it was dark. But I think it was white. If I'm going to guess, I'll say white. But all I know is that I was just walking and it was raining and I was so mad at the world. I saw two or three people that evening and I just wanted to just lash out. As I came upon Sims, I just lashed out," Wardrip said.

"Do you recall what you did with the knife that was used?" Little asked.

"No," Wardrip said, looking at Little questioningly. "It could be laying anywhere. I'm surprised it wasn't there."

"You didn't bring the knife with you?" Little asked.

"I—I can't remember if I had a knife or not. I don't think I did," Wardrip said, somewhat confused.

"Did you ever own a black-handled hunting knife?" Little asked.

"No, I never was a hunter or nothing."

"Did you ever carry a boot knife?"

"No, not that I recall. I never did carry a boot knife," Wardrip said.

Wardrip either failed to remember or deliberately chose not to tell Little and Smith about giving his brother Bryce a broken-handled, lock-blade knife as his brother and parents were leaving for a trip to the races in Altus, Oklahoma.

"I want to give you this," Wardrip had told Bryce. "A friend lost it out of his back pocket."

Bryce had taken the knife from his older brother, but lost it himself on the Oklahoma trip.

"Okay, that's fine," Wardrip had told Bryce when he told him about the missing six-inch knife.

"You spoke of a rage that was building up. What was causing the rage?" Little asked as he and Smith continued their questioning of Wardrip.

"Just all the things that go on in life. I thought my family hated me. I hated them. My wife kept coming in and out of my life. She'd come to me when times were good and then when times got hard, she'd leave and I just kept turning towards drugs. I thought everybody was out to get me. The drugs made me paranoid. And I guess the way I grew up with drugs when I was a kid, the drinking, it made me have violent outbursts. It just kept with me and I kept turning to drugs and drinking to cover it up. Thinking it would go away and it never did. I would just reach a boiling point. But the crazy thing about it was, I was so mad at my wife, but I never done anything to her. But I was just so mad and so angered. Satan had a firm hold on me, boy, he had a firm hold," Wardrip said, the emotion rising and falling in his voice.

"Did you go into the bedroom with Ms. Sims?" Little asked.

"Probably. I think we were in all different parts of the house, I think," Wardrip said.

"Do you remember anything about the bedroom you were in?" Little asked.

"No, I barely remember the house," Wardrip said.

"Did you tie Ms. Sims's hands behind her back?"

"Yes."

"With what?"

"Rope. I believe it was a rope," Wardrip said.

"Could it have been an electrical cord?" Little asked.

"It could have been," Wardrip said. "I don't remember, but I remember tying her hands behind her back."

"Do you remember where you left her at when you left the house? What room?" Little asked.

"Boy, I've blocked this out of my memory for so long," Wardrip said, shaking his head slightly. "Maybe the bathroom, maybe the kitchen, maybe the bath-room."

Wardrip paused momentarily.

"Maybe the bathroom," he repeated.

"Okay, I would like to move on now, at this point to approximately a month later, January 19, 1985. Mr. Smith would like to ask you some questions about a case he is investigating," Little said.

Paul Smith moved in a little closer to his suspect.

"We are referring to a nurse that worked at the General Hospital, Toni Jean Gibbs. Do you recall that?" Smith asked.

"Yeah," Wardrip said, taking a deep breath. "Again, I was out walking. Been out walking all night. Somehow I was downtown. It was about six o'clock in the morning. Just walking. And I started walking home. It was starting to get daylight and, uh, I was walking up towards the hospital. Toni knew me and she asked me if I wanted a ride and I said, 'Yeah,' and so we got in the car and she gave me a ride. I started basically in on her. I started seeing images of anger and hate, and it just clicked off and I told her to drive out the road there. I don't re-member which direction we were going, I just told her to drive. We drove out the road and I just grabbed her and started trying to sling her around the car and she swerved off the side of the road and we ended up on the side of the road and she turned down a dirt road and I still had her by her jacket and I was just slinging her, trying to sling her and I was screaming as loud as I can at her. I told her to stop and she stopped. I did the same thing. I took off her clothes and I stabbed her."

"Can you describe the location where this hap-pened?" Smith asked.

"Just a dirt road in a field." Faryion shrugged.

"Was there some kind of a structure out there in the field?" Smith asked.

"Maybe trees. Trees, that is the only thing I can think of, would be trees," Wardrip said.

"What did you do with the clothing?" Smith asked, trying to get their suspect to remember the burned-out bus where Gibbs's clothing was found.

"They should still be right there. I don't remember doing anything with the clothing," Wardrip said.

"Do you remember the weather that day?" Smith asked.

"It was cold," Wardrip said.

"Do you recall if there was some kind of an old bus body or trolley car body or something there?" Smith finally asked directly.

"No, I just . . . some of it," Wardrip said, apparently confused. "It took me a long time to remember a lot of different stuff because when I was in those rages, I just blacked out. I just don't remember. I don't remember that."

"Do you recall what you did with the knife in that case?" Smith asked.

"Probably it stayed right there. I don't remember doing anything with the knife, anything specific. It probably stayed right there," Wardrip said.

"How was Toni dressed?" Smith asked.

"Uh—" Wardrip hesitated, his eyes shifting to the left as he thought. "She was in her nurse's uniform."

"What color was this leather jacket? Do you remember?" Smith asked, pointing to a photo.

Wardrip took a deep breath and closed his eyes momentarily. "Brown maybe. Black. Black. I tried my best to envision it."

"How did you strip her clothes off?" Smith asked.

"I guess in the car, just pulling on her. Yeah, just wantin' to sling her around," Wardrip said.

"Do you remember where you were at, at that point?"

"We started at the car. I think she got away from me and got out the door, I'm not sure. Started to run, that's how we got in the field. I'm not sure," Wardrip said, shaking his head in puzzlement.

"What kind of car was Toni driving?" Smith asked.

"A white car. I think it was a Camaro."

"What happened to the car?"

"I drove it down the freeway and just parked it. Got out and started walking," Wardrip said.

"Where did you park it?"

"Oh, I can't remember the name of the street. I just remember coming off the freeway and just pulling up and stopping somewhere off the side of the freeway," Wardrip said.

"Was it close to where you were living?"

"Oh, it could have been," Wardrip said. "I think it was close to that McDonald's there at the end of the freeway. I think it was somewhere around there, around McDonald's," Wardrip said with more clarity.

Paul Smith leaned closer to Wardrip, staring closely into his deep-set brown eyes.

"Did you have sex with Toni Gibbs?" Smith asked.

"I don't really remember. I remember screaming at her, screaming at her that 'I hate you.' I don't remember if I had sex. I just remember screaming how much 'I hate you!' How much I hated everybody," Wardrip said.

"You said that Toni knew you. How did you meet Toni?" Smith asked.

"From the hospital. I met her there. She never had anything to do with me. I just knew her from there. It could have been anybody, she just happened to be in the wrong place at the wrong time. It could have been anybody. I never set my sights on anybody. I would just get so mad and I would just get out and walk, be in such a rage. I would just scream at the sky, scream at the trees, scream at God. Then I would just lay down for a while and sleep and then I'd see it on the news and I realized that something must have happened real bad. I tricked myself. I tricked myself into thinking it wasn't me. And I'd hear all these things. At first that she was shot and I knew it couldn't have been me. I never shot. I had no gun. I hear she got abducted from her apartment and I thought that couldn't be me. I haven't been way out there at her apartment. So I just tricked myself into thinking it wasn't me. The same with Terry. They say all kinds of reports that she was some kind of karate person and it must have been a gang or something. And all these reports kept coming in, and they just convinced me more and more that it wasn't me. I just blocked it out of my mind, wouldn't even want to think about it for a long, long, long time," Wardrip said, his chin dropping toward his chest.

"I'd like to talk to you about another case that I'm investigating at this point," John Little said as he resumed his questioning. "About the disappearance and murder of Ellen Blau in September, I believe, September 20, 1985. Do you know anything about that?"

"Yeah," Wardrip said, his head still tilted downward.

Little paused his questioning of Wardrip long enough to go into the hall outside the jail library/study room where loud noises were disturbing the interview.

"Okay, Faryion, if you would, would you tell me about the murder of Ellen Blau?" Little said on his return.

"Same thing," Wardrip said matter-of-factly. "I'd just be out walking, just walking."

"Where were you walking?" Little asked.

"Down the highway, coming up to the stoplight there by the base where the McDonald's is. There's a stoplight there. Just walking up to the stop sign. She pulled up and turned into the store, so I turned into the store, too. And she pulled up to the side of the building and I walked up to the side of the building and asked her what she was doing. She said she was looking for somebody, and I just grabbed her and pushed her back into her car. We drove out to a road and got about maybe a mile or so out the road, and I just started grabbing her and screaming at her, 'I hate you.' We went off the road and turned on a dirt road and went down a little further. I drug her out of the car, took her in a field and stripped her clothes off, but I don't remember how she died though. I didn't rape, I don't believe I raped her. I don't recall. I don't really remember how she died. She probably broke her neck because I sure was slinging her. I was just so mad and angry. I was screaming at her," Wardrip said.

"Did you try to have sex with her?" Little asked.

"No, I don't . . . no, I was too mad. I was so angry at her. She was just in the wrong place at the wrong time. If she had never even came up to that stoplight I would have just kept right on walking," Wardrip said, almost implying that it had been Blau's fault, not his, that she died.

"You forced her back into the car," Little stated.

"Yeah, I pushed her into the car. Wasn't nobody around. I just grabbed her and slung her up on the side of the car and pushed her into the car and told her to take a ride. So we went for a ride. I got so mad at her, I just started grabbing her and shaking her. She went off the road and we just turned and went on some dirt road. We only went about a mile or so," Wardrip said, expelling a deep sigh.

"Can you describe the field or pasture that you took her in?" Little asked.

"No, it was just a field," Wardrip said, shrugging. "I never really paid attention. It could have been anywhere. I just stopped and drug her out of her car and started slinging her. It was so weird. I was so mad, but I never hit them. I just slung them, just grabbed them and slung them. I never struck her. Just like my ex-wife, I never hit her, but I was so mad at her. I know a couple of times I'd see her face and I'd just get even more mad, go shoot up some drugs."

Wardrip's face was twisted by the painful memories, the bad choices, the addictions.

"Whose face were you seeing?" Little asked.

"My ex-wife's. I hated her so much," Wardrip said with a touch of the bitterness he had felt fourteen years earlier. "It was just like with Tina [Kimbrew]. I was screaming at her and I had my arm across her throat. I was screaming at her, bloody murder. I didn't see Tina's face, I saw Johnna's. I was so consumed with hatred. I never hit them though, that's what really threw me. I wonder why I didn't, but I never struck. I just grabbed and slung and yelled at her."

Little gave Smith a lingering glance. According to the autopsy reports on the four women, they had been struck, beaten. Either Wardrip couldn't remember the full details of his crimes or he was attempting to portray himself as a less-than-brutal killer. Little's attention returned to Wardrip.

"What kind of car was Ellen Blau in?" Little asked.

"Small one. I remember it was a small car," Wardrip said.

"Did you ever take anything from these women?" Smith wanted to know.

"No."

"No money, jewelry, anything like that?" Smith pursued.

"No, I never took any jewelry or anything," Wardrip said, shaking his head vigorously.

"What did you do after you killed Ellen Blau?" Little returned to his questioning.

"I started to walk down this dirt road and it was all dark and I didn't know which way to go. So I started walking and then I couldn't figure out where I was at, so I turned around and I went back and got in the car and drove it back to town. I just parked the car when I knew where I was and started walking," Wardrip explained.

"Do you remember where you parked the car?" Little asked.

"No. I got into town and saw where I was and then parked the car. I don't remember where I parked it at. I just parked it," Wardrip said with some frustration.

"When you abducted Ellen Blau, who drove? When you forced her back into the car?" Little asked.

"She drove," Wardrip said.

"Did you threaten her?" Little asked.

"No, she didn't know what . . . she didn't know nothing."

"Did you know Ellen Blau?" Little asked.

"No, no, Toni was the only one I knew, and she offered me a ride," Wardrip explained.

"Were you working anywhere when Ellen Blau disappeared, in that time frame?" Little asked.

"I wasn't holding no job down, I was mostly doing drugs, going from drug dealer to drug dealer, wherever I could get some drugs. Then I'd stop doing drugs, but the hatred had consumed me so much that it just covered everything up and made it like it never did happen in my life. That couldn't have been me, that's what I told myself. I'd see it on TV and stuff, I mean, I felt sorry. But I had just convinced myself that that couldn't possibly be me, so I would just do drugs to cover it back up. So long as I had drugs, I was all right, and I would just go some place else where there were drugs," Wardrip said rapidly. He wanted Little and Smith to understand it was the drugs. The drugs had driven him down the road to ruination.

"Was Ellen Blau in Wichita Falls when you encountered her that night?" Little asked.

"Yeah, she was out there by the base. She pulled up to the stoplight and turned into the store there when I was walking by," Wardrip said, repeating his earlier statement.

"Do you remember what the store was? The name of the store?" Little asked.

"Just the store there at the light. Might have been a Circle K or could have been a 7-Eleven. I don't know," Wardrip said, sounding confused.

Little took a deep breath, stared Faryion Wardrip in the eye, and asked again, "Did you kill Ellen Blau?"

"Yeah. I don't remember how, might have broke her neck. I don't know because I was slinging her around. She wasn't very heavy at all," Wardrip said.

"Did you kill Toni Gibbs?" Smith asked.

"Yeah," Wardrip said, lowering his head.

"Did you kill Terry Sims?" Smith asked.

"Yes," Wardrip said, his shoulders drooped, his head bowed.

Little reached across the table to push the OFF button on the recorder. He stopped, his hand poised in the air over the machine, as Wardrip spoke again.

"My conscience has to keep going. There is one more," Wardrip said.

The investigators looked at one another in surprise.

Had they forgotten to question Wardrip about some-one?

"It ain't here though. This is in Fort Worth," War-drip announced. He had to get the truth out. The whole truth. He had waited fourteen years to purge his soul, he couldn't stop now.

"I had left Wichita and I went to Fort Worth, went to a club or something. There was this girl there and we were dancing and then she was being real . . . com-ing on to me and entertaining me and we decided to leave. We went out to the parking lot around back, and I made my advance towards her and she said no. She slapped my face, and when she did that I just snapped. I grabbed her and I slung her around, and I done the same thing to her that she did to me. And I killed her," Wardrip told the astonished detectives.

After a momentary pause to collect his thoughts, Little finally asked, "How did you kill her?"

"I think I strangled her. I had her on the ground and I think I used my forearm," Wardrip said.

"This was in Fort Worth," Little stated for the re-cord.

"Yeah. I believe her name was Debra Taylor. I'm not sure, but I think her name was Debra Taylor. This had to have been in '86," Wardrip said as if trying to recall the details as he spoke. "It was on East Lancaster at a club, and I was staying at the Travel Lodge trying to find a job. All I found was just more drugs. The Travel Lodge was full of people selling drugs. If I had the money instead of finding a job, I just bought drugs, shot drugs, kept shooting the drugs. I went out to that club or bar, whatever you want to call it, and her name is Debra. I believe."

"Do you remember what the name of the bar was?" Little asked.

"No, I can show you. Hell, it's even still there. I had

somebody's car, I can't remember whose car it was. Might have been someone at the motel, I think it was. And I put her in the car, took her up the interstate there off of East Lancaster, and found the first road and just threw her out," Wardrip said with no visible sign of emotion.

"Did you kill her in the parking lot or out there where you dumped her?" Little asked.

"In the parking lot, I think. In the back of the parking lot," Wardrip said.

"Do you remember what time of year in 1986?"

"No, it might have been 1985. I don't know," Wardrip said, his brow wrinkled in thought.

"Was it before all of the murders in Wichita Falls or after?" Little asked, trying to get a fix on the specific date that the Fort Worth murder had occurred. He and Smith would have to notify the Fort Worth Police Department. The Cowtown cops could check out the information against any unsolved murders they had that fell into that time frame.

"It was after, it was before. It was after Ellen, Toni, and Terry, and before Tina Kimbrew. So it was, it was after Ellen," Wardrip answered.

"After September of 1985?" Little prodded.

"I don't know the date," Wardrip said sharply. "It had to be after Ellen because Ellen was the last one besides Tina, and then I packed my bags and took off hitchhiking and I went to Fort Worth."

Paul Smith stepped forward. "Faryion, if we were to get the sheriff's authorization to take you from the jail, could you take us to each one of these places? Do you think you could find these places where these murders took place?"

"Oh, probably, but I don't know. I'm doubtful. I've drove through Wichita Falls a lots of times. It might be hard," Wardrip said.

"Would you be willing to try?" Smith asked.

"Yes, but I don't want to be followed by a bunch of the media," Wardrip anxiously warned.

"I'll assure you, you won't be followed by the media," Little interjected.

"Because, if I see media following us, I'm just going to shut up. I've done said—I had to say what God told me to say and what I'm supposed to say to confess my sins and that's what I've done. And I'm not going to be a circus, 'cause I'm not one," Wardrip said, the words pouring out of him.

"Believe me, we don't want it to be that way either," Smith reassured Wardrip.

"My parents don't deserve this, my wife doesn't deserve this, my children don't deserve this, my brothers and sisters . . . it's because of those damn drugs and the hatred that I had in my heart. I caused so much pain to the victims' families—but I don't want to burn in hell."

Wardrip was distraught. All he had worked for in the eleven years he was in prison and the two years he had been living in Olney was gone. He began to babble about his loss.

"God told me that you think I'm kidding you, but He revealed when He gave my wife to me like He did for a couple of months. I asked her today to forgive me. I told her what I was going to do, not in so many words, because I know they listen, but I just asked her to forgive me. She said, for what? I said for all the lies, the lies that I told you. She said, what lies? I said because I brought you into my life knowing that this thing very well could happen. I didn't care, I knew I'd never get away with it. I did know that this day would happen. I realized it when I went to prison the first time. I knew this day would happen. Man, but yet, I still took a wife, and she's a beautiful Christian woman. I don't know if you've ever seen her, but she's a beautiful Christian woman. She didn't deserve this. Nobody does. Nobody does. I don't care what happens to me. If they want to put me to death, then so be it. 'Cause I'm tired of living on this earth, tired of pain and suffering that Satan brings to people, no matter how hard you try. No matter how good of things you do . . . it always seems to mess up.

"If you don't follow what God tells you to do, it's going to happen to you, I guarantee it," Wardrip said, looking straight into the eyes of the men who had cost him his freedom. "I tried to tell that to my little brother because he drinks and he's got three kids, and he's got a temper, too. And I tried to be an example, just like you said, John." Wardrip spoke directly to Investigator Little as he listened closely.

"You saw what I was doing, I was trying to. I really thought I could do it, live my lie, but God knew it. God knew this was coming, that is why He gave me the opportunity to repent and to see what it was like to live in a community with good Christian people. People that will love you no matter what. And that's what He's done. He told me this. He gave me Glenda. He gave me that community. All those people, no matter what I've done, they didn't care. They love me. Nobody ever told me that before, and I had people who love me. Oh, Lord, just do whatever to me. Forgive me. If you love your children, you will tell them that Satan is alive and the devil will get you with drugs and alcohol. If you do not live your life the way you should, he will get you. You will burn, as I have burned for so long. He is so real. He is so real. And I just wish I would have learned this a long time ago. Why is this now? Oh, my God, what have I done?" Wardrip said, placing his head in his hands.

"I'm so sorry. My parents didn't deserve this. God, they don't deserve it," Wardrip moaned.

"Faryion, will you be willing to cooperate with authorities in Tarrant County or Fort Worth to help them with that case?" Little asked, referring to the unsolved murder of Debra Taylor.

"Yeah, it's over with. I already feel all the relief gone. I'm so sorry, all the guilt, all the shame, it's all gone. I've done what God said, God said to confess your sins. I'm just tired. I have a headache," Wardrip said as he rested his head in his hands.

"Faryion, was this statement you gave to me today voluntary?" Little asked.

"Yes."

"Were you promised anything in return for giving me this statement?" Little asked.

Wardrip looked into Little's cool eyes. "Eternal life with God is what I was promised. I was promised that I won't burn in hell."

"And what you told me and Mr. Smith here today is all the truth?" Little asked.

"It's the truth," Wardrip said, his eyes dark and soulful. "It's over with, I give up. I can't go no more. You can kill me now. I don't care."

Chapter Eighteen

Investigator Little glanced at Smith questioningly. Smith shook his head slightly.

"At this time, I'm going to terminate the interview," Little said. "The date is still February 16, 1999. The time now is 11:18 A.M. That will conclude the interview."

Fifty minutes from the time Faryion Wardrip began his confession, Little turned off the recorder. He ordered a written transcript of the eighteen-page sworn statement that he, Smith, and Wardrip signed before it was delivered to the district attorney's office.

Back in his cell, Wardrip was falling into deeper depths of despair. He requested to use the phone and dialed his younger brother.

"Bryce, I did it. I did it all," Wardrip said through sobs. "I've been living with this guilt all these years. I feel so much better now. I want to be put to death. I want my life to be over. Tell Mom and Dad."

Bryce held the phone receiver to his ear. Not speaking or moving. *What is Faryion saying?* Bryce wondered. *He told me he didn't kill those women. He told me it was all a lie. I went on television to defend him. What does he mean, he did it all?*

"I wanted to be like you," Wardrip said. "You have a perfect life. I'm so proud of you."

Bryce could hear his brother crying as his own cheeks reddened with anger. Bryce felt used by his older brother. He felt like a fool.

"It's not the perfect life. It's knowing right from wrong!" Bryce shouted.

Bryce's anger at his brother grew. Faryion's laziness and drug use had kept him from doing anything worthwhile with his life. He'd drifted from job to job, never settling down until he had been released from prison for the murder of Tina Kimbrew.

Bryce, on the other hand, had begun work in the oil fields when he was only sixteen years old. He took home six hundred dollars a week, giving most of it to his parents to pay for rent, utilities, and food while his father was in intensive care recovering from a heart attack. With the exception of Roy, another drug-and-alcohol-addicted brother, the other seven Wardrip children had grown to be good citizens and responsible adults. They had all pitched in when their parents fell on hard times. But where had Faryion been when their parents needed help? Bryce winced as he thought of the answer. His brother had spent his youth stoned on drugs and most of his young adulthood in the state prison for murder.

Bryce's thoughts jumped from Faryion to his parents. Once again Faryion had left it up to him to be the bearer of bad news. At that moment Bryce hated Faryion. Their parents had helped his older brother so much. They had signed papers for him to have a car and he failed to make the payments. They raised him to be independent, yet he continually sponged off others. They provided clothes, toys, food, shelter for all their nine children. Yet Faryion was never happy.

The day of Faryion's arrest for the murder of Sims, their father had made a public statement that his son was not guilty.

"We're right now in the process of trying to find an attorney to take his case. I promise you this is not true. He didn't do this thing," George Wardrip had said. His voice had been laced with pain. He'd wanted the press, friends, the community to know his son was not guilty of such a ghastly crime.

Surprisingly, George Wardrip had also stated that he believed Faryion was innocent of Kimbrew's murder, a murder Faryion had confessed to and served eleven years at TDCJ for.

"We didn't have the money at the time to hire an attorney and he ended up with a plea bargain," the elder Wardrip had said. "He did that because he didn't want to put us through a trial. He did his time, he got out, and he started a new life. He doesn't drink or smoke anymore, and he's been clean from drugs for at least the last twelve years. He goes to church and teaches Sunday school. He's there every time they opened the doors."

Bryce hung up the phone and sat down at the table in his modest kitchen. His father was fighting cancer. He was at the Veteran's Administration hospital five days during the week for treatment, only coming home to his family on weekends. But instead of worrying about his health, he had been out trying to raise money and find a lawyer willing to handle Faryion's case. Bryce knew Faryion's confession would be a blow to his father, a shock he might not recover from.

Bryce picked up the phone and called District Attorney Barry Macha's office. Before putting his parents through another living hell, he needed to know if what his older brother had told him was true.

"We have pretty strong evidence," Macha told

Bryce. "We have a partial thumbprint and DNA. It doesn't look good for your brother."

"If I can help you, just let me know," Bryce said bitterly.

Bryce was back at work when Macha called.

"I've got some more questions I want to ask you," Macha said. "Can you come to Wichita Falls tomorrow?"

"I'll be there," Bryce said.

When Bryce arrived at the Wichita County courthouse, he cleared the metal detectors and was escorted upstairs to meet with Macha, Assistant District Attorney Jerry Taylor, and Investigator Paul Smith.

"We have a taped confession, Bryce," Macha said. "I'll just need to ask you a few questions. Are you ready?"

Bryce stared at Macha in bewilderment. He believed they had tape recorded his telephone conversation with Faryion without his knowledge. The oral confession of murder made to him would now be used against his brother.

"Yeah," Bryce replied, then followed Macha to the district courtroom down the hall from the DA's office.

"Sit here," Smith directed him.

In a matter of minutes, twelve people filed in from a courtroom side door and sat in the chairs reserved to the left of the judge's bench. Bryce's brow wrinkled as he studied the grand jury questioningly. He nervously fiddled with the brim of the Western hat he held in his hands. Bryce had expected to be speaking to Macha and the investigators. No one had said a word about being questioned before the grand jury.

For the next two hours, Bryce Wardrip answered questions about his brother. Convinced that his phone conversation with Faryion earlier that morning was the confession Macha had earlier referred to, Bryce was filled with resentment mixed with guilt.

News of the arrest of Faryion Wardrip, an ex-con who lived less than fifty miles away, sent shivers down the spines of residents who'd lived in the Wichita Falls area during the mid-1980s. Even Tina Wardrip, Faryion Wardrip's own sister-in-law and a high school student at the time of the murders, hadn't been allowed to go into Wichita Falls during the eighteen-month crime spree. Her father had feared for her safety. Now, fourteen years later, Tina recalled the number of times her brother-in-law had been in their home and played with their children. She'd never suspected that her children's fun-loving uncle was capable of killing.

Random updates from the DA's office and knowing that there was no statute of limitations on murder, a period of time in which judicial action must be taken, had been the only hope the families of Sims, Gibbs, and Blau held that their loved ones' killer would be found after nearly fifteen years. The families rejoiced in the news of Wardrip's capture.

"Thank the Lord they found him," a grateful and weeping Alma Sims, Terry's grandmother, told *News-Record* reporters. "I just prayed that they would find him. I prayed about it every day so that one of these days they would get him, so he could never do this to another little girl. She [Terry] died a horrible death, and you can never put that out of your mind. When it's that terrible, it just stays with you forever."

One of Alma Sims's biggest regrets was that her husband, Jack, hadn't lived long enough to see his granddaughter's killer brought to trial.

Sims's aunt, Delinda Bridgens, was more cautious in accepting the news that Terry's killer had finally been caught. "We just want to make sure they've got the right person. We were really disheartened with the initial police work. We felt things were missed."

Sims's sister, Catherine Reid, was relieved to hear the news of Wardrip's capture. "It feels good to know that someone was still looking into the case. My sister deserves it. My sister deserves justice, even though it's been a long time. We think about it every day. Anybody who knew my sister knows she wasn't just an ordinary twenty-year-old person. She was an old soul. She was always helping people, always friendly, a good person," Reid said.

Toni Gibbs's brother was equally elated. "I'm happy about it," Jeff Gibbs said. "It's on your mind every day, even though it's been fourteen years. It never goes away. It just gets a little bit easier with time."

Area law-enforcement officials who had worked on the Sims, Gibbs, and Blau cases were shocked. They had never suspected any of the four Wichita Falls women's slayings were connected. Sheriff Callahan, a deputy at the time of the Blau slaying, told reporters Wardrip had never been a suspect.

"His name never came up in the Blau investigation," Callahan said. "This is one of the things that is troubling."

It was equally disturbing to those on the Wichita Falls police force, who had passed on information in 1986 when he was arrested for the murder of Tina Kimbrew, that Wardrip had admitted knowing Blau. They wondered why the sheriff's department failed to interview Wardrip then. It was easier to understand why the sheriff failed to acknowledge the reference fifteen years later, after Wardrip's apprehension.

Although other law-enforcement agencies had doubted that one man could have been responsible for the three killings, Barry Macha had always suspected that one person, or related persons, may have been involved. Macha had driven by the house where Terry Sims had been murdered, the street where Toni Gibbs's car was abandoned, and an apartment where Ellen Blau had lived. Because the three locations had been in a relatively confined area, Macha had long believed the murderer had some connection to that part of Wichita Falls. Finally, his suspicions were validated. And at last, he would have the chance to vindicate the deaths of three innocent women.

As dumbfounded as authorities seemed over Wardrip's arrest and confession, the people of Olney were overwhelmed.

"I feel shocked. He's been an excellent worker for us, and did a good job. He seemed like a heck of a nice guy," Brad Duncan, the president of Olney Door and Screen said in reaction to Wardrip's arrest.

Duncan, his parents, Fred and Betty Duncan, owners of the factory, as well as Dave Collard and others at Olney Door and Screen, had no reason not to believe Wardrip when he told them he had been in prison for vehicular manslaughter. They'd had no idea Wardrip was a convicted killer until word of his arrest hit the news.

The Duncans continued to stand by their decision to give Wardrip a chance.

"We knew he was an ex-con, but he seemed to be a model employee and model citizen. I don't ever recall seeing him get angry, and he always had a smile on his face. He always did what he was told.

"If he is acquitted of these murders, he's got a job waiting here," Duncan said. "I can't believe he's the same person as the one they are saying murdered and raped all those young women. He has certainly changed, or else he's a very good actor and should be in Hollywood.

"However, if he really did what they say, he needs to be hung out to dry. He must pay the consequences if he's guilty."

Dave Collard was heartsick. How could he have misjudged Faryion Wardrip so completely? Wardrip had seemed more like a son than an employee.

Dave walked to the pole barn and the wooden shelf that had served as a chest-high desk for Wardrip as he calculated purchase orders. The color drained from Dave's face as he stared at a crudely drawn figure of a knife with blood dripping from the blade. He felt nauseated. The childish prank by a fellow employee pierced his heart.

News of Wardrip's arrest spread through Wichita Falls, then on to Colorado where Danny Laughlin's mother had continued to cling to the hope that someday the real killer of Toni Gibbs would be found. The news of Wardrip's confession was like a two-edged sword. She was elated that at long last her son had been exonerated for the murder of Toni Gibbs, and furious that Danny's life had been made wretched because of suspicion and innuendo.

Wilma Hooker received a letter from Roger Williams, Danny's former defense attorney, telling her of Danny's decisive exoneration. But the letter from Williams was not enough for Danny's mother. She wanted more. She wanted the state to formally apologize for the living hell they had put her son through. She wanted Cody, Danny's son, to be able to read the letter and know beyond a doubt that his father wasn't a killer.

"It was different back then [in the 1980s]," District Attorney Tim Cole of Archer County said. "There wasn't the technology. There are times in a case like this where you form an opinion about suspects. It's unfortunate those things happen. Sometimes it takes twelve people to make that decision. Keep in mind, he wasn't convicted. The system didn't convict him."

That wasn't enough for Wilma Hooker. The jury may not have convicted Danny, but they hadn't acquitted him either. She wanted full vindication for her son. He'd lived with a cloud of suspicion over his head for years. Hooker wanted his name cleared so he could finally rest in peace.

Hooker didn't get a letter of apology or any formal statement clearing Danny of murder. She would have to settle for knowing that the DNA technology that cleared her son was the same science that put the real killer behind bars. A killer who had coincidentally shared a multicell section of the Wichita County Jail with her son while Wardrip was confined on a misdemeanor charge.

"Danny's purpose may have been for Faryion Wardrip to get caught," Hooker said, trying to find a reason for her son's persecution and untimely death.

Heartsick, George and Diana Wardrip faced the fact that their oldest son was guilty of not one, but five vicious murders. The headline of their Olney weekly newspaper read SUSPECT IN MURDERS ARRESTED, with a two-by-four-inch, red-etched box declaring in bold red headlines FLASH: HE CONFESSES.

The ailing older Wardrip and his wife refused any further interviews. They sought seclusion in their small apartment, eventually fleeing to Florida and the temporary refuge of their daughter's home.

Faryion Wardrip was on his own. If he was to defend himself against four counts of capital murder, he would have to rely on the public defender's office for help. George Wardrip's belief in his son was gone, destroyed by lies and half-truths.

Assistant District Attorney Jerry Taylor worked closely with investigators Little and Smith from the beginning of the inquiry into the murders of Sims and Gibbs. As pleased as he was that their own cases against Wardrip were rapidly developing, it was with great pleasure that he called the Fort Worth Police Department.

"We've got your guy," Taylor told FWPD detectives. The same words Wichita Falls authorities had heard from Galveston police fifteen years earlier.

The day after Wardrip's confession, Sergeant Dave Loftis, an investigator assigned to the Debra Taylor murder in 1985, and Lieutenant Mark Krey, a supervisor with the Fort Worth Police Department's Violent Crimes Unit, made the trip to Wichita Falls to talk with Wardrip and possibly clear the cold case file.

Like Wichita Falls, Fort Worth had experienced a rash of female homicides in a nine-month period that started in September 1984. Ten of the unsolved murders were around the time Wardrip claimed to have killed Debra Taylor.

Although the term "serial killer" was not widely used at the time, Wardrip fit the standard FBI definition of a killer who hunts human beings for the sexual thrill it gives him and who will do it over and over again, believing he can outsmart the police and never expecting to be caught. It was believed Faryion Wardrip was one such body hunter.

Fort Worth and Wichita County authorities alike were concerned that there was a gap of time between the killing of Ellen Blau and Tina Kimbrew. Time that could have been filled by more killings, more bodies.

Wardrip talked with Loftis and Krey matter-of-factly about the night he killed Debra Taylor. He told them about going to the bar, meeting Taylor, dancing, and making a sexual advance in the parking lot.

"She rejected him, slapped him," Krey later reported. "He has a very volatile temper that sets him off. . . . He ended up strangling her."

For the time being, Loftis and Krey were pleased that information derived from Wardrip gave them enough to charge Wardrip with Taylor's murder. Although they were unable to link Wardrip with any of the other unsolved murders in their area, it was a break Fort Worth law officials never anticipated.

"I was surprised that somebody would come forward in this type of circumstance. It's not common to come forward and give voluntary statements," Lieutenant Krey said. "Hopefully, it will give Taylor's family some sense of peace."

In fact, it had been bittersweet news for Ken Taylor. Relief and shock flooded over him. For fourteen years, he had lived knowing Debra's family blamed him for her murder. He was finally absolved, but the price he had paid for Wardrip's years of silence had been too great.

On February 17, 1999, four days after his arrest, Faryion Wardrip faced the Wichita County grand jury.

District Attorney Barry Macha presented the evidence against Wardrip, which included fingerprint comparisons, DNA testing, and Wardrip's own oral confession.

The jury returned two indictments. One for the murder of Terry Sims, the other for Toni Gibbs. Faryion Wardrip was bound over for trial and Public Defender John Curry was appointed as his counsel. The process of filing briefs with the court and preparing a defense began.

For nine months, Wardrip languished in the Wichita County Jail awaiting trial. Visits from his wife lifted his spirits momentarily, but he was plunged into the depths of depression each time she left.

Initially, Wardrip took Prozac, hoping it would help control the crying and intense feeling of despondency, but he decided the antidepressant drug was not helping, so he stopped taking it. "I put my faith in Him," Wardrip said, referring to God and His healing powers.

Reverend Scott Clark helped Wardrip stay connected to his faith by visiting him weekly at the Wichita County Jail.

Wardrip had to rely on God *and* John Curry in preparing for his murder trial. The state had already announced they intended to seek the death penalty.

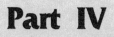

Part IV

Part IV

Chapter Nineteen

The indictment of Faryion Wardrip for the 1980s murders of Terry Sims, Toni Gibbs, and Ellen Blau became the talk of the town in local coffee shops, beauty salons, radio broadcasts, and on the nightly television news in Wichita Falls. The defense was convinced the court would be hard-pressed to find a prospective juror who hadn't heard of Faryion Wardrip and the brutal rapes and murders of the young North Texas women.

Carroll Wilson, editor for the *Times-Record News,* reminded everyone in his February 19, 1999, editorial that anyone accused of a crime in Texas is assumed innocent until proven guilty, even if the accused hands over a confession. Wilson reminded his readers that until a judge or jury determined Wardrip guilty, he must be presumed innocent.

"Working under the assumption that the public does not yet have all the details of the cases being developed both by the prosecutors and the defense counsel, and acknowledging that the law-enforcement agencies working on these cases have been wrong in the past, we might be premature in offering congratulations to the agents and agencies involved," Wilson wrote.

The editor went on to applaud the teamwork of 97th District Attorney Tim Cole, who pursued DNA testing; John Little, investigator for Wichita County District Attorney Barry Macha; Paul Smith, investigator in Cole's office; and District Attorney Barry Macha, who worked hand in hand with Cole.

Wilson ended his editorial with "Now, let justice be done."

Certain that his client couldn't get the justice Wilson wrote about in Wichita Falls, John Curry petitioned Judge Bob Brotherton of the 30th District Court for a change of venue. As a practicing attorney, Brotherton had represented Danny Laughlin in his plea bargain with the state on perjury charges and had represented Johnna Wardrip during her divorce from Faryion fifteen years earlier. Now that he was a presiding judge, Brotherton was slated to officiate the capital murder trial of Faryion Wardrip. The district judge agreed with Curry and ruled that the trial be held in Denton, Texas, about one hundred miles southeast of Wichita Falls.

Much preparation was necessary before the trial could take place. The move to Denton meant that Wardrip would have to be housed in the Denton County Jail and that prosecutors, defense attorneys, and court personnel would have to lodge in a Denton hotel.

Denton, about thirty miles from both Dallas and Fort Worth, was part of the North Texas region known as "the Golden Triangle." Ranked as one of the fastest-growing counties in the country, Denton's population had spiraled from seventy-five thousand in 1970 to over two hundred thousand in 1990. Alliance Airport and Texas Motor Speedway, one of the largest sports and entertainment facilities in the world, had helped the southern portion of the county prosper, while the northern region remained centered on horse ranches and farming. The University of North Texas and Texas Woman's University made the city a major center for higher education.

Wardrip's trial would be held in the two-year-old Denton County courthouse. Unlike the historical Wichita County courthouse, the Denton courthouse was ultra modern with concrete walls, chrome banisters, and glass partitions. The up-to-date building replaced the 1896 brick courthouse built in the center of the town square, which had been transformed into the Denton County museum.

The court staff was happy to be headed for a building with the latest in courtroom innovations, including a separate viewing room for the media. It was a far cry from the days of Denton's meager beginnings of the early 1900s, when court was held under a large oak tree.

Judge Brotherton scheduled the capital murder trial of Faryion Wardrip to begin October 4, 1999, nearly nine months after the accused killer's capture.

As Faryion Wardrip waited in the Wichita County Jail for his day in court, investigators continued to build their case against him.

After several weeks of careful analysis by the Department of Public Service lab in Austin, it was determined that the second set of fingerprints taken from Wardrip after his arrest matched the print taken from the shoe of Terry Sims.

"It wasn't a standard print you would get when you're printed in jail," Little explained. The print on the shoe was of a lower finger joint or partial palm print. Little claimed that was why the print taken from Sims's shoe was never compared to Wardrip's fingerprints from his 1986 conviction for the murder of Tina Kimbrew.

The news of a serial killer's apprehension in Wichita Falls set off a flurry of calls from police agencies from across Texas. Little was bombarded from officers who wanted to find out if Wardrip could be tied to any of their cold cases.

"You should look through your cases for any DNA evidence and send it to Gene Screen," Little told them.

As other agencies contacted Wichita Falls authorities, Fort Worth continued to investigate their own nine unsolved female homicides, utilizing their city's crime lab for possible matches to Wardrip.

While Little fielded inquiries about Wardrip and his possible link to other murders across the state, Wardrip's public defender was petitioning the court to have his client's confession ruled inadmissible.

In a hearing held August 27, 1999, John Curry asked detention officer Paul Martinez about the day he escorted Wardrip back to his jail cell on February 16, three days after his arrest in connection with the slaying of Terry Sims.

"He wanted to talk to the DA guy, John, 'before I change my mind. Tell him to hurry before I change my mind,' " Martinez told the court.

Curry then asked John Little about Wardrip's demeanor during their conversation and if Wardrip appeared to have been under the influence of any drugs.

"He seemed upset, but didn't seem to be under the influence of medication or lack of medication," Little said.

Little further explained that after eating his lunch and getting an insulin shot for his diabetes, Wardrip drove with Little and Smith to the locations of Sims's and Gibbs's murders.

"He offered to show us where each of the murders had occurred," Little testified.

Nine relatives of three of Wardrip's victims sat silently in the courtroom as Little recalled the day Wardrip had taken them to the murder sites. Debra Taylor's daughter clung tightly to her husband's hand. Terry Sims's two sisters wiped tears from their eyes. Tina Kimbrew's father, mother, and a close friend sat stone-faced, staring at the killer. Marsha Bridgens, Terry Sims's mother, a tattoo on her right shoulder that read IN LOVING MEMORY OF TERRY, rocked gently in her seat.

The relatives of the victims were relieved and Curry was not surprised when Judge Brotherton ruled the confession admissible.

"They seemed to have done what the law required them to do," Curry said. Although he accepted the ruling, Curry knew that the video and audio tapes of Faryion Wardrip confessing to killing four women in the mid-1980s would have a devastating impact on the jury, and his client.

Chapter Twenty

On the morning of October 4, 1999, Wichita County Sheriff's deputies transported Faryion Wardrip from the Denton County Jail to the Denton courthouse for the first day of jury selection. Wardrip walked briskly into the courtroom, clad in a light blue, button-down-collar shirt and Dockers. He sported a short haircut, with a touch of gray at the temples. He was clean shaven. For the first time in his various court appearances, Wardrip wore glasses. Except for the white plastic identification band on his left wrist, Wardrip more closely resembled the Sunday school teacher from Olney than the accused Wichita Falls killer. He appeared healthy, rested, and ready for the first day of what would be a long process of jury selection.

Wardrip took his place behind the defense table, his public defender sitting at the opposite end. John Curry was a large man. He rested with his arms folded over his massive stomach, his body pouring over each side of his blue upholstered chair. The young, dark-haired attorney, who could be heard breathing heavily from the back of the courtroom, didn't speak to his client. Curry and Wardrip waited in silence for Judge

Brotherton to enter the courtroom and begin the proceedings.

Judge Brotherton had opted not to conduct jury selection in his formal black robe, but in the more casual attire of tan jacket, white shirt, and brown tie.

The judge took his place behind the bench in a cordovan chair embossed with a gold seal of the state of Texas. On the wall above his head, a gold star with a black background was encircled with a gold ring. Leslie Ryan-Hash, Brotherton's court reporter, was seated below him and to his right.

Seven hundred and fifty potential jurors were originally called for the Wardrip trial. District Attorney Barry Macha estimated that it would take about four weeks to choose a jury of twelve.

There were about seventy exemptions that could have been claimed by potential jurors, including stay-at-home parents caring for children under the age of ten, and full-time students. Several jury candidates took advantage of some of the exclusions. Two were excused because they said they had formed an opinion of the case, and two women were eight months pregnant. The process of eliminating those who could not serve, for one reason or another, took most of the first week of Wardrip's scheduled trial.

Week two began with a scaled-down jury pool of three hundred. These were interviewed as possible panel members. Once the potential jury pool reached fifty, prosecutors and public defenders then exercised their fifteen preemptive strikes. The remaining panelists would make up the jury seated to hear Wardrip's case.

On Monday, October 11, 1999, Wardrip was upbeat, smiling and laughing with deputies who sat close behind him in the courtroom. The unarmed officers could easily be identified as Wichita County Sheriff's deputies by the black jeans, large silver belt buckles, and tan shirts with neat stitching spelling out WICHITA COUNTY on the left breast and SHERIFF'S OFFICE on the sleeve.

The courtroom was nearly empty. Curiosity seekers and victims' families seldom attended the tedious process of jury selection, except for Elaine Kimbrew Thornhill. The attractive, dark-haired mother of Tina Kimbrew sat in the empty jury box waiting for potential jurors to be questioned. She occasionally glared at Faryion Wardrip, trying to catch his eye. She wanted him to be aware of her presence. While Wardrip's pending trial was for the murder of Terry Sims, Elaine felt like it was Tina's trial, too. The trial she never got. Elaine sought closure.

Wardrip's demeanor changed to serious concentration as John Wyatt, a retired heating-and-air-conditioning technician with graying hair and metal-rimmed glasses, approached the witness stand. The first of many potential jurors, Wyatt was prepared to answer questions posed by the prosecution and the defense.

District Attorney Barry Macha approached Wyatt, a warm smile on his face.

"Have you ever served on a jury, Mr. Wyatt?" Macha asked.

"Yes. I served on a DWI case seven years prior," Wyatt replied.

Macha took a chair and placed it about twelve feet in front of the witness box. He casually sat as he explained what constituted the death penalty in Texas. He carefully noted that a capital offense was the murder of a public safety officer, fireman, or correctional employee; murder during the commission of a specified felony (kidnapping, burglary, robbery, aggravated rape, arson); murder for payment; multiple murders; murder during prison escape; murder by a state prison inmate; and murder of a child under the age of six, or murder of a person over the age of sixty-five.

"How do you feel about the death penalty, Mr. Wyatt?" Macha asked, leaning forward in his chair.

"I've seen some cases that seem are right for the death penalty, but I've seen some that don't. I'm not for it or against it," Wyatt answered.

All eyes in the courtroom were fixed on Wyatt, judging his response. All but the defense attorney's, who avoided looking at the possible panelist.

Macha stood and walked to the prosecution table. He took a large white chart with black lettering and set it on an easel. Pointing to the chart the DA read the numbered list. "One, can vote for the death penalty. Two, against the death penalty. Three, philosophically opposed to the death penalty, but could serve with others who do believe in it."

Macha turned and faced Wyatt. "What category do you put yourself in, Mr. Wyatt?"

"Number one," Wyatt answered.

Macha continued the jury interview by describing the two phases of the upcoming trial—guilt or innocence, and penalty. He then placed a second chart on the brown wooden easel to help him in defining the term "intentionally." The DA explained that intent was a state of mind wherein the person knows and desires the consequences of his act. Wyatt pushed his glasses up on the bridge of his nose, leaned forward as if to read the chart, then nodded to indicate he understood.

Macha, careful not to intimidate the jury prospect, pushed back his light brown jacket and slid his right hand casually into the pocket of his dark brown trousers in a nonchalant manner as he approached Wyatt.

"Mr. Wardrip is assumed innocent today," Macha

said. Then he read the indictment of Faryion Wardrip for the murder of Terry Sims.

As Macha's two assistant district attorneys sat at the prosecution table talking to each other, Macha moved closer to the witness box.

"The burden of proof is on the State," Macha said. "A burden of proof beyond a reasonable doubt."

Macha clarified that reasonable doubt referred to the degree of certainty required of a juror before he could make a legally valid determination of the guilt of a defendant. That innocence was to be presumed unless the jury could see no reasonable doubt of the guilt of Faryion Wardrip. Macha said the term did not require that proof be so clear that no possibility of error existed; it meant that the evidence had to be so conclusive that all reasonable doubts were removed from the minds of the jurors.

Then Macha again changed the chart resting on the easel to one that denoted special issues that would be addressed during the penalty phase of the trial. Wyatt sat expressionless as Macha went through the first issue. The district attorney contended that Wardrip had deliberately caused the death of Terry Sims. He emphasized the differences between deliberate and intentional, stating that "deliberately requires more thought process than intentionally" when it came to murder.

"Can you see the distinction between 'intentionally' and 'deliberately'?" Macha asked.

Wyatt said nothing. He merely nodded. He crossed his arms and listened closely as Macha continued.

"The second special issue to address is future dangerousness. Ask if this man would probably commit other crimes on society," Macha said. "You with me?"

"Yes, sir," Wyatt said as he nodded again.

The third issue dealt with mitigation.

"Is there something about the facts of this offense or about the defendant that would warrant a reduction to a life sentence? Anything to reduce his moral blame?" Macha asked.

"No, no, yes to these issues means a life sentence. Yes, yes, no equals the death penalty," Macha continued.

As Wyatt nodded to indicate his understanding, one of the sheriff's deputies yawned, leaned his head against the wall, and closed his eyes.

"If you are selected to serve and sat on the jury and I did prove guilt and I did satisfy the issues for the death to be imposed, can you do that?" Macha said, looking Wyatt in the eye.

"Yes, sir," Wyatt said with conviction.

"The people of Denton County have been nice to us," Macha said. "I appreciate your service."

The tall handsome district attorney returned to his seat at the prosecution table and waited for the public defender to interview the potential juror.

John Curry remained in his seat throughout the questioning.

"You've had back surgery," Curry said softly, referring to the written questionnaire completed by Wyatt. "Would that affect you sitting on the jury?"

"No," Wyatt said as he turned to face Curry.

"You said you were uncomfortable at the DWI trial because it was drawn out. Will the length of time that it will take for this case cause you a problem?"

"No," Wyatt answered.

"It seems you've done some thinking about the death penalty," Curry said. "Do you have a special interest?"

"No special interest. I've just seen cases in the news. I've thought about it for a long time," Wyatt replied.

"You only get one shot at it. There's no chance to come back when you sentence someone to die by lethal injection," Curry said.

Wyatt kept his eyes on Curry. He didn't notice Wardrip staring at him, waiting for a reaction.

"Based on the evidence, can you apply the definition of deliberate?" Curry asked.

"Yes, sir."

"On future dangerousness, if a person is in prison and he'd never been in trouble and his behavior is controlled with medication, can you conceive that person could be dangerous in the free world, but not in a controlled environment of prison?" Curry asked.

"Yes, sir."

"When younger, people are more prone to violence. When they are older, they are more self-controlled. Are people capable of change?" Curry asked.

"Sure," Wyatt said.

"All things considered, if the circumstances indicate the death penalty is not appropriate, the third special issue allows you to say life is more appropriate. Can you do that?" Curry asked.

"Yes, I can do that," Wyatt said.

"I'm sure you've heard the term 'parole.' You won't hear information about parole here. Your decision shouldn't come down to concern about being released sometime. If instructed not to consider parole, can you?" Curry asked.

"Yes, sir," Wyatt said.

"On behalf of Faryion and myself, I want to thank you for coming today," Curry said.

Judge Brotherton spoke to Wyatt before excusing him for the day.

"We will continue to speak to potential jurors. We'll call fifty back and let you know the twelve who

will serve, plus two alternates," Brotherton said.
"We'll take a break now."

When court resumed, each juror was questioned
just as John Wyatt had been. Some, like the young
man who followed Wyatt, were excused. The clean-cut
young man was scheduled to report on November 17
to Provo, Utah, for missionary training. He would
spend the next two years as a missionary for the
Church of Jesus Christ of the Latter-Day Saints.

Both Macha and Curry agreed to excuse the potential juror, noting that the trial might very well go
longer than the November 17 date he was scheduled
to report.

Macha walked to the witness box and extended his
hand.

"Good luck," Macha told the soon-to-be missionary.

And so it went with each of the fifty possible jurors
called in the Faryion Wardrip trial, both the prosecution and the defense competing for jurors who would
be honest, fair, and sympathetic to their side.

Chapter Twenty-one

Dana Rice, investigator for the Wichita County Public Defender's Office, had been dealing with the Faryion Wardrip case for nine months. Not only was the pretty, former parole officer responsible for interviewing witnesses, but for keeping Wardrip reasonably in line as well.

Rice's path had crossed Wardrip's before. She had first seen him in the 1980s when she frequented the Stardust Club and he checked IDs at the door. She hadn't really known Wardrip personally, but since she had taken over the investigation of his case for Public Defender John Curry and second-chair Defender Dorie Glickman, Dana had become quite familiar with Wardrip and many of his idiosyncrasies.

"Who died for our sins?" Wardrip had asked Dana Rice on their first meeting.

Rice had stared at Wardrip questioningly. *Is this a trick question?* she'd thought.

The question had been one of many religion-based inquiries Wardrip had made during their meetings. But when the trial proceedings began, Wardrip had concentrated his dialogue with Dana on requests for snacks and treats. Because of his diabetes, Faryion had to have orange juice during the court breaks, as well as an occasional milk shake. Wardrip loved milk shakes—and he loved to be waited on. Because of his nervous snacking, he was confined to the jail infirmary every night with his blood-sugar levels reaching erratic highs and lows. Rice wondered if he would even live through the trial.

November 1, 1999, the first day of scheduled trial testimony, Dana Rice was leaving the Radisson Hotel with Dorie Glickman. Dorie, an attractive young woman in her thirties, wore a black conservative suit; Dana, a black-and-white-checked jacket with black pants.

The prominent skyscrapers that rose from the campuses of the University of North Texas and Texas Women's University were shrouded in fog. Temperatures were in the mid-fifties.

"Wait a minute," Glickman said, hurrying back into the room. The bright young female defense attorney picked up the hotel Bible from the bedside table and tucked it neatly under her arm. In her right pocket was Wardrip's wedding ring. She had obtained special permission from Judge Brotherton for her client to wear the ring in court but, because jewelry wasn't allowed in the Denton County Jail, she was responsible for bringing it to her client each day.

Wardrip and Glickman may have thought the ring gave the impression of a stable, normal married man, but in the world of serial killers Wardrip was more the standard than the exception. A serial killer's continuing success largely depended on an ability to look like an average Joe, and Wardrip was as average as one would have expected. Even his marriage didn't exempt him from falling into the serial-killer profile—a large number were married, leading the darkest of double lives.

The Wardrip defense team of Curry, Glickman, and

Rice arrived at the Denton County courthouse ready for trial. They got there early enough to capture parking spaces in the courthouse complex, while others were forced to park in the residential area adjacent to the facility.

As Glickman entered the courtroom, she handed the Bible to Wardrip, who was already seated at the defense table.

"What am I suppose to do with this?" he asked.

"I don't care. Just open it. Pretend to read it," the crafty defense attorney replied.

District Attorney Macha and his assistants, Rick Mahler and Jerry Taylor, sat at the prosecution table closest to the jury box. Across the aisle from them was the defense. Public Defender John Curry and District Attorney Barry Macha had tried capital murder cases together before. They had an easy esprit de corps that made working on opposite sides of the legal system run smoothly.

The ever-present Wichita County Sheriff's deputies, in black jeans and green knit shirts, sat behind Faryion.

Once Judge Brotherton entered the court and settled into his chair, he explained that there were only two punishments for the case of Faryion Wardrip: life in prison or death by lethal injection. Any plea bargain that might be reached would be for life only.

Judge Brotherton then asked Faryion if he understood the punishments and how he would plea to the charge of capital murder.

"I'm fully aware of all my rights and my decision is made," Faryion stated, as he stood before the judge. "I plead guilty."

Unknown to anyone outside of the defense, Faryion had decided the week before the trial was to begin that he would plead guilty. He felt at peace with God.

He felt that he had to come clean and be up-front with God in order to truly repent. It was a natural flow from the confessions.

Murmurs spread through the courtroom as confused spectators asked what the unexpected plea meant to the outcome of the trial. Their baffled conversations continued as the jury entered the courtroom and took their seats in the jury box to the left of the judge.

In essence, Wardrip had forfeited any appeals to pretrial motions and errors. It more or less shut him down.

It wasn't evident on the faces of Macha or his assistant district attorneys if Wardrip's admission of guilt took them by surprise. Macha was well prepared. He was more than ready to ask the four men and eight women jurors to give Wardrip the death penalty.

Brotherton restated the procedures to the jury and Barry Macha read the indictment against Faryion Wardrip accusing him of the sexual assault and murder of Terry Sims. All eyes of the jurors remained on Brotherton and then on Macha as each man spoke. No juror looked at the defendant sitting fifteen feet away.

"Again, I am instructing you not to talk to anyone, or read anything, or watch television concerning anything about this case," Brotherton warned. "I want you to keep an open mind."

It was time for opening statements. The scheduled two-phase trial of guilt or innocence, and punishment, had suddenly become only a question of life or death after Wardrip's guilty plea. District Attorney Barry Macha launched right into a short statement, telling the jury that they would hear evidence that Terry Sims had been raped before Faryion Wardrip brutally stabbed her to death. The State was asking the jury to sentence Wardrip to death for the capital offense.

Macha returned to his seat next to his fellow prosecutors. With the announcement by John Curry that the defense reserved the right to make an opening statement later in the trial, Macha was back on his feet calling his first witness to the stand.

"The State calls Leza Boone," Macha announced.

From the back of the courtroom a blond-haired woman entered through the double doors. Wearing a black jacket and white blouse, Leza Boone took the stand without glancing toward Wardrip.

In a voice laced with nervousness, Boone told the jury that she had worked with Terry Sims at the Bethania Regional Heath Care Center. She had ridden to work with Terry; then after their shift, they had gone to their friends, the Whitakers, to exchange gifts about 11:25 P.M. They were at the Whitakers about an hour; then she took Terry to her house. Then she went back to work a second shift.

"Terry planned to stay at my house to help me study for finals and to help me stay awake," Boone said. "She had stayed at my house occasionally."

Boone described her house as a small, two-bedroom, one-bath home on Bell Avenue.

"We got to my house close to twelve-thirty A.M.," Boone said. "I drove Terry's car because my car was out of gas. I was poor. My car was parked at the side of the house. There were no lights on inside. The porch light was on outside. Terry went in with my house keys. I left her there and went back to the hospital."

Leza explained that the next morning, December 21, 1984, she got off work at 7:15. She drove home and knocked on the door because she didn't have her keys; she had given them to Terry. There was no answer, so she went to her landlord's house two doors down from her place to get an extra key.

"I opened the door. The living room was in disarray. I yelled Terry's name, but there was no answer. I ran. I was scared. [I] ran back to the landlord's. I said, 'Something is really wrong.' He followed me back to my house and he went in," Leza said, a touch of fear still present in her voice.

She explained that she was hysterical. The police were called and she learned that Terry had been murdered.

Barry Macha moved the wooden easel used during jury selection closer to the jury. The large white poster board with black markings depicted a diagram of the streets around Boone's house.

"Will you please step down here, Ms. Boone?" Macha asked.

Boone pointed out her street, her house, and a red-brick apartment house nearby.

Macha exchanged the poster with one diagramming the layout of Boone's house. She pointed out the two bedrooms, the bath, and the combined kitchen and dining room.

Macha asked Boone to return to her seat in the witness box, then moved to his desk where he took several minutes to flip though a number of eight-by-ten photos on the table.

"Can you tell the jury what you see in these photos?" Macha asked.

"In this one, Terry's glasses are on the floor," Boone said as she began to flip through each of the pictures. "The keys are on the floor here. The speaker is turned over. This is the bed in the front bedroom of the house. This is a pillow in the bedroom."

As Boone flipped to the next photo, her voice began to break. She spoke in a hushed tone. "This is an extension cord that was in the bedroom. It was yellow. It ran from the outlet to the waterbed."

Macha took the photos from his witness and handed them to Curry for the defense's inspection. For several minutes, Curry and Glickman reviewed the photos, as Faryion carefully looked at each one, expressionless.

Spectators sitting on the wooden, pew-style benches in the courtroom strained to see the pictures of what Boone had described. However, the photos were too small to be seen in detail.

During the lull in testimony, while Curry and Glickman reviewed the pictures numbered State's exhibits six through thirty-five, two young student court reporters rested from the practice they were getting covering the trial. Leslie Ryan-Hash, Judge Brotherton's official court reporter, had graduated from the Court Reporters' School of Dallas and had invited her instructor to send a couple of students to the trial.

After the acceptance of the State's evidence by the defense and the judge, Boone again stood next to the easel in front of the jury. She described each picture for the jury: the screen door, the wooden door, the two locks that were secured with the same key and automatically locked when the door closed, a yellow Kleenex on the coffee table, a Kleenex box on the headboard of the waterbed.

Wardrip watched Boone intently as she spoke to the jury. With each photo, she seemed more in control. Until she came to her friend's clothes, spotted with blood, under the coffee table.

Boone's voice was low, barely audible to the courtroom spectators as she described Terry Sims's purse and wallet on the waterbed and the bloodstained, crumpled sheets.

"Those stains were not on there when I last saw the bed," Boone said softly.

As Macha turned to the picture of the bloody bathroom, Boone was close to tears. Wardrip was busy writing on a legal pad as Glickman chewed on the end of her pen and Curry watched the witness closely.

"Those cleaning materials were usually under the bathroom sink. The towels were usually on the towel rack," Boone explained.

Boone returned to the witness box as Macha gathered three brown-paper grocery bags and carried them to her. Carefully, he opened each sealed bag using a staple remover, then tugged on white latex gloves before reaching into the first bag.

Macha lifted out a pair of white leather, Nike tennis shoes. They were marred by a blue powdery substance. The strings were still tied securely.

"Are these the shoes worn by Terry Sims on December 21, 1984?" the district attorney asked.

"Yes. She wore them to work," Boone answered.

Next Macha reached in bag number two and pulled out a pink smock with small flowers, the sleeves turned inside out.

"Do you recognize this garment?" Macha asked.

Taking a deep breath before answering, Boone said, "Yes. Terry wore that at the health-care center. She was wearing it December 21, 1984."

Boone also identified a pink shirt with small flowers as what Terry Sims wore to work under her smock on the night before her murder. Macha held each garment so that all jurors could see it clearly.

Macha pulled from the last bag a pair of pink pants, turned inside out, with underpants rolled into them.

As Macha held up the uniform pants and panties, a reporter sitting in the gallery heaved a long, moanful "Oh."

Again, Boone identified the garments as those worn by her friend on December 21, 1984.

Macha passed his witness.

"Mr. Curry," Judge Brotherton said, indicating that the defense could question Boone.

"No questions," Curry said, remaining seated.

"The State may want to recall this witness later, Your Honor," Macha announced. Then Boone was excused.

Wardrip looked at his lead defense attorney questioningly. It was obvious he was wondering why Curry had asked no questions.

By the end of Boone's testimony, spectators had relaxed. They seemed to understand that although the proceedings had skipped right to the penalty phase of the trial, Macha was presenting all the evidence he had scheduled prior to Wardrip's admission of guilt. The jury would hear exactly how he had raped Terry and then killed her. In addition, the jury would hear declarations of other offenses. Testimony that would have a marked effect on them.

Joe Shephard, chief of police of Seymour, Texas, approached the witness stand as the State's second witness. The stocky, former Wichita Falls police officer with thinning hair and thick mustache swore to tell the truth in a loud voice with a slight Texas drawl.

Shephard was assigned to the Detective Division of the Wichita Falls Police Department in December 1984, when he was dispatched to a Bell Avenue address.

"The house appeared to be ransacked," Shephard said. He described blood found in the bedroom, the bloody Kleenex on the coffee table, a nude body found on the floor of the bathroom.

"There was blood on the floor and walls of the bathroom. The body was lying naked, hands tied behind her back. She was on her left side. A yellow cord bound her hands," Shephard testified.

"The State would like to submit State's exhibit number five, a video tape of the residence," Macha said.

With no objection from the defense, Macha told the judge it would take him a few minutes to set up for the tape to be shown to the jury.

"We'll take a morning break," the judge announced.

Glenda Wardrip arrived late at the courthouse and sat directly behind her husband in the second row of the gallery. Wardrip smiled broadly.

Neither Glenda nor her husband was smiling as Macha asked Chief Shephard to stand in front of the jury, upon their return, and describe what they were seeing in the crime-screen video.

Some of the two dozen spectators moved to the far right of the courtroom in an effort to see the video, but their view was mostly obscured by the awkward position of the television set.

All twelve jury members and two alternates remained stoic as they watched the video of Leza Boone's disheveled small house. There was no change in their expressions as the camera panned to blood that had splattered on the bathroom counter and then to the bloody, nude body of Terry Sims, her swollen hands bound behind her with the yellow electrical cord. A puddle of dark blood surrounded her body. Stab wounds were visible in her slender back. Her head was resting near the cat's litter box and her legs were outstretched.

The jury remained controlled, but members of the spectator gallery flinched as Shephard described the murder scene as it unfolded in video for the jury.

Members of the Sims family shed tears of sorrow and clung to one another for emotional support.

Once the video was completed, Macha introduced State's exhibits numbers twenty-six through twenty-nine, still photos of the crime scene. The pictures showed blood on the edge of the bathtub and on the wall behind the tub, blood on the chest of drawers and the bathroom light switch, and blood that had run down the side of the tub. As Shephard talked about the photos, Faryion Wardrip sat staring at the open Bible in front of him. No one knew for sure if he was reading passages or making a show of faith for the jury's benefit.

Snapping a clean pair of latex gloves on his hands, Macha pulled the electrical cord used to tie Terry Sims's hands behind her back from another brown-paper sack. The cord, discolored from the powder used to dust it for fingerprints, was a shocking reminder of the brutality used to subdue Sims.

Glenda Wardrip's stare never drifted to the evidence in the prosecutor's hands. She remained stone still, her total attention directed toward her spouse.

Macha took the bloody Kleenex found on Boone's coffee table and held it up for the jury to see. He asked Shephard what was done with the tissue. The officer stated that it had been sent to Southwest Institute of Forensic Sciences for testing.

"Was a knife or other sharp instrument found at the scene?" Macha asked.

"No, sir," Shephard answered.

"Did you look for one?" Macha asked.

"Yes, sir," Shephard responded.

"Were oral swabs taken of Miss Sims?" Macha asked.

"Yes, sir. They were sent to Gene Screen for DNA screening," Shephard said.

"In 1984–1985 was Faryion Wardrip ever developed as a suspect?" Macha inquired.

"No, not to my knowledge," Shephard said.

"No arrests were made in the Sims murder prior to Faryion Wardrip?" Macha asked.

"No, not to my knowledge," Shephard responded.

"Pass the witness, Your Honor," Macha stated before returning to his seat.

"No questions, Your Honor," Curry said softly.

Wardrip shot a sharp glace at Curry. He hurriedly scribbled a note and passed it to his attorney. Curry seemingly ignored his client's message.

"The State calls Dr. Allen Stilwell," Macha announced loudly.

The short, stocky, retired forensic pathologist walked to the front of the courtroom, a briefcase clutched in his right hand, a loud black tie with orange pumpkins around his neck.

Dr. Allen Stilwell told the court he was a graduate of Wayne State University in Detroit, Michigan. He had done his postgraduate work in general surgery and pathology, with pathology his specialty. He had practiced in Michigan, Texas, and Alabama, was board certified in forensic pathology and anatomical pathology, and had performed more than six thousand autopsies.

From July 1, 1984 to June 30, 1985, Stilwell had worked for the Dallas County Medical Examiner's Office. He had been responsible for performing the autopsy on Terry Sims.

"Miss Sims had sustained several points of injury," Dr. Stilwell told the jury. "Eight on the front of her chest, three on the right side of her back, and an additional stab wound to the left upper arm. Plus, there were what I call defense wounds.

"She had actually gripped the knife, causing cuts

on her hand. One cut was at the base of her little finger.

"She sustained blows to the facial area, the bridge of the nose, and bruises on the left side of the face and eye. Her hands had been tied together behind her back.

"There were stab wounds on her chest that varied in size. The majority were one and one-fourth inches to one and one-half inches in width. They were approximately the size of the stabbing instrument that caused the wounds. Several other smaller wounds are what I would classify as tease wounds. They just broke the skin. They weren't deep."

Dr. Stilwell's testimony infuriated Wardrip. He turned to Dorie Glickman. "Look, he's giving his personal opinion. He's only speculating here. You aren't going to stop this?"

"We don't want to make the jury mad," Glickman whispered to her client.

"Were any swabs or smears taken during the autopsy?" Macha asked Dr. Stilwell.

"Yes. A swab, or Q-tip, was used to pick up any substance from the mouth, vagina, or anus. A smear was done with a cotton swab rubbed across a slide and then sent to be viewed under a microscope," Dr. Stilwell replied.

"Was that done for the purpose of seeing if there was the presence of semen, for example?" Macha asked.

"Yes," Dr. Stilwell said.

"Were you able to determine the cause of death?" Macha asked.

"Miss Sims died from two items. One, at least one stab wound injured an artery of the heart. Two, stab wounds opened portions of the right and left lungs.

Both lungs collapsed. She couldn't breathe," Dr. Stilwell explained.

Terry Sims's sisters fought back tears as they listened to the doctor explain how Terry had bled to death alone in her friend's house.

"Would death have been immediate?" Macha asked.

"No. There wasn't one fatal single blow. It was a combination of bleeding and lung collapse. It took two to four minutes," Dr. Stilwell said.

"Would she have known she was dying?" Macha asked.

"Oh, yes," Dr. Stilwell said emotionally. "At least while fighting she would have known what was about to happen. She struggled several minutes with her assailant."

Glenda Wardrip hung her head. She couldn't bring herself to look at the doctor as he characterized how Terry Sims had suffered before her death.

"Dr. Stilwell, will you look at these photos and tell the jury what you see?" Macha asked.

Dr. Stilwell put on his glasses, took the eight-by-ten photos from Macha and studied them momentarily. He began to again describe the wounds to Terry Sims as he looked at each photo. A woman in the audience released a low moan as he talked about Sims's defensive wounds, where she obviously had grabbed the knife of her assailant, trying to save her life.

After taking the photos from the doctor, Macha gave them to the defense attorneys before passing them to the jury. As Curry and Glickman shuffled through the pictures of Sims's battered and wound-riddled body, Wardrip kept his eyes focused on the Bible before him. His wife's eyes remained downcast.

"No objection, Your Honor," Curry announced after reviewing the photos.

Dr. Stilwell continued his testimony regarding the wounds suffered by Terry Sims.

"On her left hand there were cuts to the middle, ring, and little fingers. They were caused when she grabbed the knife and it was jerked away," Dr. Stilwell explained.

The detailed account of Terry Sims's wounds and her suffering was too much for some of the jury. An older man with graying hair covered his mouth as though sickened by the doctor's testimony. A woman dressed in blue denim wrinkled her brow and frowned at the vivid details of Sims's death. But the gruesome description continued.

"There were eight stab wounds to her chest. The small cuts to her skin are believed to have occurred first," Dr. Stilwell continued. "The speculation was that he did those to get her attention. And there were several wounds grouped around her breasts. That indicates some sexual activity of the killer.

"I believe the wounds occurred in this order: first, the face blows, then the defensive hand wounds, stabs to the chest, and then she was rolled over and stabbed. Her arms were tied behind her when the chest and back wounds were done. There was not enough blood on the bed to be from a chest wound. Perhaps it came from her hands," Dr. Stilwell stated.

Faryion Wardrip showed the first sorrowful response of the trial. First dabbing his cheeks with a Kleenex, then wiping tears from his eyes and glasses. Dorie Glickman reached over and put her arm around him, as though to comfort her client. The attorney knew that the gesture would show the jury that she was a petite, young woman who wasn't afraid of Faryion Wardrip.

"From the large amount of blood on the bathtub," Dr. Stilwell continued, "she must have been over the edge of the tub at some point. It couldn't be all splatters. I think she was on the ledge of the tub at some time, either during the back or chest stabs."

Dr. Stilwell pointed to a diagram of Terry Sims's body, noting each of the stab wounds, as well as the defensive wounds of the victim.

"Can you tell what kind of weapon was used?" Macha asked.

"Someone from the Wichita Falls Police Department came to my office and asked the type of weapon used. I made a drawing, although I'm not an artist. It was my *attempt* to help them," Dr. Stilwell answered.

Macha showed the jury the crude drawing made by Dr. Stilwell as he described what he believed to be the murder weapon.

"It was four inches long. Something struck the body. I believe it was a knife guard," Dr. Stilwell said. "It was a deadly weapon."

Macha passed the witness to the defense, who only had one question.

"Could the shallow wounds have been incurred while Sims was defending herself?" Curry asked.

Dr. Stilwell reluctantly responded, "Yes."

Macha recalled Leza Boone to the stand and asked her how the death of her best friend had affected her.

"Terry's dad died when she was one. Terry died at twenty. Her mother is in the courtroom and so is her sister Catie," Boone said tearfully.

"You were going to buy Catie a bike for Christmas. You didn't get to do that, did you?" Macha asked.

Boone momentarily broke down, tears flowing from her eyes. While she wiped them away, Macha waited patiently. She muttered a muffled "No."

"This has changed my life completely," Boone said sadly. "I still won't go into a house by myself. I was an underachiever. It took me five more years to finish school. I miss her terribly."

The tears of regret and sadness spilled from Leza Boone's eyes as she left the stand and walked slowly past her best friend's killer.

Chapter Twenty-two

After a short recess, District Attorney Macha said loudly, "The State calls Jeff Gibbs."

A fortyish man with brown hair took the witness stand and told the jury that he was the older brother of Toni Gibbs. Jeff, his older brother, Walden, and Toni were raised in Clayton, New Mexico. In 1985, he had been living in Wichita Falls, not far from Toni. She had graduated from Midwestern State University and worked as an RN at Wichita General Hospital.

"On January 19, 1985, Toni was working at the hospital," Jeff Gibbs testified. "It was a Saturday morning. She got off at 7:30 and she was scheduled to go back at 10:45 P.M. I was notified on Sunday that Toni was missing. I called my older brother and he came down. We were told Toni hadn't shown up for work. That was highly unusual. We went to her apartment. She wasn't there. We went to the police and reported her missing. We went back to her apartment, the Rain Tree Apartments on Barnett Road, but Toni still wasn't there. Her car wasn't there either. I feared the worst. Toni had told me she had gotten some obscene phone calls. She didn't go into specifics, but she was very upset and very scared."

Several jurors stared at the witness with wrinkled

brows. It was as if they were asking themselves, "Who is Toni Gibbs and what does she have to do with the murder of Terry Sims?"

Jeff Gibbs identified photos of Toni and her 1984 white Z28 Camaro. He told the court that when her car was found on January 22, 1985, he didn't recall seeing any blood in the car.

Gibbs tilted his head back and took a long, deep breath before telling the jury that Toni had been found in a field in Archer County. She had been raped and murdered.

"How has Toni's death affected you?" Macha asked.

Gibbs closed his eyes and moments later cleared his throat. In a raspy voice that strained to hold back the emotions that welled within him, he said, "I'm sorry." He sobbed while he held his hand to his mouth a full minute before regaining some degree of composure and continuing his testimony.

"I don't think words could explain what I felt or my family felt. It was a horrific nightmare." Then the loving brother of Toni Gibbs broke down and cried.

As Jeff Gibbs left the courtroom, his eyes still filled with tears, Bill Gerth, a retired Department of Public Safety Texas Ranger, was called to the stand. The large man pulled on the bottom of his black-and-white-checked coat as he settled himself in the witness chair.

Gerth testified that a woman's body was found in Archer County one mile south of the Wichita Falls city limits and the Wichita county line. The body was in a pasture at the southwest corner of Highway 281 and West Gents Road.

Toni Gibbs's car had been found legally parked on Van Buren Street in Wichita Falls. The car was processed and photographed. A small smear of a red sub-

stance had been found on the inside door handle and
on the outside door handle on the driver's side.

"On February 15, 1985, I went with the chief deputy, Ed Daniels, and Trooper Miller to the crime scene
around an abandoned bus. Two individuals made
crime-scene drawings. There was an evidence-recovery
team and an evidence-search team. A list of all the
officers at the scene was made.

"The first thing we did was check out the nude body
of a female. She was on her back. The victim's hands
and arms were above her head. Her head was turned
to the south. There were wounds to her upper and
lower chest. There were distinctive paw marks on her
thighs and breasts. Part of her upper leg, arm, and
lower calf had been eaten by animals."

The description of Toni Gibbs's wounds caused by
wild predators visually disturbed some of the courtroom spectators. Some flinched; others covered their
mouths with their hands. Jeff Gibbs hung his head;
his shoulders shook from the painful thought of his
beautiful young sister devoured by animals.

"The bus sat in a pasture. The motor and wheels
were gone," Gerth said. "It was open-ended to the
south. You could see the floorboard, pipes, debris, and
a stained nurse's uniform.

"Bloodstains, splatters, and drops were inside the
bus. The directions were erratic. Cast-off blood was on
the left and right sides of the bus. Whatever happened
there, there was a lot of violence."

Gerth told the jury that the body was found four
hundred and thirty feet off of Highway 281. There was
an offset metal gate, and on the east side, a downed
barbed-wire fence. At the scene, two Bic pens were
found, one blue with a cap and one red. Ten feet
north of the gate a crumpled, weathered one dollar

bill was found. Inside the bus there was a lady's white bra, still clasped, located among the pipes.

Macha asked Gerth to step down from the stand and point out the location of the crime scene on a map he had set on the easel.

Gerth's strong voice carried throughout the courtroom as he pointed out the mesquite tree, the body, and the place where the dollar bill was found in front of the locked metal gate.

"The bus resembles a trolley car," Gerth said. "Clothing could be seen under the floorboard of the bus. There was a lot of action in that area of the bus."

"Was a weapon found?" Macha asked.

"Thirty-five officers made up the search team. They walked side by side. We used metal detectors. We found nothing that looked like a weapon," Gerth replied.

"I'd like to present a videotape of the crime scene," Macha said, placing the tape into the machine that had been moved in front of the jury.

"Is this a fair and accurate presentation?" Macha asked before pressing the PLAY button on the video machine.

"Yes, it is," Gerth said.

For the second time that day, the jury sat in their places in the jury box and viewed a disturbing crime-scene video.

Macha and Gerth pointed out scrub brush, tire tracks, white nurse's shoes, dark blood splatters, blood on pipes, broken windows, and the burned-out bus.

While the jury watched the video, some slight confusion registered on their faces. Faryion Wardrip stared at the Bible Dorie Glickman had taken from her hotel room.

The camera moved across the crime scene and focused on the body of Toni Gibbs. She lay faceup. Her arm had been eaten at the elbow. Dried blood was visible across her right forearm. She had two holes in her chest, and her left knee had been eaten away. There were bruises on her left hip.

A male juror shook his head, signaling his disbelief at the sight of Toni Gibbs's mutilated body. Another put his hand to his mouth. A reporter from the Wichita Falls newspaper abruptly left the isolated media room where the video could be clearly seen. "I think I've seen all of this I need to," she said.

Gerth continued to explain the scene. "You can't see the body unless you know it's there, or happened on it," he said.

There was a slight incline from the bus down to the body and the body was lying between the bus and a pole. Businesses outlined the distant skyline above the nearly barren pasture.

"What was done with Miss Gibbs's body?" Macha asked.

"Justice of the Peace C. D. Cox of Archer City pronounced her dead and ordered an autopsy. We covered the body with a sheet, put her in a body bag, and she was picked up by All's Funeral Home," Gerth said.

After returning to the witness box, Gerth flipped through a stack of photos handed him by the district attorney. He handed them back to Macha, who then gave them to the defense counsel for their review. Curry and Glickman studied each of the photos for a long time. Wardrip kept his gaze riveted to the book in front of him.

"No objection, Your Honor," Curry said as he handed the photos back to Macha.

Wardrip's mood was clearly deteriorating. His shoulders were lowered and his head nearly rested on the Bible. Glenda hadn't come to the afternoon trial session, and Wardrip's mood reflected her absence.

As Macha and Gerth stood before the jury to go over each of the still photographs, a couple of the jurors in the back row stood for a better view.

Gerth casually put his right hand in the pocket of his black pants and stood with his weight shifted to one side while he described the photos for jurors. Again the jury had to listen to a description of Toni Gibb's wounds and look at the gruesome pictures of her tortured body.

"Her feet were toward the west, her hands over her head to the east," Gerth said. "There were several bruises under the chest wound. There was a defensive wound on her right wrist. A scratch ran from her hairline down her cheek. She was wearing a gold necklace."

"Was anyone ever arrested for the murder of Toni Gibbs?" Macha asked after Gerth had moved back into the witness box.

"Danny Laughlin was arrested and tried. It was a hung jury. The charges were dismissed," Gerth answered.

"Was any DNA testing done?" Macha asked.

"In 1985–1991, it was attempted to have DNA testing done. Miss Gibbs had been vaginally and anally raped. DNA testing was done to see if Laughlin was the perpetrator, but the technology just wasn't there," Gerth said.

"Was Faryion Edward Wardrip ever a suspect?" Macha asked.

"Faryion Wardrip was never a suspect," Gerth replied.

"The State passes the witness," Macha said.

"No questions, Your Honor," Curry said.

Glenda Wardrip had silently slipped into the courtroom. She faced forward, not looking at anyone until defense investigator Dana Rice moved over and sat beside her, giving her client's wife a smile of encouragement.

"The State recalls Dr. Allen Stilwell," Macha announced.

The pathologist took the stand for a second time during the first day of Wardrip's capital murder trial.

"Did you perform an autopsy on Toni Gibbs?" Macha asked.

"No, Dr. Roger Fosum performed the autopsy. Dr. Fosum is now dead," Dr. Stilwell responded.

"Can you tell us about what was in Dr. Fosum's autopsy report?" Macha questioned.

"Yes. Toni Gibbs was five-foot, one-inches tall and weighed ninety-four pounds. She was dead for some time because there was some decomposition, insect and animal activity. Her injuries consisted of stab wounds by a sharp instrument, three areas on the front of the chest, three areas on the left side of the back, a slice on the back of the left forearm, and a defense wound to the base of the left thumb. There were six stab wounds, two or three defense wounds. There were bruises to the leg area, particularly the left leg, and scratch marks by an animal. There were contusions on the chest. One stab wound to the lower portion of the mid-chest caused damage to a lung. It was consistent with a knife wound," Dr. Stilwell testified.

Dr. Stilwell told the jury that sperm was found in both the vagina and anus of Toni Gibbs. Swabs were taken from Gibbs's mouth, vagina, and anus. Privately, Dr. Stilwell had been personally astounded, and pleased, that the swabs had been preserved for fifteen years, awaiting the capture of a suspect.

"Are there any similarities between the death of Miss Gibbs and Miss Sims?" Macha asked.

"Several aspects of wounds were almost identical," Dr. Stilwell said. "One aspect is dissimilar—the depth of the penetration of the blade. The maximum depth of wounds to Miss Gibbs was six inches, to Miss Sims, four and one-half inches. Those numbers are explained by the strength of the person being stabbed and the stabbing person. The width was the same, one and one-half inches to one and one-fourth inches."

"Did Miss Gibbs struggle with her assailant?" Macha queried.

"Yes, in some respect," Dr. Stilwell answered.

"How long did it take Miss Gibbs to die?" Macha asked.

"Only one lung was punctured. She didn't die as quickly as Miss Sims. She lived five to ten minutes before she died from a loss of blood. She obviously had difficulty breathing."

"Did she know she was dying?" Macha asked.

"She knew she was seriously hurt. I have no way of knowing if she knew she was going to die," Dr. Stilwell said.

"Was it possible for her to have wound up from the bus to the location of the body on her own?" Macha asked.

"Yes, it's possible," Dr. Stilwell said.

"Could the injuries on her knees have been caused by trying to get to this location?" Macha asked.

"I believe so," Dr. Stilwell replied.

"I pass the witness," Macha said.

"No questions," Curry said.

Once Judge Brotherton had recessed trial proceedings until the following morning at nine o'clock, Wardrip jerked the knot of his tie and began to remove it from around his neck as he approached Curry.

"Why aren't you doing anything?" Wardrip asked irritably. "You're just sitting there. Why don't you object or something?"

"We didn't want to keep him on the stand any longer than necessary," Curry answered, knowing the doctor's testimony would have a negative impact on his client.

Wardrip, who either refused to admit it or truly believed he hadn't sodomized Gibbs, wanted his attorney to ask the doctor if gravity couldn't have caused the sperm to travel to the anus. Curry just shook his head.

Wardrip wasn't satisfied. He wanted his attorneys to ask questions and dispute testimony. But his defense team knew they were facing a wall that was unscaleable. A wall built with the bodies of five innocent women violently slain by their client.

The jury, who had been selected to hear the evidence concerning the murder of Terry Sims, had already been exposed to one more killing than they had expected. They were visibly shaken from the testimony. What would be their reaction when they heard about the deaths of Blau, Taylor, and Kimbrew?

Chapter Twenty-three

On the second day of Faryion Wardrip's murder trial spectators filed into the courtroom, choosing their seats much like guests at a wedding. Prosecution supporters on the right, defense backers on the left. The right side of the courtroom was nearly filled, while, except for a few reporters, Glenda Wardrip sat alone behind the defense.

As usual, Faryion Wardrip was escorted into court by deputies from the Wichita County Sheriff's Department. He had abandoned the tie he had worn the first day of court for the comfort of a red-and-white-striped, open-collared shirt and Dockers. His mood appeared solemn, until he noticed Glenda sitting two rows back.

"Mornin'," Wardrip said to Glenda with a smile. "You all right?"

Glenda nodded.

"Good," Wardrip said.

Wardrip studied the people in the gallery, looking for new faces. He spotted Floyd and Pauline Jackson, his first wife's parents.

"What are they doing here?" Wardrip asked Dorie Glickman irritably.

"Who?" Dorie asked.

"The Jacksons. Johnna's parents," Wardrip snapped.

"I don't know," the defense counsel responded.

Wardrip's attention was redirected to Judge Brotherton as he entered the court, followed by the jury.

The State called Banita Harwood Robbins as their first witness of the day.

"Would you tell us where you are from and what you do, Ms. Robbins?" Macha instructed her.

The attractive, well-dressed witness replied, "I live in Flagstaff, Arizona. I've been a forensic serologist for twenty-one years. I have a BA from the University of Texas and I've had some FBI training."

"Where were you working in 1984 and 1985?" Macha asked.

"At Southwest Institute of Forensic Science in Dallas," Robbins said.

At Macha's request, Robbins explained testing she had performed in relationship to Terry Sims and Toni Gibbs.

In the Terry Sims case, Robbins had tested vaginal and oral smears and swabs, bed sheets, pillows, blood samples from the bathtub, a Kleenex, a bar of soap, and Sims's clothing for both blood and body fluids.

In the case of Toni Gibbs, Robbins tested vaginal and anal swabs and smears. She found semen present. Blood from four galvanized pipes, a bra, a rubber hose, a floor mat, a left shoe, a stick, and a steel angle brace were examined by Robbins, and all were found to have been splattered with type-B blood, the same type as Ms. Gibbs.

"Ms. Gibbs had sexual intercourse prior to death, both vaginally and anally," Robbins testified. "Ms. Sims had semen present in both her mouth and vagina."

"Did you perform any DNA testing?" Macha asked.

"No. The first case for DNA in court was in 1987.

I now do DNA testing as part of my regular duties," Robbins answered.

"No further questions, Your Honor," Macha said. "Pass the witness."

From his seat at the end of the defense table came John Curry's familiar response, "No questions."

Ken Taylor slowly walked to the front of the courtroom. He appeared shaken by his mere presence in court. It had been fifteen years since his wife's death. So much had happened to him. All because Faryion Wardrip hadn't confessed to Debra's death when he admitted killing Tina Kimbrew. Taylor had lost everything dear to him; now he had to relive the nightmare for the Denton jury.

"Mr. Taylor," Macha said, "tell the jury where you were living in 1985."

"I lived in Fort Worth with my wife, Debra Taylor. We had been married five years. We had two girls, Tarrah, seven, Debra's daughter from a previous marriage, and Jennifer, four," Taylor said, his voice shaky.

"What happened on March 24, 1985?" Macha asked.

Taylor told the jury about Debra wanting to go somewhere that evening with her cousin. She'd left the house after he'd gone to sleep and he had never seen her again.

"On March 25, 1985, I reported my wife was missing to the Fort Worth Police Department. On March 29, 1985, she was found dead in a field," Taylor said.

"How old was your wife?" Macha inquired.

"She was twenty-five at the time of her death. Her date of birth was April 5, 1959," Taylor said.

"How was your wife's body identified?" Macha asked.

"I went to the morgue to identify her," Taylor said, his voice breaking. Taylor took off his glasses and rubbed his eyes.

"I met the police there. I viewed the body. I couldn't identify what I saw, I could only identify her from the jewelry she was wearing—her wedding rings and a necklace I had given her for Christmas," Taylor replied.

As they watched their father break down on the stand, Tarrah and Jennifer sobbed in their seats in the gallery. One of Taylor's relatives shook uncontrollably as he tried to hold in his tears, occasionally emitting a sob that wrenched his body. Spectators speculated that the man was either Debra's father, or Ken's. Two jurors looked at the emotional members of the family with sympathy in their eyes.

"How were you treated by the police?" Macha asked.

"The Fort Worth Police Department treated me as a suspect. They interviewed me and searched my home on several occasions," Taylor said, his voice laced with bitterness as he emphasized "several."

"And how did that affect you?" Macha questioned.

"Her family, her father in particular, blamed me and threatened me. It was a long time before we could even talk to each other again," Taylor said. "It was a nightmare from day one."

The frustrating years of suspicion showed on Taylor's ruddy face. He wiped the back of his hand across his red beard and mustache; then he rubbed tears from his eyes.

"Did you know Faryion Wardrip?" Macha asked.

"No, and I doubt very much that my wife knew him," Taylor said.

"No one was ever arrested for the murder of your wife?" Macha asked.

"True," Taylor said softly.

When Macha passed the witness to the defense, it was obvious they wanted to get the grieving husband of Debra Taylor off the stand as quickly as possible.

"No questions," Curry announced.

Taylor left the stand without looking at the man that had cost him his wife, his family, and fifteen years of his life.

Ray Sharp, retired from the Fort Worth Police Department after thirty-one years, was a homicide investigator at the time of Debra Taylor's death. He told the jury that he had been called to the scene at Randal Mill Road, west of Loop 820. He'd observed the scene, and coordinated with patrol and crime-scene units.

"The body was in a clump of trees one hundred and seventy-five feet south of Randal Mill Road and two hundred feet east of new road construction. At that time there was one apartment unit under construction. Nothing else was there.

"The body was bloated, decomposed, and nude. We found clothes northeast of the body, about eighty-four feet. They were laying together in a pile.

"The body was sent to the Tarrant County Medical Examiner for an autopsy," Sharp testified.

Sharp stepped down from the witness stand and joined Macha in front of the jury. He identified aerial photos of the crime scene and pictures of the body of Debra Taylor.

"Paper sacks were put on her hands to preserve any evidence on her hands or under her nails," Sharp explained.

All twelve jurors and two alternates remained visibly unemotional while viewing the gruesome photos of Taylor. Had they become numbed by the parade of graphic depictions of death?

"Were any weapons found at the scene?" Macha asked.

"No."

"Was anybody ever arrested for the offense?" Macha queried.

"No."

"Was Ken Taylor considered a suspect?" Macha asked.

"Yes."

"Was Faryion Wardrip ever considered a suspect?" Macha questioned.

"No," Sharp said, concluding his testimony.

A tall, handsome man with graying hair and mustache pushed open the short swinging doors that separated the court from the gallery and took his place in the witness chair.

Dr. Mark Krauss was the Deputy Chief Tarrant County Medical Examiner. A graduate of Texas A&M University, Krauss had attended Southwestern Medical School. He was a member of the American Board of Pathologists and had performed more than ten thousand autopsies.

After referring to his notes, Dr. Krauss began to tell the jury about his autopsy of Debra Taylor.

"The body was sixty-four and one-half inches, one hundred and ten to one hundred and twenty pounds. When I received the body, it was nude. There were two rings on her left hand.

"There was moderate decomposition with considerable insect infestation. She was not recognizable. We identified her by dental records.

"On my external examination I found that the scalp, right ear, face, and neck had received some trauma that seemed to have accelerated the decomposition. There were no lacerations. There wasn't much tissue behind the right ear, which indicated some type of head injury. There were bruises to both sides of the face and hemorrhaging on both sides of the neck and thyroid gland. There was a blunt-force injury—something hitting her, or her head striking something.

"The cause of death was manual strangulation," Krauss said.

Tears poured from the eyes of Taylor's loved ones. The man who had cried during Ken Taylor's testimony sobbed, his body shaking violently and, yet, not making a sound.

"Oxygen deprivation must be five to ten minutes, maybe fifteen minutes to cause death. A minimum of five to seven minutes. In thirty seconds, you could lose consciousness.

"There are two types of strangulation, manual or with ligature. This death was caused by manual strangulation," Dr. Krauss said.

In answer to an inquiry by Macha, Dr. Krauss told the jury that Debra Taylor's genitals were so infested with larva that he could not tell if she had had sex before her death.

When the district attorney passed the witness to the defense, there were again no questions.

The jury had heard the grim details of three murders. Witness testimony, still photos, and videotape assaulted their sensitivities. As each victim's plight was presented, the twelve member panel, plus the two alternates, could be seen physically slumping farther down in their seats. The body count seemed to be pressing them under. Only time would tell how they would handle the weight of two more victims.

Chapter Twenty-four

As testimony continued on the second day of the trial, Janie Ball was called to testify for the State. The forty-two-year-old mother from San Antonio, Texas, had lived in Wichita Falls in 1985, and had been the best friend of Ellen Blau.

Janie told the jury that, although she was seven years Ellen's senior, the two women had become close friends while they both worked at Bennigan's Restaurant. They had spent a lot of time together and Ellen had visited Janie and her husband, Danny, in their apartment, a four-unit, two-story complex on Bell Street.

Barry Macha approached Ball holding a photo in his hand.

"Is this a photograph of Ellen Blau?" Macha asked.

Janie answered in a soft, low voice, "Yes."

Janie Ball described Ellen riding her bike everywhere she went: to work, home, even in the rain. "She even named it Trigger," Janie said with a smile. "Then she got a Volkswagen Rabbit convertible."

"Would you describe Ellen Blau? How tall was she and how much did she weigh?" Macha asked.

"My guess is that Ellen was five-foot, three-inches tall and weighed about one hundred and twenty pounds. She had dark brown hair, almost black, and brown eyes," Janie Ball said, fondly remembering her friend.

"Can you tell us what happened on September 20, 1985?" Macha asked.

"In the morning I received a phone call from work that Ellen was supposed to have opened the store, Subs N' Suds. She had worked the night before. She didn't come home, and she was supposed to open between nine and nine-thirty. I was worried. We had an agreement that she'd give me a call if she was not coming home so that I wouldn't worry," Janie explained, her voice quivering slightly.

Ball explained to the Denton jury that Subs N' Suds was close to Sheppard Air Force Base. She'd called to make certain that Ellen was scheduled to open that morning.

"Ellen was very responsible," Janie said. "She would have been at work. I was very, very worried.

"I got a call from a bread delivery man, who serviced the Subs N' Suds. He said he had seen Ellen's car parked at the Country Mart. I told him I would be right there.

"I found the car parked in front of the store on Burkburnett Road, with the keys in it, her pocketbook, and a spot of blood on the driver's seat.

"I was very upset at that point. Someone else called the police while I called my husband. I organized a search around the city," Ball said.

Taking a deep breath and brushing back her frosted brown hair, Janie added, "Her body was found on October 10, 1985."

The jury listened without expression as they heard about yet another young Wichita Falls woman who had been killed in the mid-1980s.

"I understand you keep in contact with Ellen's parents," Macha stated.

"Yes, they live in Gilford, Connecticut. They're elderly. Mr. Blau has a heart condition that keeps him from being here. Ellen was their only daughter.

"They lived in Saddle River, New Jersey, before moving to Connecticut when Ellen was in her late teens. Ellen was very intelligent. She attended the Choate School. JFK went there.

"Ellen had become involved with a man in Connecticut who was from Texas. She followed him here. Her parents disapproved," Janie told the court.

"Can you identify this photo?" Macha asked.

"It's the apartment where we lived in Wichita Falls. We lived in apartment D on the far left, the second floor," Janie said, identifying the photo for Macha and the jury.

Ball continued her testimony by telling the court that Faryion Wardrip had lived on the bottom right of the same apartment complex, in apartment A. He'd lived with his wife and a small child and his wife had been pregnant at the time.

Ellen Blau often visited the Balls at their apartment and it was very possible she had visited them while Wardrip was living there. She recalled that Wardrip had made her extremely uncomfortable.

"We talked about him once," Ball told the jury. "I told her if he was out of his apartment not to talk to him, but to come right up."

"Can you identify Faryion Wardrip for the court?" Macha inquired.

"Yes, he's sitting there," Janie Ball said, pointing to the defendant. "He looks older, but his eyes are distinct."

"Dating back to the late 1980s, was anyone ever arrested for the murder of Ellen Blau?" Macha questioned her.

"No."

"Did Mr. and Mrs. Blau run an ad in the local paper twice a year offering a reward?" Macha asked.

"Yes. There was a photo of Ellen and a reward for information. It ran on her birthdate and on the date she disappeared," Janie answered.

Macha handed his witness a copy of a newspaper ad and asked her to identify it as one that had run soliciting information concerning the disappearance and death of Ellen Blau.

"How has your life been since Ellen's death?" Macha asked.

"Ellen was the kindest person. She was nonjudgmental. She always wanted to be liked. It's been extremely difficult since she died. I spoke to her the day she died. I told her, 'If you ever die on me, I'll kill you,' " Janie said, with tears filling her eyes. "I have a little girl named after her. She lives on in my life."

As the jury listened to Janie Ball's heartfelt words about her dear friend and namesake of her daughter, they'd sunk even lower in their seats. The weightiness of Ellen Blau had been added to the growing victim count.

Following Ball's emotional testimony, Judge Brotherton called a well-timed recess for lunch.

During the lunch recess, Ken Taylor stood at the entrance of the Denton County courthouse and spoke to Dana Byerley of KFDX-TV.

"What do you think about Wardrip's confession?" the young reporter asked during her interview.

"It's really nice to be vindicated," Taylor said. "I

think Mr. Wardrip should be very glad these guys got him before I did," he added bitterly.

"How do you feel right now?" Dana questioned.

"It's a great relief he got caught. I've lived with it every day for fourteen years. The image in the morgue is burned into my brain," Taylor said with sorrow.

Before the afternoon session of court convened, Faryion Wardrip waited at the defense table to be joined by his attorneys. Nervously, he tinkered with his chair.

"Looks like Tim the Tool Man is adjusting the chair," Dorie Glickman told Dana Rice as she and her investigator approached their places in court.

"Faryion, quit fuckin' with stuff!" Dana snapped.

Rice's patience was wearing thin. When Wardrip wasn't asking for juice or milk shakes, he was constantly joking with the deputies, fiddling around with papers on the desk, or demanding she get his laundry done.

Wardrip's perfectionism was at its height when it came to his clothes. His shirts, even his socks, had to be laundered to his specifications. Just that morning, when she had picked up his laundry, the jailer had reminded her, "He's particular about his socks."

"He's particular about everything," Rice had shot back. *Everything except those ugly shirts,* she had thought.

Dana Rice had taken away two of the shirts Wardrip had picked out to wear during his trial, but the remaining ones were equally unattractive to the young investigator whose job it was to see that he arrived in court each day properly attired.

Wardrip and his defense team settled down as the jury entered the courtroom. Barry Macha called Sheriff Tom Callahan to the stand.

Except for his graying hair, Callahan looked much like he had in 1985 when he investigated the death of Ellen Blau. His large belly hung over the top of his dark blue suit pants, bracketed by his unbuttoned jacket.

Callahan, then a deputy with the sheriff's department, had been in charge of the criminal investigation of the death of Blau. Since the news that he and his department had failed to follow up on a lead that Wardrip had claimed to have known Blau at the time of his arrest in 1986, Callahan had been criticized by the media and his lack of action scrutinized by fellow lawmen.

Callahan told the jury that a decomposing body had been found under a mesquite tree beside the wall of a stock pond in rural Wichita County. There was one sock on the body. A pile of clothes, including blue jeans, tennis shoes, one sock, a bra, and a yellow-and-white T-shirt, was found on the far side of the pond.

Again Macha requested the permission of the court to show a crime-scene video, this one relating to the case of Ellen Blau.

As Macha rolled the television in front of the jury box so that jurors would have a clear view of the screen, three sheriff's deputies moved in front of the media room window to obscure the vision of reporters. The press was furious. How could they report what was shown to the jury if they were unable to see it themselves? Who had ordered the window blocked, and why?

Reporters later discovered that Judge Brotherton had issued the order out of anger when a Wichita Falls television station aired film of an earlier crime-scene clip, one in which the nude body of one of the victims had indiscriminately appeared. He was taking no chances that another victim would be so irreverently displayed.

As the Blau crime-scene video rolled, jurors saw a blackish body with skeletal head. Just like Gibbs's body, Blau's had been eaten away by animals. Flies swarmed around the decaying corpse.

Macha pushed the cart holding the TV and VCR away and asked that still photos of the crime scene be introduced into evidence. As the defense and Wardrip looked at the photos, the jury scanned the gallery.

Ken Taylor's mother, a prim, neatly dressed older woman with gray hair, put her arm around her son and rubbed his shoulder. Appearing at the trial of Debra's assailant was unmistakably difficult for Taylor whose eyes remained filled with tears most of the time.

Obviously absent from the afternoon trial session was Glenda Wardrip. Speculation was that the details of Ellen Blau's death were more than the conservative Christian could handle.

After the defense announced that they had no objection to the photos being placed into evidence, Macha asked Callahan, as he had other investigators, to join him in front of the jury box to describe the pictures.

The sheriff adjusted his glasses and began to tell jurors what each photo depicted at the location where Blau's body was found in 1985. The jury showed no visible signs of their reactions.

Janie Ball couldn't look up. She sat with her head bowed and her eyes closed. Not until Sheriff Callahan returned to the witness seat did she again focus on the trial.

"You conducted a vigorous investigation, but you weren't able to arrest anyone. No suspects?" Macha asked.

"That's right," Callahan replied, not mentioning

the communication sent to his office by the Wichita
Falls police concerning Wardrip's initial statement.

"No further questions," Macha said, already returning to his seat.

"No questions," Curry declared.

Outside the courtroom, Callahan refused to answer
questions from reporters concerning the 1986 Wardrip statement.

Back in the courtroom, the previous confused expressions seen on the faces of the jurors when victim
after victim had been introduced into court were not
evident after testimony concerning Ellen Blau began.
It appeared the jury had finally realized that they
weren't dealing with a man who had committed one
horrible crime, but with a person who had repeatedly
preyed on young women and viciously stripped them
of their lives. The only question seemed to be, how
many victims were they going to see?

The horrors that the women Wardrip was accused
of killing had suffered had been vividly brought to life
in the courtroom by the numerous forensic pathologists. Drs. Stilwell and Krauss had described the horrific deaths of Sims, Gibbs, and Taylor. Then the State
called to the stand Dr. Fielder.

The petite doctor, dressed in a conservative dark
suit and white blouse, began her testimony by telling
the court that the body of Ellen Blau had been so
badly decomposed that dental records had to be util-
ized in order to make a positive identification.

"On my external examination, I found the body
was badly decomposed. Those changes were in part
caused by the warm weather," Dr. Fielder said. "The
skin was tough. The body was exposed to animal
predators and there appeared insect changes in the
body.

"Animals had eaten away at the left leg and upper

portion of the arm. The body had been exposed for twenty-one days in an open field. The changes in the body were consistent with a death in September. There wasn't much skin on the face and only some on the right side of the body. There was a hole in the left side of the neck by the blood vessel. The outside surface of the skin showed no clear evidence of injury."

"What do you mean by no evidence of injury?" Macha asked the pathologist.

"There were no foreign objects such as bullets or knives," Dr. Fielder replied. "There were no broken or cut bones. The cartilage in the body was intact. There were animal artifacts found in the body, including in the genital area. It was obvious that something happened to the body before decomposing."

"Did you take any swab samples from the body?" Macha asked. The seasoned prosecutor, who tried almost exclusively capital cases, was methodical in his approach to presenting evidence he wanted the jury to hear.

Dr. Fielder looked over the top of her glasses and stared at the prosecutor. "Trying to take swabs where nothing was there didn't make sense," Dr. Fielder said, referring to the condition of Blau's body.

"Could you determine what caused the death of Ellen Blau?" Macha continued.

"Looking at the whole scene, Ellen Blau died of undetermined homicidal violence. A violent death inflicted by another person," Dr. Fielder replied.

Before turning the witness over to the defense, Macha admitted into evidence the medical examiner's report, State's Exhibit 122.

As had become customary throughout the trial, John Curry had no questions.

* * *

The trial was clipping along at a speed that even surprised Barry Macha. If the trial continued at the pace he had set, the case would go to the jury by Friday.

"The State calls Shelly Kelly," Macha said loudly.

Kelly, an attractive woman in her mid-thirties with reddish-brown hair and a medium build, was the cousin of Tina Kimbrew. Only thirteen months apart, the two young women had been more like sisters than cousins as they grew up in Vernon, Texas.

Macha asked Kelly to tell the jury what occurred on May 6, 1986.

A few of the jurors took long, deep breaths, as though bracing themselves for yet another barrage of facts and photos concerning the death of one more young North Texas woman.

"On May 5, 1986, Tina's mom had back surgery in the Wichita Falls hospital," Kelly began her account. "I went to see her May 6, 1986, with my grandmother. I drove my grandmother and Amy, my two-year-old daughter. We were at the hospital at two o'clock or three o'clock P.M. Tina was expected, but we didn't see her. We assumed she was on her way to the hospital when there was no answer on the phone.

"My grandmother wanted to go by Tina's apartment to check on her. 'She needs to get up there and see her mom,' my grandmother said. She had been there the night before and said she'd be back.

"We drove over to the Park Regency Apartments on Seymour Road. I had a key to Tina's apartment. I knocked on the door, but there was no answer. Her car was there, so I thought she'd gotten a ride with someone.

"Amy had made a mess on her face from some candy. My grandmother said, 'Let's go in and clean Amy up.'

"The dog met me at the door, jumping up. I glanced to the right and noticed a table and lamp had been knocked over. I told my grandmother, 'Look what that dog did to this apartment.' Then I noticed Tina on the floor on her back. I thought she was unconscious. I thought she had fallen. I went straight over to her, but knew something was wrong. I grabbed Amy and backed up against the wall. Amy had seen Tina and my first reaction was to move my daughter. I was scared. Tina was faceup with one leg bent, leaning against the table. Her nightgown had been pulled up above her waist. I don't recall if she had on anything under her gown. I just stared at her face in shock.

"My grandmother got on the floor and tried to wake her up. There were bruises on her face. My grandmother said, 'Shelly, she's dead. I can't look at her like this, let's get something to cover her up.'

"I got a sheet, covered her, then called the police," Kelly continued.

"Did you touch anything?" Macha asked.

"No, I didn't touch anything. I was in a state of shock. I didn't know what to do. I just sat and waited for the police," Kelly said, reliving her worst nightmare.

"Will you describe Tina Kimbrew for the jury?" Macha asked.

Tina's mother dabbed her eyes with a tissue as she watched her niece talk about her only child, the daughter that Faryion Wardrip had ripped from her life.

"Tina was five-foot, seven-inches tall and about one hundred ten to one hundred and twelve pounds. She had brown hair and brown eyes. She was very petite," Kelly said, remembering her pretty young cousin.

"Was Tina's death difficult for you?" Macha inquired.

"To this day it's the worse day of my life. It's never gotten any better. It seems it's always going to be there," Kelly replied, her voice laced with sadness.

Shelly Kelly had done what she had been asked to do, tell the jury about Tina. She had held it together, for Tina. But as Kelly returned to her seat by Tina's mother, she broke down and cried.

With no questions from Curry, William Stephen Pruitt, a nineteen-year veteran of the Wichita Falls Police Department, took the stand. As an investigator for the Crimes Against Persons Division in 1986, Pruitt had been called to Kimbrew's apartment at the Park Regency Apartments.

Upon arrival, Pruitt had found another officer checking the body of a white female for life signs. Finding none, Pruitt had removed the sheet and noticed that the woman was wearing a light-colored nightgown. Her genitals were exposed, there was bruising on her face, neck and legs, and he'd noticed her panties close to her body.

Pruitt located a witness in the apartment complex who reported seeing a tall, lanky, white male wearing a ball cap knocking on Tina's door earlier in the day. Then the description was put out over the television asking for information.

"Did the Wichita Falls police receive a phone call from the Galveston Police Department?" Macha asked.

"Yes, they said a white male subject had called the Galveston police threatening suicide. When they responded, they made contact with Faryion Wardrip," Pruitt replied.

Macha asked Pruitt to tell the court what Wardrip had told the Galveston police.

"He made a statement admitting to killing Tina Kimbrew. He said he had struck her and beat her about the face, then strangled her. He said he had known her, that they met when he was a bouncer at the Stardust country-and-western club. He said he was the one described on TV. Then we went to Galveston to pick him up," Pruitt said.

"Can you identify that man?" Macha asked.

Pruitt pointed to Faryion Wardrip sitting at the defense table next to Dorie Glickman.

"When did you take his statement?" Macha probed.

"We took his statement in Galveston. His hand had been injured, but he didn't know how," Pruitt said, continuing with a description of the injury to the hand as the knuckle of the middle finger and some bruising. "He told us his nickname was 'Gonzo,' but never told us why."

From the back of the courtroom, Bryce Wardrip flinched slightly. He recalled his brother telling him how he had gotten the unusual nickname from friends who thought he looked like the fictional character with the same name in the *M*A*S*H* television series. Bryce bristled at the thought of Faryion believing he looked like a TV personality. It was so like Faryion to think he was important.

Bryce was having difficulty dealing with the trial and dealing with all the lies Faryion had told him and his family over the years. He was torn between family loyalty and seeing justice done. Faryion was his brother, but he believed that if a person did the crime, he should be punished. That included Faryion.

"Did he tell you he went out with Tina Kimbrew two times, but not again because he met other girls?" Macha queried.

"My recollection is two times," Pruitt said.

The police detective then told jurors that, based on Wardrip's statement to authorities, an arrest warrant was issued and he'd been taken back to Wichita Falls where their witness picked Wardrip's picture out of a photo lineup.

"Did he indicate he knew Ellen Blau?" Macha asked.

"Yes, he indicated he knew Ellen Blau," Pruitt said.

"Did he confess, plead guilty, and receive a thirty-five-year sentence?" Macha inquired.

"Correct."

"He was never considered a suspect in the Sims, Gibbs, or Blau cases, is that correct?" Macha asked.

"He mentioned he knew Ellen Blau and that information was passed on to the Wichita County Sheriff's Office for their investigation," Pruitt explained.

As spectators hummed with the realization that the murders of Ellen Blau, and perhaps Sims and Gibbs as well, might have been solved fourteen years earlier if only the sheriff's department had followed through with questioning Wardrip.

The State's last witness of the day prepared to testify. Dr. Gillium, the pathologist who had performed the autopsy on Tina Kimbrew, took his oath to tell the truth. As Dr. Gillium talked passively about the compression of blood vessels in the neck, and how it had taken between ten and thirty seconds for Tina to have lost consciousness, Tina's mother wiped tears from her eyes.

"You must keep applying pressure for several minutes to cause death," Dr. Gillium explained, adding that Tina had known for some time what was happening to her.

Still photographs of Tina Kimbrew's lifeless body were passed to the defense team for their review.

Curry and Glickman studied the photos as their client looked away. Their investigator sat behind them.

Dana Rice remembered Tina Kimbrew well. They had gone to school together in Vernon, Texas. She remembered Tina's father and his interest in Palomino horses, and Tina's mother, the attractive woman who sat on the front row behind the prosecutors each day.

Dr. Gillium stepped down from the witness chair and stood with Macha in front of the jury. He pointed to photos and diagrams of the victim as he described her injuries.

"There were finger marks on her body, as though she had been grabbed," Dr. Gillium said. "On the left side of her face, there is bruising on the forehead, eye, and cheekbone. There is a mark on her chin consistent with a chain. That mark moves up and is impressed on her cheek," he said, pointing to a photo of Tina Kimbrew's face.

"It is not easy to see pinpoint hemorrhages. Some of the skin marks are not injuries," he explained.

He told the jury that marks found on Kimbrew's elbows were consistent with contact with a rough surface, such as the carpet.

Again, there were no visible or audible signs from the four men and eight women of the jury to indicate how they had assimilated the impact of victim number five.

And, as usual, there were no questions from Curry or Glickman for the defense.

As court adjourned early for the day, DA Investigator John Little stood and suppressed a smile of satisfaction. The trial had progressed just as Macha had planned. A hint of a dimple showed on Little's handsome face. He knew that his turn to testify was fast approaching and he was ready. With his testimony, Little was prepared to nail the lid shut on any hope that Faryion Wardrip could generate some degree of mercy from the Denton jury.

Chapter Twenty-five

It was the third day of his capital murder trial and things weren't going well for Faryion Wardrip. Not his court case. Not his personal life. Wardrip's belt was missing. When Dana Rice arrived at the jail that morning, he was in a dither.

"My belt is missing," he said anxiously.

Rice looked at him with disbelief. Wardrip was on trial for his life and all he could worry about was his belt.

"Why worry about that?" Rice asked.

"Now, that was a nice reversible belt. Glenda gave it to me," Wardrip said.

Dana Rice shook her head and left for court. She wondered how Wardrip could be more concerned with a belt than with the possibility of dying.

At the front of the Denton County courthouse, Rice saw Dorie Glickman vigorously shaking out her jacket.

"What are you doing?" Rice asked.

"I'm looking for Faryion's ring," Glickman said.

"You lost Faryion's ring?" Rice asked, concern mixed with laughter filling her voice.

Glickman began rifling through the low hedge that lined the walkway.

"I have my ex-husband's ring, we can give him that

one later. We'll tell him his is in the room. We have to get to court," Rice said, encouraging Glickman to give up the search.

As soon as the women entered the courtroom, Wardrip knew immediately something was wrong.

"I think Dorie lost my ring," Wardrip told Rice. Then, turning to Glickman, he said, "You lost my ring, didn't you?"

"Why do you think that?" Glickman asked innocently.

"The way you look," Wardrip said with a touch of hostility in his voice.

"I lost fifteen dollars. I've been looking for it," Glickman lied.

Wardrip settled down and waited anxiously for the court session to begin.

Dorie Glickman stepped behind the railing that separated spectators from the court and looked unhappily at Dana Rice.

"I think I really lost Faryion's ring," she said.

"I know, Faryion figured it out, but he bought your lie," Rice said, in an attempt to make her boss feel better and redirect her attention to the trial.

Later Dorie Glickman found Wardrip's ring, gave it to him, and he was content, for at least a little while.

Jill Hill from Little Rock, Arkansas, was Barry Macha's first witness of the day. The FBI special agent, assigned to the Violent Crimes Squad, was a DNA specialist.

The tall, thin, attractive blonde explained to the jury that DNA is a chemical located in the cells of the body. All DNA cells are the same throughout a person's body and everyone's DNA is distinct, with the exception of twins.

"There are several tests available for testing DNA," Hill explained.

"RFLP is an older test not used much anymore. The test requires a good amount of the DNA sample and it must be in good condition.

"PCR is a method where DNA can be copied to increase the amount for analysis."

Hill told the court that in 1996 DNA testing was done on vaginal and rectal smears from Toni Gibbs, as well as her white uniform top. They were compared with DNA from Danny Laughlin. From the vaginal smear a sperm fraction was found—meaning a female portion and a male portion. From those tests, on March 29, 1996, Hill had been able to exclude Danny Laughlin as the sperm donor.

A few weeks later, Hill had been sent items from the Sims's case: a tennis shoe, yellow Kleenex, a hair from Sims's head, and blood samples from a police suspect.

Hill discovered a fingerprint in blood on the heel of the left shoe. She took swabs from the shoe for testing, then transferred the shoe to the Latent Print Division for fingerprint analysis.

Hill said that the Kleenex she tested appeared to be blood soaked, as if someone had been holding it.

Hill tested the vaginal and oral swabs from the Sims case and was able to exclude the police suspect at that time.

With no questions from the defense, Barry Macha called his key witness.

John Little walked to the witness stand with confidence. The dark-haired, well-built investigator had been the topic of numerous news articles since breaking the fourteen-year-old case. His name was familiar to everyone in the courtroom, with the exception of the Denton jurors.

"How long have you been an investigator with the district attorney's office in Wichita County?" Macha asked.

"Six and a half years," Little said in a slow Texas drawl.

"What did you do before that?" Macha asked.

Little twitched slightly, as though he preferred not to answer the question. He hadn't arrived at the district attorney's office by the usual route of prior law-enforcement experience; he had been a bricklayer.

Little's wife had been expecting twins at the time of his decision to enter police work. "She told me to go out and get a job," Little had told friends.

Bricklaying was seasonal work. With a rapidly expanding family, Little needed the security of a regular paycheck. Each morning before work, he had stopped at a local convenience store for a cup of coffee. He often talked to the Texas Highway patrolmen who were taking their morning breaks. They encouraged him to take the entrance test and go to work for the Wichita Falls police. But Little had a problem. He failed the eye exam. He decided to have RKO eye surgery to improve his vision. He completed his law-enforcement training, and redirected his desire for security and his interest in the law to the district attorney's office. No one was more pleased with Little's decision than Barry Macha.

Little didn't mention that he had been somewhat involved in the Gibbs case years earlier. Little's wife and Gibbs had once been members of the same college sorority. He had been invited to a party at the woman's house, and although he didn't know her, Little had liked her. When he had heard of Gibbs's disappearance and the urgent need for people to help with the search, Little immediately called his brother and they both volunteered. John Little and his brother crossed frozen fields near Gibbs's apartment, up and down alleys, and through empty parking lots. They found no trace of the pretty young nurse. Now, nearly fifteen years later, he could finally help the Gibbs family.

Little explained to the jury that Macha had requested that he take the cold case files of Sims, Gibbs, and Blau and study them. He had driven to locations important to the case and read and reread each of the files, knowing that the Sims and Gibbs cases were connected because of DNA testing and suspecting that Blau's murder was linked as well.

Two weeks later, Little determined that he wanted to talk to Faryion Wardrip. Little had read a report in the file that Lieutenant Callahan had been informed that Wardrip knew Ellen Blau. Then, he read a report from Janie Ball, linking Faryion Wardrip to her apartment house. Callahan had even taken a photo to Janie Ball, which she recognized as Faryion Wardrip, a man living in the same building across the hall.

Little had further connected the slain women with Wardrip when he checked employment records at Wichita General Hospital. The work records indicated that Wardrip was employed at the hospital during the time of the murders of Sims on December 21, 1984, and Gibbs, less than a month later.

City water service accounts from the apartment house on Bell Street indicated that water service was initiated in apartment A, Wardrip's unit, on October 12, 1984, and cut off for nonpayment on April 18, 1985. During that time period both Sims and Gibbs were murdered.

"The decision to locate Faryion Wardrip and get a

saliva sample to be used in DNA testing was made," Little testified.

"I located Faryion Wardrip in Olney, Texas, at an apartment complex on Mockingbird. I went to Olney on February 1, 1999. Originally, just to see where he went during the day. Where he lived. Where he worked. I followed him around town."

"Can you point Faryion Wardrip out for the jury and describe him?" Macha asked.

"Right there at the end of the table," Little said, pointing to the defendant. "He's six-foot, six inches tall and weighs about two hundred pounds. He worked at the Olney Door and Screen Company."

Little explained how he watched Waldrip from his car and how he would change cars so the defendant wouldn't notice he was under surveillance.

"I watched Wardrip from the laundry across the street from his work. I'd go in and watch through the plate-glass window. On February 5, 1999, I was watching from the laundry. He would go in and out of the yard and drive a forklift.

"A little after nine o'clock A.M., Faryion was loading a trailer. He then walked from the yard to the main building. He was in the building five minutes. His wife and a small child drove up to the west of the gate in front of the building. Faryion came out with a coffee cup and a package of cheese crackers. He opened the gate, then closed it, holding the cheese crackers in his mouth.

"Faryion sat in the passenger seat. I watched him eat and drink for about fifteen minutes. He got out, sat the cup on top of the car, opened one side of the gate, then walked to a green, fifty-five-gallon drum and pitched the cup into the can. He then opened the gate fully."

John Little then told the jury the story everyone in the courtroom had read about or heard on the news.

"I walked over and asked Faryion if he had a cup—a spit cup. We walked over to the trash can and got a cup. It had cracker crumbs on the rim," Little said regarding retrieval of the State's primary piece of evidence.

Little explained that he then labeled and packaged the cup, completed his paperwork, and took the cup to Judy Floyd at Gene Screen for testing.

As Little testified to the events that led to the apprehension of Faryion, Glenda Wardrip arrived at court. Forty-five minutes late, she took her seat behind Faryion. He scribbled on a piece of paper, folded it, and handed it to his wife. The note read "I love you."

The coffee cup Little rescued from the trash, photos of the cup, barrel, and Wardrip's workplace were all admitted into evidence.

Little described the fax he had received from Judy Floyd stating that Faryion Wardrip couldn't be excluded as a donor for the DNA found on the oral swab in the Sims case. He told the jury that an arrest warrant had been issued on February 12, 1999, for the offense of capital murder. The warrant authorized the gathering of a blood sample and fingerprints from Faryion to be compared to evidence found at the scene of the Sims murder.

"On February 12, 1999, we interviewed Faryion Wardrip, advising him of his rights. We asked about the case of Ellen Blau because we had DNA for Sims and Gibbs. We wanted to talk about Ellen because of the lack of physical evidence in the case," Little said.

"I object, Your Honor," John Curry said loudly from his seat. "I object to this line of questioning."

"Overruled," Judge Brotherton responded.

"Did he deny knowing Ellen Blau or having anything to do with her death?" Macha asked.

"Yes, he did," Little answered.

Little informed the jury that he arrested Wardrip for the capital murder of Terry Sims. He obtained a blood sample, and again Little submitted Wardrip's blood to Judy Floyd at Gene Screen. Little had also obtained a second search warrant for an additional set of prints.

"Judy called and said she was able to collect saliva from the cup for DNA testing," Little said.

Glenda Wardrip sat quietly in her place behind Faryion. Her face red and splotchy, Glenda appeared to have spent the night crying. The trial was hard on her. She found it difficult to listen to testimony that described a man she'd thought she knew. A man she loved.

Macha told the court he had no further questions for John Little, but would be recalling him later. He then called Judy Floyd to the stand.

"I would like the record to reflect my objection to this testimony based on evidence collected by the search warrant," Curry stated.

"The record will so reflect," Judge Brotherton responded.

Judy Floyd approached the court dressed in a dark gray suit, her frosted brown hair neatly shaped. Floyd was a professional, having testified more than two hundred times in court for matters concerning DNA evidence.

Floyd began her testimony in the Wardrip case by discussing Terry Sims. In a report dated February 12, 1999, Floyd said that DNA tests she ran showed that the saliva from the coffee cup provided by John Little matched the sperm from the oral swab taken from Sims.

"The frequency of occurrence is one in every one billion, two hundred million," Floyd said. Meaning that only one person out of one billion, two hundred million people could be a possible match. That made the odds of the sperm being Wardrip's nearly certain.

In the Toni Gibbs case, Floyd stated that the genetic profile of the vaginal swab and the saliva were a match.

Then Floyd referred to a report she had prepared on May 13, 1999.

"I compared the oral swabs to the paper cup with saliva and blood that had been drawn from Faryion Wardrip. There were a total of ten markers on each item of evidence," Floyd said.

"Did he have unusual genetic markers?" Macha asked.

"Yes. Mr. Wardrip had several uncommon high numbers for frequency of occurrence," Floyd answered. "The frequency for the North American Caucasian population was one in 3.23 quadrillion. The sperm from the oral swab is unique in only the individual who could have left the sperm."

Floyd told the jury that the results were the same in her official report for the Sims case. In that case, she had tested the oral swab and blood from Wardrip.

"Is it most likely that the sperm deposited in Toni Gibbs was deposited by the defendant?" Macha asked.

"Yes."

Macha had successfully connected the saliva-traced cup taken by John Little from the Olney Door and Screen Factory to the sperm found in the bodies of Sims and Gibbs. He dismissed his witness.

There was no cross-examination by the defense.

"The State calls Glen Unnasch," Macha said.

"I object, Your Honor," Curry announced. "This

witness is going to testify to matters I have previously objected to. I would like the record to so reflect."

"Your objection is so noted and overruled," Judge Brotherton responded.

Unnasch, a supervisor with the Latent Fingerprint Division of the Texas Department of Public Safety, testified that he had been asked to examine a pair of shoes submitted to him by the Wichita County DA's office.

"I used a dye-staining technique," Unnasch said. "When the amino dye came in contact with the blood, it turned a reddish brown or black to enhance it. I photographed the print first, then took additional photos of the print after it was stained. Then I began the comparisons."

Unnasch pointed out the fingerprint on the left side of the heel of Sims's left shoe as the print he tested.

"Did you take prints from a man on March 12, 1999?" Macha asked.

"Yes, from the man at the end of the table in the light blue shirt," Unnasch answered.

"Did you compare those prints to the tennis shoe print?" Macha inquired.

"Yes. After comparing the latent print of the shoe and Mr. Wardrip's prints, I determined he was the only one who could have left that print," Unnasch said.

"Was the print left in blood?" Macha asked.

"Yes, what appeared to be blood from the amino black testing," Unnasch responded.

The DPS fingerprint examiner then told the jury that he had compared the various ridges of Wardrip's print and the print from the shoe.

"I'm one hundred percent sure the print was left by Faryion Wardrip. His left middle finger, the third joint," Unnasch stated.

Macha then had his witness stand before the jury

and show them where the fingerprint had been left on Sims's shoe. He indicated the location by pointing to Macha's shoe as the district attorney held his leg in the air.

As with the DNA evidence, Macha had successfully linked the bloody fingerprint on Sims's shoe to the defendant.

Neither Curry nor Glickman had any questions for the expert witness.

Chapter Twenty-six

John Little was called to return to the stand.

"After the arrest of Faryion Wardrip, did you file a probable cause affidavit with the appropriate court?" Macha asked his investigator.

"Yes."

Macha had Little tell the jury that the local media had been given a copy of the affidavit, which included DNA evidence that linked Wardrip to Sims. The information had been subsequently released to the public.

"On February 16, 1999, did you receive a call from Captain Foster at the jail annex?" Macha questioned.

"Yes. I was in my office. Captain Foster advised me that a couple of jailers said when they were escorting Wardrip to his cell he told them he wanted to speak to 'John, the DA guy.' He also said, 'He better get out here before I change my mind,'" Little testified.

Little related how he and Paul Smith had driven south of Wichita Falls to the jail annex to talk with Wardrip. As they met in the jail library, Wardrip told them he had talked to his wife that morning, then decided he wanted to talk to them. Little advised him of his Miranda rights and asked if he wanted an attorney. When Wardrip waived his right to an attorney, Little had again given him the Miranda Warning. He then recorded the interview on audio tape.

"Were all the statements given without inducement?" Macha asked.

Little shot a quick glance to Wardrip, then answered, "Yes."

"Did he knowingly and voluntarily waive his rights?" Macha queried.

"Yes."

Macha asked that State's Exhibit Number 133-A, the audio confession, and State's Exhibit Number 134, a written transcript of the audio confession, be admitted into evidence.

The usually quiet Curry once again objected to the admission of the evidence for the record. Judge Brotherton acknowledged the objection, but again overruled the defense.

John Little remained in the witness chair facing the jury with a copy of the transcribed confession in his hands. Across from him sat Barry Macha with another copy of the transcript. Hearts of the victims' families raced as they anticipated the reading of Faryion Wardrip's statement. They had been reliving the events of their loved ones' deaths for the past three days. Now, with John Little and Barry Macha reading the confession to the jury, they would have to endure the horrors again, through Wardrip's own words.

" 'Okay. Faryion, what I would like to do is just kind of go back to the beginning in your own words and start the events surrounding December 21 of 1984, if you would. This would be in reference to the death of Terry Sims,' " Little read his own words to the jury.

Macha responded by reading Wardrip's words from the confession. " 'I don't recall the dates to be exact.

I do know at that time I was under heavy drugs. Intravenous drugs caused a lot of dysfunctional activities in my life. All it did was create hate in my heart and I was out walking, actually walking home, and I had been in a fight with my ex-wife. Drugs had just totally taken control of my life and as I was walking, she was at her door. I went up to the door and forced my way in. Well, just ransacked her, just slung her all over the house in a violent rage. Stripped her down and murdered her.' "

Tears welled in the eyes of Terry Sims's sisters while anger grew in their hearts as they heard the words of their sister's killer. The courtroom was silent. No one talked. No one moved. It was as though the spectators were riveted to their seats by the steely cold words of the defendant.

For the first time since his brother's arrest, Bryce Wardrip learned that Faryion had given the investigators a confession on his own. For more than nine months, Bryce had lived with the regret that he had been responsible for his brother's confession falling into the hands of the district attorney.

He'd believed that Faryion's phone call from the Wichita County Jail in which he told Bryce that he had indeed killed five women in the Wichita Falls area had been taped. With the reading of Faryion's confession, a burden of guilt was lifted from Bryce.

However, Bryce Wardrip's feelings of relief quickly turned to rage and resentment when he heard his brother imply that his family hated him. There had been nothing but loving support from their parents, even when he had been arrested and imprisoned for the murder of Tina Kimbrew. Bryce couldn't speak out. He could only sit and listen to the lies his brother had told Little and Smith.

In the pew-style bench in front of Bryce and Tina

Wardrip sat the parents of Johnna Wardrip, Faryion Wardrip's first wife. Paulette and Floyd Jackson wept as their former son-in-law's words ripped at their hearts. They had done everything possible to help Faryion and Johnna while they were married, but Wardrip's drug use had stripped the couple of everything the Jacksons had given them. Although he had been abusive with Johnna on a couple of occasions, he had never raped Johnna or forced himself on her in any way. The person they heard described in court was not the one they had known. The only similarity was the blame he placed on others for his own wrongdoing.

Little continued to read passages from the transcript. He read where he turned the Wardrip interview over to Investigator Smith for questions concerning Toni Jean Gibbs. Smith had asked Wardrip if he remembered the incident.

" 'Yeah. Again I was out walking all night. Somehow I was downtown. It was about six o'clock in the morning. Just walking. And I started walking home, it was starting to get daylight and I was walking up towards the hospital, and Toni knew me and she asked me if I wanted a ride.' " Macha continued to read Wardrip's confessing.

Tears fell from Jeff Gibbs's eyes. It was no comfort to know that Faryion Wardrip had only happened on his sister. Toni was showing her usual compassion by giving Wardrip a lift in the rain. He had repaid her by stripping away her vibrant life.

The confession moved from the death of Toni Gibbs to the murder of Ellen Blau as Little read questions asked of Wardrip during his disclosure.

The faces on the jury reflected the stress felt by everyone in the courtroom. It had been an exhausting, burdensome three days for the jury. Photos of dead bodies, emotionally damaged friends and families, and now the words of the killer himself were all weighing heavily on the hearts and minds of the jurors.

Luckily, Ken Taylor wasn't present in court the day Wardrip's confession was read. The stark reality of Wardrip's matter-of-fact confession may have been too much for him to endure.

Little and Macha continued to read from the transcript, pinning down the time frame in which each of the young victims had been slain. Then Macha reached a point in the confession that emotionally stirred everyone in the courtroom.

" 'My parents don't deserve this, my wife doesn't deserve this, my children don't deserve this, my brothers and sisters. It's because of those damn drugs and the hatred that I had in my heart. And I caused so much pain to the victims' families—but I don't want to burn in hell. God told me that, you think I'm kidding you, but He revealed why He gave my wife to me like He did for a couple of months. I asked her today to forgive me. I told her what I was going to do, not in so many words, because I know they listen, but I just asked her to forgive me. She said, for what? I said for all the lies, the lies that I told you. She said, what lies? I said because I brought you into my life knowing that this very well could happen. I didn't care, I knew I'd never get away with it. I did know that. I knew this day would happen,' " Macha read.

Emotion overcame Faryion Wardrip as he dropped his head on the defense table and cried. His shoulders shook with each gut-wrenching sob. He covered his face with his hands, trying to hold back the flood of tears. His sobs could be heard across the courtroom and his head could be seen bobbing up and down with each painful breath he took in.

A female juror wiped tears from her eyes several

times during Wardrip's torrid confession of apparent regret. A male juror covered his mouth with his hand and another stared at Faryion questioningly.

" 'I realized it when I went to prison the first time. I knew this day would happen. Man, but yet, I still took a wife, and she's a beautiful Christian woman. I don't know if you've ever seen her, but she's a beautiful Christian woman. She didn't deserve this. Nobody does. I don't care what happens to me. If they want to put me to death, then so be it. 'Cause I'm tired of living on this earth, tired of pain and suffering that Satan brings to people, no matter how hard you try, no matter how good of things you do . . . it always seems to mess up. If you don't follow what God tells you to do, it's going to happen to you, I guarantee it.' "

Macha continued to read until the very last words. " 'Oh, my God, what have I done? I'm so sorry. My parents didn't deserve this, God, they don't deserve it.' "

There were few dry eyes in the courtroom by the time Little and Macha completed the reading of Wardrip's confession. There were tears of sadness from the families. Tears of anger from Paulette Jackson, who believed Wardrip was blaming her daughter, Johnna, for his vicious behavior. And tears of regret from Faryion Wardrip.

Wardrip continued to cry as he removed his glasses and wiped away his tears. Tina Kimbrew's mother and cousin wept as they clutched hands. Tina's father rubbed his eyes with the back of his weathered hand. Terry Sims's sisters dabbed their eyes with tissues. Janie Ball lowered her head and left the courtroom, obviously too disturbed to hear the remainder of Little's testimony.

Barry Macha laid his copy of the powerful confes-

sion on the table. He and Little approached the jury
with large diagrams that indicated the routes Wardrip
had taken in each of the murder cases.

Videotapes taken the day Little and Smith had
driven Faryion Wardrip around Wichita County as he
pointed out how he had reached the house where
Sims was killed and how he had escaped were admitted
into evidence.

Judge Brotherton wisely announced a lunch recess.
Everyone attending the trial needed a break. They
needed to collect themselves for the remainder of the
day's testimony.

At the break, Dorie Glickman approached Judy
Floyd who had remained in the courtroom following
her testimony.

"It's too bad Texas doesn't have life without parole," Glickman said. She believed her client was a
perfect candidate for the nonexistent penalty. He had
obviously changed his life. Evidently dedicated himself
to God. But the jury would have to decide between
life in prison, which meant incarceration for fifteen
years before Faryion would be eligible for parole, or
death by lethal injection. Dorie knew in her heart that
it would be difficult for any jury that had just been
presented with a signed confession of five brutal murders to vote for life. She held out slim hope.

The afternoon session began at 1:40 with John Little
describing the tape of the route Faryion Wardrip took
to the house where Sims was murdered. The jury
watched the video without expression while Judge
Brotherton leaned against the wall to the right of the

jury for a better view of the television set. Unable to clearly see the video, some in the audience dozed.

Macha then entered into evidence various items relating to Wardrip: his booking photo, penitentiary packet, Marion, Indiana, school records reflecting that he dropped out after the tenth grade, and his armed forces records showing he had received a "less than honorable" discharge.

Curry took several minutes to review the exhibits before stating for the court that he had no objections.

Macha stood behind the prosecutor's table and confidently announced, "The State of Texas Rests."

Chapter Twenty-seven

As the defense prepared to present their case, court-room onlookers wondered if Faryion Wardrip would take the stand in his own defense. But they would have to wait. John Curry had other witnesses he planned to question.

John Dillard, Wardrip's parole officer, was the first to take the stand in his defense. Dillard described Wardrip as a model parolee, in fact, as his "best client in the intensive electronic-monitoring system."

Dillard told the jury that when Wardrip was released from prison in December 1997, he had to wear an ankle bracelet that monitored his movement. He and Wardrip had worked out a schedule every week and the parolee couldn't stray from that plan. In addition, at least once a week, Dillard would surprise Wardrip with a visit and monitor his whereabouts by checking out his workplace and residence.

Dillard testified that Wardrip never violated the conditions of his parole and attended mandatory anger-management classes and Alcoholics Anonymous and Narcotics Anonymous meetings regularly.

"Did Mr. Wardrip go to AA and NA meetings beyond the time that was required?" Public Defender John Curry asked.

"Yes, he did," Dillard replied.

When it was time for the district attorney to question Dillard, he asked if Wardrip had requested to be released early from the monitoring program.

"Yes," Dillard said. "Wardrip requested several times to be released from the electronic-monitoring system."

Dillard didn't mention in court that no one had ever been released early from the monitoring system.

Curry's second, and last, defense witness was called to the stand.

Fred Duncan, owner of the Olney Door and Screen Company, walked slowly to the stand. He had volunteered to speak on behalf of his former employee. Duncan had always liked Wardrip. He found him to be dependable and hard working. Even after Wardrip's confession had become public, and his guilty plea at the beginning of the trial, Duncan found it difficult to believe he could be responsible for the ghastly murders.

When Duncan first learned of Wardrip's arrest he had been furious. He had even considered taking action against the DA's office for trespassing on his property in order to obtain the paper cup needed for DNA testing. But time and information had softened the senior Duncan.

Duncan told the court that in the fourteen months Wardrip had worked for him he had never missed a day of work.

"He was an excellent employee," Duncan said. "We moved him on up, and he was learning purchasing."

Duncan stated that his opinion of Wardrip as an employee hadn't changed much since his arrest.

Under cross-examination by Macha, Duncan admitted that he was never told that Wardrip had been in prison for the murder of Tina Kimbrew.

"We understood that he went away because of a vehicular homicide," Duncan said.

"Has your opinion of Wardrip changed since you found out he confessed to killing five women?" Macha asked.

"I'm not here to get involved in that decision. I'm here to tell you what he did for me," Duncan responded.

It was clear that Fred Duncan had thought highly of Wardrip as an employee. Macha decided not to press the witness further. Duncan was dismissed.

Testifying in court had been hard for Duncan. Tears swelled in his eyes as he made his way to the courthouse parking lot.

John Curry stood and addressed the court.

"The defense rests, Your Honor," Curry said.

Speculation about Wardrip's testifying had been answered. He would remain silent.

Initially, Wardrip had expressed his desire to testify before the court.

"The DA will ask how you felt when you killed this one, then that one," Dorie Glickman had advised her client.

"Can they do that?" Wardrip asked, agitation in his voice.

Glickman didn't want her client on the stand. She feared he would show hostility toward the prosecution and play right into the DA's hands by demonstrating that the anger he claimed to have overcome still lay just below the surface.

There wasn't much more Curry and Glickman could have done. They had called the witnesses they believed would benefit their contention that Faryion Wardrip was a changed man who deserved to live, a point that Curry planned to argue during his closing argument.

But Barry Macha had four rebuttal witnesses that would cast a shroud of doubt over Wardrip's alleged change.

Sheriff Tom Callahan again took the stand to tell the jury that while he was escorting Wardrip to his jail cell after his February arrest, Wardrip told him he was innocent.

Then the first of three emotionally charged witnesses was called.

Robert Kimbrew, a small weathered man with a big hurt in his heart, told jurors about the 1996 and 1997 mediation sessions with Wardrip in which Wardrip had told him and Tina's mother that he had never killed anyone before smothering their daughter.

The pain Kimbrew had carried with him for fifteen years showed on his face.

"Did he look you in the eye and say he never hurt anyone before Tina?" Macha asked.

"Yes," Robert said bitterly.

"Did he tell you that he was never so under the influence [of drugs and alcohol] that he didn't know right from wrong?" Macha questioned.

"Yes," Kimbrew responded.

Kimbrew was obviously embittered by Wardrip's deception during the mediation sessions.

"It's so important to be truthful and then find out it was a total lie," Kimbrew said.

As Tina's father left the stand, he looked toward his daughter's killer, hoping to make eye contact with him. But Wardrip's eyes remained on the open Bible in front of him.

"I call Elaine Kimbrew Thornhill," Macha announced.

Elaine and Robert Kimbrew had divorced prior to

Tina's death, and Elaine had remarried. She had been in the front row of the Wardrip trial each day, lending support for the prosecution. Although Wardrip had served time for killing her daughter, Elaine appeared determined to see that the five-time killer was taken out of society.

From the stand Elaine talked about how she and her first husband had both been told they would never have children. Then she got pregnant. During a difficult delivery, Robert Kimbrew had been forced to decide between saving the life of his wife or his child.

"But I had a special doctor," Elaine told the court. She and Tina both pulled through, creating an exceptional bond between them.

"I know everyone in the courtroom in here won't understand what I'm talking about, but the mothers will," Elaine said, crying. "On May 6, 1986, I woke up and felt her body leave my body. I knew something bad had happened to my baby. I said somebody has to go and see about her."

There wasn't a dry eye among spectators or jurors. The pain and anguish of a mother who'd lost her only child cloaked the courtroom in misery.

Elaine's testimony hit Wardrip hard. He jotted a note to his counsel asking if there was any way to stop her testimony, to stop the pain she was obviously going through.

While Macha and Curry approached the judge's bench for a sidebar discussion, Elaine Thornhill stared at Faryion Wardrip, willing him to look at her. Only three feet away, Wardrip kept his eyes down, avoiding Elaine's cold, hard stare.

The prosecution's last rebuttal witness was Catie Reid, the younger sister of Terry Sims.

Reid was only fourteen at the time of her sister's

death. The girls had been close, with Terry often looking after Catie.

"She taught me to ride go-cars and took me to mov-
ies," Reid said fondly. "She was at every swim meet
and softball game."

Reid told a touching story about how she was em-
barrassed to use a wooden tennis racket when she
joined the school tennis team.

"We didn't have a whole lot of money," Reid said.
"I was the only one on the team who used a wooden
racket. I made quite a fuss about it. And then, one
morning before I left for school, there was an alumi-
num racket waiting at the front door. Terry bought
it."

Reminiscing about her sister brought tears to Reid
and her other sister, who sat in the audience.

The four rebuttal witnesses had brought to life the
slain victims of Faryion Wardrip. Tina Kimbrew and
Terry Sims became real people, not just statistics of a
drug-addicted serial killer.

Macha had presented all his witnesses, all the evidence he believed necessary to obtain a death sentence for Faryion Wardrip. He returned to the
prosecution table and waited for his turn at closing
arguments.

The shrewd district attorney had deliberately not
introduced all the victims in his opening statements.
His instincts had been right on target. The impact of
presenting one victim at a time had visibly shaken the
jury. As they deliberated, they would remember victim
after victim laid at their feet. All casualties of Faryion
Wardrip.

Because the burden of proof rested with the State,
John Curry was the first to present arguments to the
jury.

Curry, who had remained in his seat throughout

the trial, stood and ambled over to the jury box. Breathing heavily, the rotund public defender began by talking about Faryion Wardrip and the changes he had made in his life since the murder of Tina Kimbrew. He cited his attendance at AA and NA and reminded jurors of the words of Wardrip's parole officer, John Dillard.

"He was Dillard's best client in the intensive electronic-monitoring system," Curry reiterated.

Then, to most everyone's surprise, John Curry began to cry. His emotional conduct surprised many in the courtroom, not least of all his client.

Wardrip was glad that Curry had become so emotionally involved with his case, but believed his attorney should have bridled his emotions while addressing the jury. He wondered what effect it would have on the outcome of his sentence.

" 'I know I'm responsible,' Faryion said. Does that mean he's a changed man? I don't know," Curry remarked. But the defense wanted jurors to believe Faryion was changed. That he would no longer be a threat to society.

In far less than the time allotted by the court, Curry completed his closing. He returned to his seat and began writing a note.

"I'm sorry, Faryion. I didn't do a good job for you," Curry wrote, folded the paper, and passed it to his client.

The statement and Curry's emotional presentation to the jury both surprised and irritated Wardrip. Curry had let his emotions take over. He'd shown the jury how personally painful the case had been. His attorney's sensitivity made Wardrip believe he didn't have the kind of lawyer he really needed to defend him.

Barry Macha stood, buttoned his suit jacket, then walked to the wooden easel he had used throughout the trial. As he turned the easel to face the jury, a large poster board with five eight-by-ten glossy photographs was a glaring reminder of the victims. In the center was a graduation photo of Terry Sims, surrounded by pictures of Tina Kimbrew, Ellen Blau, Toni Gibbs, and Debra Taylor.

As Macha began his closing arguments, jurors stared at the faces of the once-vibrant young women whose lives had been extinguished by Faryion Wardrip.

"There are five witnesses," Macha said as he motioned toward the photos. "You didn't get to hear from them."

Macha emphasized that, in both the murders of Sims and Gibbs, Wardrip took a knife with him and left with it, implying his intention to kill.

"Terry tries to defend herself," Macha said. "She's screaming, fighting. What's he doing? He's ripping her clothes off. He can't get them off fast enough. He cuts a cord to tie her hands. He forces his penis into her mouth. He does the same thing vaginally.

"If you're like me, you'll never forget what he did to her in that bathroom. No question, she was stabbed in that bathroom."

The reliving of Terry's brutal murder was overwhelming for the Sims sisters. The tears poured from their reddened eyes faster than they could wipe them away.

"Three weeks later, he finds a nurse. What do nurses do? They help people. She sees him and asks if he needs a ride. He no longer works at that hospital. Ask yourself, why is he there at seven-thirty in the morning? Why is he carrying a knife? He took her to that field because he wanted to rape her and murder her," Macha said angrily.

Macha reminded jurors that it had been more than fourteen years since the deaths of Sims, Gibbs, Blau, and Taylor. That in that time an innocent person had been charged and tried for the Gibbs murder. And in spite of the time lapse, Wardrip still remembered all the names of his victims. He knew exactly what he had done.

"This isn't about rape," Macha said. "This is about power and control over women. Not so much sexual power, but to make them do what he wanted them to do."

He reminded jurors of Debra Taylor and how Wardrip was forced to dump her body in the open field because people in the club had seen them together. How Taylor's body had lain exposed to the elements for days while her family searched for her.

"Having your loved one missing twenty-one days, twenty-eight days. You can't imagine what has happened to her," Macha said as he slapped his hand on the jury rail. "I can't imagine the anguish.

"Toni was left outside in weather so cold that it preserved her body. Preserved the sperm inside her.

"Who convicted him? These girls did. I hope you listen for their screams. You know their names," Macha said, looking at the pictures of the five smiling faces.

The eyes of everyone in the courtroom were transfixed on the photographs of the victims. Everyone's but Faryion Wardrip's.

"Sims had two sisters and one brother. Her dad died when she was one. Debra Taylor's daughter is pregnant with her granddaughter. She won't be here to help raise her. Why? Because of the selfish controlling conduct of this man," Macha said, pointing to the defendant.

"On November 5, 1996, Faryion Wardrip said, 'I didn't hurt anybody for fourteen years.' It's a lie. A big lie. His whole life has been a lie."

Macha approached the jury rail and spoke softly.

"I want to remind you, five people died horrible deaths. I know this is one of the most difficult and important decisions of your life. These were citizens of our state. The defendant is not the only one who has rights. These girls have rights, too. There are no mitigating circumstances.

"Remember to use the same response this girl said," pointing to Sims picture. "She said no.

"He deserves to die for what he did. Those girls deserve to see this man forfeit his life.

"Remember, the last thing these girls saw in their lives was Faryion Edward Wardrip."

Macha's impassioned plea for the death penalty sent tears of sorrow pouring from the eyes of the victims' families. But the jury remained as they had throughout the majority of the trial, unshaken visibly.

Judge Brotherton excused the two jury alternates, thanking them for their service, then excused the twelve jurors for deliberations.

There was nothing more for Macha to do. He had built a strong case on powerful evidence. He gave most of the credit to his investigator, John Little, who through the use of high-tech DNA testing, coupled with old gumshoe investigative work, had supplied Macha with the ammunition needed to take Wardrip down.

Visibly absent was Paul Smith, the Archer County investigator who had helped Little build the case. Some say it was "politics" that had pushed Smith to the background, while others believed all the credit should go to Little. Whatever the dynamics behind Smith's absence, Macha had done an effective job of taking the evidence supplied him and presenting it to the jury.

* * *

The jury began deliberating a few minutes after nine A.M. Within two hours, they were stuck on the second question, which asked whether Wardrip could be a continuing threat to society.

The first vote was ten-to-two that Wardrip was a threat, but the vote had to be unanimous in order for the jury to move on to question number three.

During the course of the five-day trial, the families of Wardrip's victims had become close. They had stayed in the same hotel and each night had gathered together to learn about each other. Wardrip had ripped their individual families apart, yet bonded them collectively in a mosaic of comfort and caring. Now they waited for the jury to decide the fate of a killer. Holding hands, resting in one another's arms, they sought each other's compassion.

For Wardrip, only Bryce and Tina Wardrip were present to hear whether he would live or die. Glenda Wardrip had been absent in court for two days. Word had it that she had moved to Oklahoma. Living in Olney, attending the trial, had all been too much for the wife of a man convicted of five unthinkable killings. Likewise, to escape the publicity and pain of their son's trial, Wardrip's parents had fled to the serenity of their daughter's home in Florida.

As the bailiff announced that the jury was returning, people scurried to the courtroom in anticipation of a verdict. But they would have to wait. The jury had merely asked for the further definition or explanation of the meaning of "society."

Inside the jury room there was little sympathy for Wardrip. There were some tears, but more for the enormity of the task they had been asked to do, than for the defendant. All twelve jurors took their assignment seriously. They were dealing with a person's life.

As most of the families waited outside the courtroom, Elaine Kimbrew Thornhill wandered in. Faryion Wardrip sat quietly at the defense table. For more than ten minutes, Elaine stood in the courtroom, staring at her daughter's killer, never turning away.

Wardrip glanced up to meet Elaine's cold stare. *I'm sure she thinks I'm going to get away with it again,* Wardrip thought to himself. *She never wanted me to get out of prison.*

Again, the bailiff signaled that the jury was returning to the courtroom. The families moved at a slower pace, hoping that this wasn't another false alarm, that a decision had finally been reached.

Dorie Glickman asked her co-counsel, "Do you think it's the death penalty?"

Curry whispered, "Yes."

The twelve expressionless jurors took their seats. They avoided looking at the defendant as the judge asked if they had reached a verdict.

"Yes, Your Honor," the foreman said.

Dressed in an olive green shirt and brown pants, Wardrip remained seated at the defense table. He'd drunk a chocolate milk shake right before entering the courtroom and seemed more concerned about the mints he had asked for being absent than the impending verdict.

"What about my mints?" he was heard to ask Curry.

Curry reached over and patted him supportively on the back and whispered softly, "Shut up."

After five days of testimony, the jury responded to the three questions given them by Judge Brotherton.

Yes, they believed Wardrip had acted deliberately in causing the death of Terry Sims. Yes, they believed he represented a continuing threat to society. And, no, the jury did not believe there were any mitigating factors that would warrant that Wardrip spend his life in prison rather than be put to death.

By effectively answering each question, the jury had sealed Faryion Wardrip's fate. He would die by lethal injection strapped to a gurney in the Texas death chamber.

The crowd in the courtroom barely restrained their joy. There were hugs all around, with John Little receiving the bulk. Barry Macha had a smile and a hug for Sims's sisters. It was for Terry Sims's murder that Wardrip would be executed.

One of the Wichita County assistant DAs calmly walked to the front of the courtroom and turned the easel with the five smiling faces of Sims, Gibbs, Blau, Kimbrew, and Taylor to the jubilant gallery. Elaine Kimbrew Thornhill clasped her hands, raised them, and shook them in a sign of victory.

As the gallery celebrated his impending death, Wardrip stood, angrily spoke to Curry, and was led away by Wichita County deputies.

Except for his wife, Bryce Wardrip stood alone in the back of the courtroom. Torn between the satisfaction that justice was done and love for his brother, Bryce exited the courtroom, his black cowboy hat in his hands.

"Bryce," Robert Kimbrew said, stopping the younger Wardrip.

"Yes."

"Can I ask you a question?"

"Sure," Bryce said hesitantly.

"How old are you?" Robert asked.

Bryce looked puzzled. "Thirty-two," he answered.

"Well, that son-of-a-bitch. He lied to me. He told me he was the youngest in his family," Robert said bitterly.

Bryce only shrugged. He was not surprised.

After a slight delay, Wardrip shuffled back into court, his hands bound by handcuffs secured to a leather belt, and shackles encircling his ankles.

The courtroom was packed. The regular court attendees had been joined by workers from offices around the courthouse, as well as all twelve jurors.

Tina Wardrip placed her arm around her husband as the judge spoke. "Faryion Wardrip, please stand." Glickman and Curry rose to stand beside their client.

"Do you have anything to say?" Judge Brotherton asked.

Wardrip shot a quick glance toward Curry. He had asked the public defender if the judge would be asking him if he had anything to say, but Curry had told him no. Faryion had lots to say, most of all that he was sorry for what he had done.

"Don't say anything," Curry advised.

Faryion, disgusted with the system, responded with a resounding "No, sir."

Judge Brotherton announced that Wardrip would be transported from Wichita County to the Texas Department of Criminal Justice in Huntsville until the date of his execution.

Under Texas law, victims have the right to make an impact statement in court. Vickie Grimes, one of Terry Sims's sisters, chose to exercise that right.

As Grimes approached the stand, she shot a look of hatred at Wardrip. Her voice grew venomous as she told the court and Wardrip of the sorrow she and her family had experienced since Terry's death. That her grandmother gave up her will to live. That her own children would never know Terry, but through her, would know what a great person she was.

"I will be there to watch you put to death," Grimes said. "I only wish you would suffer. I do not see how you can live with yourself. I only wish you can suffer the way the girls did. I will always remember you as a coward."

Her words had an affect on everyone in the courtroom.

"All these women had so much to give. If God told you to confess, why did you wait until you got caught? You using the Bible as an excuse is a sin in itself," she told Wardrip.

"I know what it's like to watch a child die. To hold them. These women had no one to comfort them. You changed all our lives forever."

Vickie Grimes left the stand while spectators mourned the loss of the five women whose pictures remained a glaring reminder of Wardrip's carnage.

Wardrip knew in his heart the pain and suffering he had caused. He knew it before Elaine Kimbrew Thornton had testified and before Vickie Grimes had rebuked him.

Wardrip turned to his lawyers, and said, "I appreciate everything you've done for me. I'll never forget you."

Then, as he was being escorted from the courtroom, Wardrip looked at the surviving victims and in a spontaneous burst of conscience, he blurted out, "I'm sorry."

Just as spontaneously, Robert Kimbrew retorted, "You sure are!"

Epilogue

Victims of violent crimes extend far beyond the individual who suffers the wrath of the brutality. Like a pillaging hailstorm, the violence destroys indiscriminately, causing loss to some and leaving others untouched. The courts say Faryion Wardrip had five victims; in reality they are countless. The casualty list begins with Faryion himself.

FARYION WARDRIP:

Faryion Wardrip is currently on death row in Livingston, Texas. The maximum-security prison maintains optimum control by segregating prisoners in single cells composed of reinforced walls and metal doors. Only a single slot where food is passed gives Faryion contact with another human. The one hour a day he is allowed for recreation is spent alone in the exercise yard. There is no day room. No television. He passes his time reading his Bible, writing letters to his wife, and drawing.

In addition to the death sentence imposed by Denton jurors for the murder of Terry Sims, Faryion Wardrip received three life sentences after pleading guilty to killing Toni Gibbs, Debra Taylor, and Ellen Blau. The sentences, which will run consecutively, ensure that even should the thirty-nine-year-old murderer not be executed, he would serve a minimum of sixty years behind bars before becoming eligible for parole.

As Wardrip left the Wichita County courthouse to return to death row after his plea in the Blau case, he was asked by KFDX television reporter Dana Byerley how he felt after the court appearance.

"I'm glad this is almost over with and the families can put this behind them and start with some closure and some healing," a dejected Wardrip replied. His head hung low, and his shoulders were rounded as he shuffled down the hall in leg restraints.

"I have remorse every minute, every day," Wardrip said. "I start my day with remembering and I finish my day with remembering."

"How do you prepare for death?" Byerley asked, referring to the lethal injection the convicted murderer will be facing once his appeals are complete.

"You can't prepare," Wardrip said in a muffled tone. "You just do the best you can."

The depression that plagued Faryion Wardrip as a child and followed him through adulthood has a secure grip on him emotionally. Wardrip has indicated he will not seek additional appeals of his death-sentence case after the initial state-mandated appeal.

"I'm ready to go home," Wardrip said in an exclusive interview. "I told my wife I'd miss her and she'll miss me, but I told her that when my time does come, I'll be at peace."

GLENDA WARDRIP:

Before the start of Faryion Wardrip's trial for the murder of Terry Sims, Glenda Wardrip sold the poodle she gave her husband for Christmas, packed up her belongings, and moved to an undisclosed location in nearby Oklahoma. There she is in charge of a latch-key program for children.

Glenda writes to Faryion, but rarely visits. She refuses to discuss the past, something he feels a need to do. Glenda wants only to look forward, never back. Glenda is going on with her life in the service of God. Wardrip family members report Glenda has been accepted at an overseas missionary school.

BRYCE WARDRIP:

Bryce and his family continue to live in Olney, Texas. The ordeal of his brother's exposure as a serial killer has left Bryce with fewer friends and bitter memories. Bryce painfully refutes statements made by his brother regarding their parents and his declarations that he was a troubled youth, plagued by depression, learning disabilities, and misunderstanding by everyone, including his parents. Wardrip claims to have reached out to his mother and father, but says they never understood his needs. He remembers that he cried a lot and his parents just thought it was part of his personality rather than depression. He claims he sank deeper and deeper into a corner of despair.

Bryce publicly blasted Faryion for accusing his parents of mistreatment, saying, "Mom and Dad had done so much for Faryion and the other kids. I remember all the bicycles, go-carts, and automobiles they bought for us when we were growing up.

"What Faryion has said has left a black mark on their names. One of the things my father gave me was a lot of pride in the Wardrip name and in myself, and I am not going to let anyone say things about my parents which are not true. I don't care who it is.

"The thing Faryion needs to do is to take responsibility for what he's done and not blame anyone but himself. I am strongly in favor of the death penalty, and I think Faryion is going to get what he deserves."

Bryce, who has not heard from Faryion since he was sentenced, plans to attend the execution of his brother "to make certain justice is served."

GEORGE AND DIANA WARDRIP:

Faryion's parents, George and Diana Wardrip, continue to live quietly in Olney, Texas, where Mrs. Wardrip takes care of her ailing husband as he recovers from cancer.

They have written to Faryion and have traveled to see him on death row.

JOHNNA AND THE CHILDREN:

Johnna Wardrip divorced Faryion shortly before his imprisonment for the murder of Tina Kimbrew. She has remarried and lives in an undisclosed location with her husband and her two children fathered by Faryion. The children were allowed no contact with any of the Wardrip family for the fourteen years between Wardrip's arrests. There were no letters. No pictures. Since his imprisonment on death row, Johnna now feels sufficiently safe to allow both her son and daughter to have contact with their paternal grandparents, and they have written letters to their father.

THE SIMS FAMILY:

Terry Sims's parents divorced as a result of the murder of their daughter. As a consequence of Terry's death, Mrs. Sims experienced periods when she was "not well." Neither of Terry's parents lived to see their daughter's killer brought to justice.

KEN TAYLOR:

Ken suffered endless torment during the fourteen years his wife's killer was at large. He was estranged from his daughters, his in-laws, and many friends whose faith had wavered under the close police scrutiny.

Although it was a great relief that Wardrip confessed to the brutal murder of his wife, the image of Debra lying on the cold steel morgue slab is forever burned in Ken's brain.

"I think Mr. Wardrip should be very glad these guys [the authorities] got him before I did," Taylor said shortly after testifying at Wardrip's trial.

Ken has remarried and has one child.

TARRAH (TAYLOR) SHIRLEY:

Debra Taylor's oldest daughter continues to harbor the pent-up anger she feels about her mother's senseless death. Only the medications she takes help level her emotions.

"I hate the world," Tarrah said. "I have so much anger inside me."

The holidays are especially difficult for Tarrah since the suspicion of her stepdad as the killer split her family apart. Tarrah believes it may be possible that one day she can forgive Wardrip for what he did, but she will never forget. All Tarrah has of her mother is memories.

"My dad tells me all the time I'm just like my mom. She's not around for me to see that myself," Tarrah said. "The memories that I have are that she was a kind, loving person that would never hurt anybody. She definitely didn't deserve to go through something like this."

Although Tarrah was able to make a statement at Wardrip's sentencing for her mother's death, his placid demeanor gave her little satisfaction.

JANIE BALL:

The best friend of Ellen Blau continues to mourn the loss of the person she still considers her soul mate. She spoke at the sentencing hearing of Faryion Wardrip and expressed the importance of Ellen being remembered by both herself and Ellen's elderly parents. After Janie had read her victim's impact statement, Wardrip spoke an unemotional "I'm sorry."

The gesture was meaningless to Janie. "That meant nothing to me," Janie said. "You can't just come back later and say, 'Oh, I'm sorry.' "

Her best friend continues to live in the heart and mind of Janie Ball through her daughter, whom she named Ellen.

ROBERT KIMBREW AND ELAINE KIMBREW THORNHILL:

The Kimbrews divorced before the death of their only child, Tina. Together they have continued to fight the fight against Wardrip until his death sentence has been rendered. Robert Kimbrew, who owns a seed store, lives in Oklaunion, Texas. Elaine now lives in Vernon, Texas, with her second husband.

WILMA HOOKER:

Danny Laughlin's mother cannot let go of the bitterness she feels toward Wichita County and Archer County officials. Following the arrest of Faryion Wardrip, Hooker requested an official apology for the daunting harassment of her son. She one day hopes to give the expression of regret to Danny's son, Cody, along with news clippings and snips of news videotape that proclaim his father's innocence. But Wilma Hooker is not likely to receive the written statement she so deeply desires.

The oral expression of apology and pledge to "take

his job more seriously" that Wilma Hooker received from Barry Macha is not enough for the grieving mother.

BARRY MACHA:

District Attorney Barry Macha continues to represent the people of Wichita County in his elected office. He is diligently working on forming an interjurdisdictional violent crimes task force that will work together in solving crimes against people outside each member's bounds of authority. The task force would bring the various departments together to avoid the "turf guarding" that has occurred in the Wichita Falls area in the past. Macha believes that the organization of the special unit will avoid the future persecution of any innocent suspect, as well as help to expedite the apprehension of the guilty.

JOHN LITTLE:

Investigator John Little remains with the Wichita County prosecutor's office as their chief investigator.

Catie Reid, the youngest sister of Terry Sims, visited Little a few weeks after Wardrip's trial. She carried with her a token of appreciation. A red brick. The simple reminder of his past was inscribed with the words OUR HERO, JOHN LITTLE.

Each of those victimized by Faryion Wardrip has expressed a desire for closure. To experience true closure, one must find satisfying explanations and in the end view the situation in clear and stable terms. It has helped some to confront the killer, but in order for there to be complete finalization, they must let go of the emotional burden each of them has carried for fourteen years. The anger, shame, and even, in some cases, guilt they have felt must now be released to Wardrip. Only then can the hail storm be withstood, if not forgotten.

BOOK YOUR PLACE ON OUR WEBSITE AND MAKE THE READING CONNECTION!

We've created a customized website just for our very special readers, where you can get the inside scoop on everything that's going on with Zebra, Pinnacle and Kensington books.

When you come online, you'll have the exciting opportunity to:

- View covers of upcoming books
- Read sample chapters
- Learn about our future publishing schedule (listed by publication month *and author*)
- Find out when your favorite authors will be visiting a city near you
- Search for and order backlist books from our online catalog
- Check out author bios and background information
- Send e-mail to your favorite authors
- Meet the Kensington staff online
- Join us in weekly chats with authors, readers and other guests
- Get writing guidelines
- AND MUCH MORE!

Visit our website at
http://www.pinnaclebooks.com